Flash Game Development by Example

Build 9 classic Flash games and learn game development along the way

Emanuele Feronato

PUBLISHING

BIRMINGHAM - MUMBAI

Flash Game Development by Example

First published: March 2011

Production Reference: 1150311

Published by Packt Publishing Ltd.
32 Lincoln Road
Olton
Birmingham, B27 6PA, UK.

ISBN 978-1-849690-90-4

www.packtpub.com

Cover Image by Charwak (charwak86@gmail.com)

Credits

Author
Emanuele Feronato

Reviewers
Jon Borgonia
Robin Palotai
Tarwin Stroh-Spijer

Acquisition Editor
David Barnes

Development Editor
Roger D'souza

Technical Editor
Arun Nadar

Indexers
Rekha Nair
Monica Ajmera Mehta

Editorial Team Leader
Aditya Belpathak

Project Team Leader
Lata Basantani

Project Coordinator
Vishal Bodwani

Proofreader
Mario Cecere

Graphics
Geetanjali G. Sawant

Production Coordinator
Shantanu Zagade

Cover Work
Shantanu Zagade

About the Author

Emanuele Feronato has been studying programming languages since the early eighties, with a particular interest in web and game development. He taught online programming for the European Social Fund and now owns a web development company in Italy where he works as a lead programmer.

As a game developer, he developed Flash games sponsored by the biggest game portals and played more than 50 million times.

As a writer, he worked as technical reviewer for Packt Publishing.

His blog, www.emanueleferonato.com, is one of the most visited blogs about indie programming.

I would like to thank the guys at Packt Publishing for giving me the opportunity to write this book.

Special thanks go to David Barnes for believing in this project, and to Vishal Bodwani and Arun Nadar, along with the technical reviewers, for dealing with my drafts and my ugly English.

A big "thank you" goes to my blog readers and to my Facebook fans for appreciating my work and giving me the will to write more and more.

I would also mention Ada Chen from Mochi Media. I made my first Flash game after getting in touch by e-mail with her, so she has an important role in the making of this book.

Finally I want to thank my wife Kirenia, for being patient while I was writing the book late at night.

This book is dedicated to my little daughter Kimora, who always strokes random keys on my computer. The legend says most of my scripts were born this way.

I love you "bambina squalo".

About the Reviewers

Jon Borgonia is a Level 28 programmer. He hails from his home base, *Goma Games*, located on the remote Pacific island of Oahu. Jon lives and breathes games and in the few moments when he is neither playing nor programming, he enthusiastically discusses game design, game theory, and game addiction with his fellow teammates.

Through *Goma Games*, Jon has developed many mini-games for the Flash platform using haXe technology. Some titles he has released include *Polyn, Santa's Sack, Thanksgiving Kitchen Hero, Jet-Pack Turkey of Tomorrow*, and *10-10-10*.

By developing fun and original games, Jon's vision is to inspire people to respect video games as a creative interactive art. He strives to create an experience that evokes real-world change.

> Thank you Kelli, you are the light that emanates from the fire of my being. Thank you for putting lines and fills on the games we make. Thank you Will, for being my best friend to laugh, cry, and build castles with in the sandbox of our lives. Thank you Jesse, for being the active ingredient for our creativity with your new ideas and fresh perspective. Thank you friends and family, for your unconditional love and tolerance for my fanatic addiction for games. Finally, thank you Keith, for letting me win MVC2 a few times.

Robin Palotai enjoys developing flash games and utilities using haXe and ActionScript3. He is one of the authors of SamHaXe, an open-source SWF resource library assembler tool. He also runs `TreeTide.com`, providing interesting tools and articles for flash game developers.

Tarwin is a self-taught programmer (unless having his dad excitably explain what and how amazing DBase2 is) who loves the power that programming brings him, especially when used along with the WWW. He has worked as a freelance web designer and developer for almost 15 years. He also worked as a DVD author but was saved from that by the insistence of a university mate with whom he started Touch My Pixel.

Back in 1997, on Flash 2, Tarwin started to hack around in Flash after seeing the (at the time) amazing Future Splash—The Simpsons (r) website.

Tarwin has also taught Multimedia Design at Monash University in Melbourne, Australia and been part of small creating interactive artwork, some of which has been displayed internationally at the Taiwan Biennale, 2008, and another which won the prestigious Queensland Premiere's prize in 2010.

Thanks to my parents who let me pursue my own work, even though it wasn't a "real job", thanks to my peers for always pushing me to do better, and thanks for those close to me who put up with my workaholic nature. I promise I'll spend more time with you!

www.PacktPub.com

Support files, eBooks, discount offers and more

You might want to visit www.PacktPub.com for support files and downloads related to your book.

Did you know that Packt offers eBook versions of every book published, with PDF and ePub files available? You can upgrade to the eBook version at www.PacktPub.com and as a print book customer, you are entitled to a discount on the eBook copy. Get in touch with us at service@packtpub.com for more details.

At www.PacktPub.com, you can also read a collection of free technical articles, sign up for a range of free newsletters and receive exclusive discounts and offers on Packt books and eBooks.

http://PacktLib.PacktPub.com

Do you need instant solutions to your IT questions? PacktLib is Packt's online digital book library. Here, you can access, read and search across Packt's entire library of books.

Why Subscribe?

- Fully searchable across every book published by Packt
- Copy and paste, print and bookmark content
- On demand and accessible via web browser

Free Access for Packt account holders

If you have an account with Packt at www.PacktPub.com, you can use this to access PacktLib today and view nine entirely free books. Simply use your login credentials for immediate access.

Table of Contents

Preface

With the Flash games market in continuous expansion, it's no surprise more and more developers are putting their efforts into the creation of Flash games. Anyway, what makes Flash games development different from other kinds of casual game development is the budget required to make it a commercial success.

There are a lot of indie developers building games in their spare time and turning their passion into an income source, which in some cases becomes a full time, well paid job.

Being able to develop quick and fun Flash games is also a skill more and more required by employers, and with this scope comes this book: teaching you how to develop indie Flash games.

Dissecting and replicating games that made the history of video games, we'll see how easy it is to create a funny Flash game even if you are a one man development studio.

What this book covers

Chapter 1, Concentration is the simplest game ever that can be made with just an array and limited user interaction.

Chapter 2, Minesweeper is a game that can be made with an array, but shows more interesting features such as recursive functions.

Chapter 3, Connect Four is an array-based game with more complex rules and a basic artificial intelligence to make the computer play against a human.

Chapter 4, Snake is also a keyboard interaction game with simple rules but now it's a real time game, the snake never stops so the game doesn't just sit and wait for player inputs.

Chapter 5, *Tetris* is the most difficult game, featuring timers, player inputs, multi-dimension arrays, and actors with different shapes.

Chapter 6, *Astro-PANIC!* is a shooter game with virtually infinite levels of increasing difficulty and a complete score and high score system.

Chapter 7, *Bejeweled* is a modern blockbuster with combos and a basic artificial intelligence to give the player hints about the game.

Chapter 8, *Puzzle Bobble* is a match 3 game played on a non-orthogonal game field, which can also be played in multiplayer.

Chapter 9, *BallBalance* is a game I made from scratch; it's not complex but had decent success, and will show you how to make an original game.

Sokoban (online: `https://www.packtpub.com/sites/default/files/ 0904_Sokoban.pdf`) is a game where even more complex rules, keyboard interaction, different levels, and the "undo" feature makes it a benchmark for every programmer.

What you need for this book

Flash CS4 or CS5 is required for this book. You can download a free 30 days evaluation version at `http://www.adobe.com/products/flash/whatisflash/`.

Who this book is for

- AS3 developers who want to know quick and dirty techniques to create Flash games
- Flash animators who want to learn how to create games from their works with AS3
- Programmers who know languages different than AS3 and want to learn AS3 to make something more interesting and fun than the old "phone book"
- Even if you aren't a programmer, but you love Flash games, you can count on this book: you will be guided step by step with clear examples and the support of the full source code of every game

Conventions

In this book, you will find a number of styles of text that distinguish between different kinds of information. Here are some examples of these styles, and an explanation of their meaning.

Code words in text are shown as follows: "There is a call to a new function called `placeDisc` with an argument."

A block of code is set as follows:

```
package {
  import flash.display.Sprite;
  public class board_movieclip extends Sprite {
    public function board_movieclip() {
      x=105;
      y=100;
    }
  }
}
```

When we wish to draw your attention to a particular part of a code block, the relevant lines or items are set in bold:

```
public function Main() {
  prepareField();
  placeBoard();
  placeDisc(Math.floor(Math.random()*2)+1);
}
```

New terms and **important words** are shown in bold. Words that you see on the screen, in menus or dialog boxes for example, appear in the text like this: "Create a new file (**File | New**) then from **New Document** window select **Actionscript 3.0**".

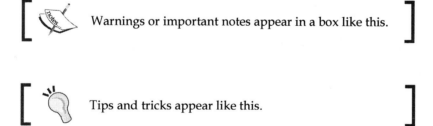

Warnings or important notes appear in a box like this.

Tips and tricks appear like this.

Reader feedback

Feedback from our readers is always welcome. Let us know what you think about this book—what you liked or may have disliked. Reader feedback is important for us to develop titles that you really get the most out of.

To send us general feedback, simply send an e-mail to `feedback@packtpub.com`, and mention the book title via the subject of your message.

If there is a book that you need and would like to see us publish, please send us a note in the **SUGGEST A TITLE** form on www.packtpub.com or e-mail suggest@packtpub.com.

If there is a topic that you have expertise in and you are interested in either writing or contributing to a book, see our author guide on www.packtpub.com/authors.

Customer support

Now that you are the proud owner of a Packt book, we have a number of things to help you to get the most from your purchase.

Downloading the example code

You can download the example code files for all Packt books you have purchased from your account at http://www.PacktPub.com. If you purchased this book elsewhere, you can visit http://www.PacktPub.com/support and register to have the files e-mailed directly to you.

Errata

Although we have taken every care to ensure the accuracy of our content, mistakes do happen. If you find a mistake in one of our books—maybe a mistake in the text or the code—we would be grateful if you would report this to us. By doing so, you can save other readers from frustration and help us improve subsequent versions of this book. If you find any errata, please report them by visiting http://www.packtpub.com/support, selecting your book, clicking on the **errata submission form** link, and entering the details of your errata. Once your errata are verified, your submission will be accepted and the errata will be uploaded on our website, or added to any list of existing errata, under the Errata section of that title. Any existing errata can be viewed by selecting your title from http://www.packtpub.com/support.

Piracy

Piracy of copyright material on the Internet is an ongoing problem across all media. At Packt, we take the protection of our copyright and licenses very seriously. If you come across any illegal copies of our works, in any form, on the Internet, please provide us with the location address or website name immediately so that we can pursue a remedy.

Please contact us at copyright@packtpub.com with a link to the suspected pirated material.

We appreciate your help in protecting our authors, and our ability to bring you valuable content.

Questions

You can contact us at questions@packtpub.com if you are having a problem with any aspect of the book, and we will do our best to address it.

1
Concentration

Concentration is a memory game you can play even without a computer, just with a deck of cards. Shuffle the cards, lay them face down on a table and at each turn choose and flip any two cards with faces up.

If they match (both cards are Aces, Twos, Threes, and so on), remove them from the table. If not, lay them face down again and pick another couple of cards. The game is completed when, due to successful matches, all cards have been removed from the table.

Concentration can be played as a solitaire or by any number of players. In this case the winner is the one who removed the most cards.

In this chapter you will create a complete Concentration game from scratch, with a step-by-step approach, learning these basics:

- Creating a Flash document
- Working with packages, classes, and functions
- Printing text
- Commenting your code
- Creating and managing variables and constants
- Creating and managing arrays
- Generating and rounding random numbers to simulate the shuffle of a deck of cards
- Repeating the execution of code a given amount of times with the `for` loop
- Creating Movie Clips to be added with AS3 and interacting with them on the fly
- Handling mouse clicks
- Dealing with timers

It's a lot of stuff, but don't worry as the whole process is easier than you can imagine.

Defining game design

Once you start thinking about programming a game, you are already making it. You are in pre-production stage.

During this process, gameplay as well as storyline and environment begin to take shape. Before starting to code or even turning on the computer, it's very important to define the game design. This is the step in which you will decide how the game will work, the rules and the goals of the game, as well as the amount of options and features to include.

I know you just want to start coding, but underestimating the importance of game design is a very common error. Usually we think we have everything in mind, and we want to start coding at once. Moreover, a game like Concentration looks really simple, with just one basic rule (selected cards match/don't match) and, last but not least, we just have to copy an existing game, so why not start typing right now?

Even a basic project like a Concentration remake may give you some troubles if you skip an accurate game design. Here are a few questions you probably would not ask yourself about the game you are about to make:

- How many players can take part in the game?
- How many cards will be placed on the table?
- I don't have a deck of cards. Do I have to buy one and scan all the cards?
- Are card images protected by copyright?
- Where can I find free card images?
- Which resolution should I use to clearly display all cards?
- Who will play my game?
- What difficulty levels can the player choose?
- Will there be any background music or sound effects?

Don't hesitate to ask yourself as many questions as you can. The more decisions you take now, the easier the game will be to make.

Making changes to basic mechanics when the game is on an advanced development stage can dramatically increase developing time. A good game design won't ensure you that you will never have to rewrite some parts of the code, but it reduces the probability of you having to do it.

Anyway, be realistic and know your limits. Questions like "Do I have to use a physics engine to add realism to card flipping, maybe introducing wind or different air resistance" are welcome since you don't want to start doing this and then realize it's not needed, but avoid thinking about features you know you aren't able to add or you will quickly turn a game you are about to publish into a game you'll never make.

At the end of this process, you must have at least a set of basic rules to define how a playable prototype should work.

So here are the decisions I made for the game we will create:

- To be played in solitaire mode.
- The game is intended to be played on a web browser by young children.
- Twenty cards placed on the table. Being for young children, a complete deck of cards could be too difficult.
- Rather than the classic deck of cards, we'll use tiles with primitive colored shapes on them, such as a red circle, a green square and so on. This will let us draw the graphics on our own, without needing a card deck.
- Player will select the cards with a mouse click.

Defining the audience of a game is very important when you are about to fine-tune the game. Being a game for young children, we'll add some educational content in it. Parents love when their children play and learn at the same time.

Setting stage size, frame rate, and background color

You are about to create a Flash game, and like all Flash movies, it will have its stage size (width and height in pixels), frame rate (the number of frames per second) and a background color.

 The area where you will add the content to be viewed is called the **stage**. Any content outside the stage will not be visible when playing the game.

The higher the size and the frame rate, the more CPU-intensive will be the game. But it's not just a CPU-based issue: you also have to set the size according to the device your game is designed to be played in. If you plan to design a Concentration game for smartphones, then a 1280x1024 size is probably a bad choice, because they don't support that kind of resolution.

Although we have decided to create a game to be played in browsers we should still put some effort into thinking about what size it should be.

Flash games are mostly played on famous game portals such as Kongregate (www.kongregate.com) or Armor Games (www.armorgames.com), that give players a wide choice of quality games. Since the games are embedded in web pages, they must fit in a pre-built layout, so you can't make your game as wide and tall as you want because most portals won't just pick it up and you won't be able to see your game being played by thousands of players.

As you can see from the picture, the game is not the only content of the page, but it's carefully embedded in a complex layout. There may be login forms, advertising, chat rooms, and so on.

A common error is thinking the bigger the game size, the better the graphics and the more information you can show. A good designer can make everything fit in small resolutions. A PSP console has a 480x272 resolution and a Nintendo DS has a 256x384 resolution split in two. Both consoles have awesome games.

Play some successful games in various Flash game portals, and you'll see the most used sizes are **550x400** and **640x480**. The former is the size we'll use for the game.

Run Adobe Flash and create a new file (**File | New**) then from **New Document** window select **Actionscript 3.0**.

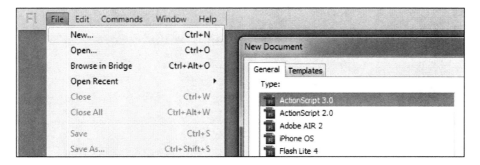

Once we create a document the first thing we should do is set its properties. Open **Properties** window (**Window | Properties**) and you'll probably see stage size is already 550x400, because it's Flash's default movie size. Click **Edit** button to see **Document Settings** window. If you don't already have these values by default, set width to **550**px, height to **400**px, background color to #FFFFFF (white) and frame rate to 24. A higher frame rate means smoother animations, but also a higher CPU consumption. In this game we don't use animations, so I just left the frame rate to its default value.

You will also need to define the Document Class. Call it Main and you will probably see this alert:

Don't worry: Flash is warning you just set the main document class for the current movie, but it couldn't find a file with such class. Warm up your fingers, because it's time to code.

Now your **Properties** window should look like this:

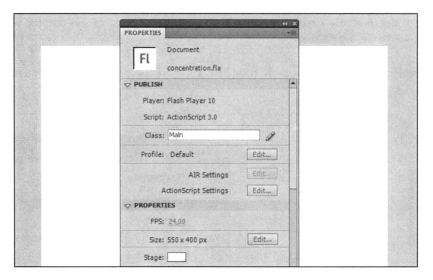

The white area in the background is the stage itself.

Your Flash document is now ready to turn into a Concentration game.

Save the file (**File | Save**) and name it as `concentration.fla` then let's code `Main` class.

Welcome to Concentration ("Hello World")

At this time we just want to make sure things are working, so we are only writing some text. It's the first script of our first project, so it's a huge step anyway.

Without closing `concentration.fla`, create a new file and from **New Document** window select **ActionScript 3.0 Class**.

You should be brought to an empty text file. If you are using Flash CS5 you'll get a box asking for the class name. Type in `Main`, then delete the default script in the text file and start coding:

```
package {
    // importing classes
    import flash.display.Sprite;
    // end of importing classes
    public class Main extends Sprite {
```

```
    public function Main() {
      trace("Welcome to Concentration");
    }
  }
}
```

Save the file as `Main.as` in the same path where you saved `concentration.fla`.

At this time the content of your project folder should look like this:

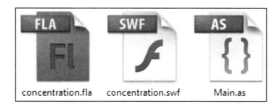

As you can see, `Main` is repeated a lot, from the name of the document class to the name of the file you just saved.

Now it's time to test the movie (**Control | Test Movie**). You will see the blank stage but in the output window (**Window | Output**) you will see:

```
Welcome to Concentration
```

You just made your first class work. At this time you may think AS3 may not be the best language for game development as it took eight lines to do what can be easily done in other languages, such as PHP or Javascript, in just a single line. But you didn't just write "Welcome to Concentration". You defined the package, the class, and the main function of the game in just eight lines. It sounds different, doesn't it?

Let's see how it works:

`package` indicates that the following block of code (everything between { and }) is a package of classes and functions.

`package` usually is followed by a name such as `package com.packagename` to ensure class name uniqueness in large libraries programmers want to distribute. Since the creation of libraries for distribution is not the topic of this book, just remember to add `package {` to the first line and close it with } in the last line.

```
import flash.display.Sprite;
```

Imports `Sprite` built-in class for later use. This class allows us to display graphics. `flash.display.Sprite` means we are importing `Sprite` class from `flash.display` package.

```
public class Main extends Sprite { ...}
```

This defines the main class of this file (called `Main`). `extends` means the class will be built based upon `Sprite` class. Basically we are adding new functionalities to `Sprite` class. This class must be set as `public` so don't worry about it at the moment. You have no choice.

 Throughout the book you will find a lot of "three points" (…). They mean the rest of the code has not been changed.

Once the class has been defined, we have to create the constructor. It's a function that is called when a new class is created, in this case when the project is run. The constructor must have the same name of the class.

```
public function Main() {...}
```

Defines the constructor function of the class. This must be set as `public` as well.

`trace()` will show any value you pass in the output window when the movie is executed in the Flash environment. It will become your best friend when it's time to debug. This time, displaying "Welcome to Concentration" in the output window, it will let you know everything worked fine with your class.

Congratulations. You just learned how to:

- Decide which size your game should be.
- Create and set up a Flash movie.
- Code, test, and debug a working class.

At this time you had a brief introduction to classes, constructors, and functions, but that was enough to let you create and set up a Flash movie, as well as testing and printing text on the debug window.

Also notice there are comments around the code. Commenting the code is almost as important as coding itself, because good comments explain what your script is supposed to do and can help to remind you what the code is meant to be doing, especially when you aren't working on the script for a while. Also, during this book, you'll be asked to insert or modify parts of scripts identified by comments (that is "delete everything between `// here` and `// there`") so it's recommended you use the same comments you find in the book.

You can comment your code with either single line or block comments.

A **single line comment** starts with two slashes `//`, and lasts until the end of the line. The compiler will ignore everything after the `//`.

```
trace("Welcome") // I am an inline comment
```

A **block comment** starts with /* marker and ends with */ marker. The compiler will ignore everything between the markers.

```
/* I am

a multi-line

block comment */
```

Now it's time to start the real development of the game.

Creating the tiles

As said, we won't use a standard card deck, but tiles with basic shapes on them. We can place any number of tiles, as long as it's an even number, because any tile must have its match. So, if you want to play with ten symbols, you must have 20 tiles in game.

That's exactly what we are going to do. We will create twenty tiles, each one represented by a number from 0 to 9. Since there are two tiles for each value, we will have two zeros, two ones, two twos, and so on until two nines.

Now you may wonder: why are we representing ten tiles with numbers from 0 to 9? Wouldn't it be better to use the classic 1-10 range? Obviously representing numbers from 1 to 10 seems more meaningful, but keep in mind when you code you should always start counting from zero.

You may also wonder why we are defining tile values with numbers when we decided to use shapes. Think about a Flash game as if it were a movie. In a movie, you see what the director wants you to see. But there is a lot of stuff you will never see, although it is part of the show. Let's take a car chase: you see two cars running fast along a freeway because the director wanted you to see them. What you don't see are cameras, microphones, mixers, storyboards, safety belts, make-up artists, and so on. You only see what the camera filmed.

A game works in the same way; the player will see what happens on the stage, but he won't see what happens behind the 'scenes', and now we are working behind the scene.

Change Main function this way:

```
public function Main() {
   // variables and constants
   const NUMBER_OF_TILES:uint=20;
   var tiles:Array=new Array();
   // end of variables and constants
```

```
// tiles creation loop
for (var i:uint=0; i<NUMBER_OF_TILES; i++) {
  tiles.push(Math.floor(i/2));
}
trace("My tiles: "+tiles);
// end of tiles creation loop
}
```

Test the movie and in the output window `trace(tiles)` will print:

My tiles: 0,0,1,1,2,2,3,3,4,4,5,5,6,6,7,7,8,8,9,9

Let's see what we have done:

First, we created a constant called NUMBER_OF_TILES.

In AS3, you can declare constants and variables. A constant represents a value that will never change during the script. A real world example of a constant is the number of minutes in an hour. No matter how you are using minutes in your code, you will always have 60 minutes in an hour. A variable holds information that may change during the execution of the script. Referring to previous example, the amount of minutes I play Flash games each day changes according to the amount of my spare time.

Since the number of tiles will never change during the game, we defined it as a constant. But we need to give a better definition to our constant. We know NUMBER_OF_TILES is a number that can only be positive. That is, an unsigned integer.

AS3 provides three ways to define a number.

- `int` — represents an integer that can be positive or negative, called signed integer.
- `uint` — an unsigned integer that is used to represent numbers that can only be positive.
- `Number` — (uppercase "N") is used to represent whole and fractional numbers, no matter if positive or negative. You can use it if you are unsure about `int`/`uint`, anyway you should always know which values could be stored in a variable.

As you can see, I named the constant NUMBER_OF_TILES, but I could have named it A or EXTERNAL_TEMPERATURE. You can give variables and constants any name you want, but naming them with descriptive words will help you to remember their role in your script.

Also, the name is ALLCAPS. There's nothing special in `NUMBER_OF_TILES` constant to be written ALLCAPS, it's just a convention to quickly distinguish constants from variables. In this book, all constants will have ALLCAPS names.

Now we need a way to manage all tiles. There is no easier way to store an ordered set of data than using arrays.

 Think about an array as a container holding any number of individual values in a single variable. Any individual value (called element) will have a unique index to allow an easy access.

An array representation of a normal deck of 52 cards would be this one:

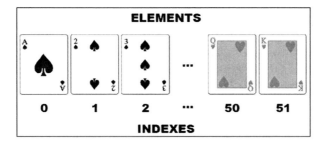

Note in AS3, as with many other programming languages, array indexes start from zero. This is why we earlier talked about the cards 0 to 9.

So we declared an `Array` variable called `tiles`.

```
var tiles:Array=new Array();
```

This will create an array with no items in it. But we are about to populate it.

Notice constant name is uppercase while variables is lowercase. This is not mandatory, but it's recommended to write names in a way that allows you to easily recognize a variable from a constant. The scripts on this book will follow this rule.

As said earlier, the tiles will contain shapes easily recognized by children. But we won't populate the tiles array with red squares or green circles. What if tomorrow we needed to replace red squares with angry ducks?

We are working behind the scenes so let's just fill it with a pair of numbers from zero up to (but not including) `NUMBER_OF_TILES/2`. This way we can easily associate any symbol with any number without rewriting a single line of code.

```
for (var i:uint=0; i<NUMBER_OF_TILES; i++) {...}
```

This is a `for` loop. It's used to repeat the same code a given number of times. Let's see in detail how it works:

`var i:uint=0;` is simply declaring a new unsigned integer variable called `i` and assigning it the starting value of `0`.

`i<NUMBER_OF_TILES;` means the loop will reiterate as long as the value of `i` is less than the `NUMBER_OF_TILES` value.

`i++;` means `i` is increased by `1` at the end of each iteration. The same thing can be done with `i=i+1` or `i+=1`.

It's easy to see that everything in the `for` block will be executed twenty times, since we defined `NUMBER_OF_TILES` as `20`.

```
tiles.push(Math.floor(i/2));
```

This is how we populate the array. `push()` method adds an element to the end of the array, while `Math.floor()` method returns the floor of the expression passed as parameter. In programming languages, you get the floor of a number when you round it down.

 Any action that the object can perform is called a method. Methods in AS3 are called with `objectname.method(arguments)`.

So at every `for` iteration a new element is added at the end of `tiles` array. This element contains the floor of `i/2`, that will be `0` for `i=0` (0/2 is 0) and `i=1` (1/2 is 0.5 and the closest number below that is 0), `1` for `i=2` and `i=3`, and so on.

Adding randomness: shuffling the tiles

Now we managed to have a numeric representation of the tiles, but it's very easy to guess the content of each tile. We already know 0th and 1st tile values are 0, 2nd and 3rd are equal to 1, and so on.

We have to add randomness to the game by shuffling the tiles. Randomness is very important in games. Except for some genres such as adventures and puzzles that require the player to retry the same identical level until he solves a specific problem, randomness adds variety to games that would instead offer the same, boring, challenge. Just think about a card solitaire in which you know where each card is. Or a minesweeper game where you know the position of each mine. That's why the generation of random scenarios is a very important game feature.

A series of numbers is truly random if it is completely unpredictable. In other words, if we have absolutely no way of knowing what the next number is in a series of numbers, then the series is completely random. Since computers are 100% predictable, generating true random numbers is not an easy task. Applications like online casino software and security- programs (that is password generators, data encryption, and more) demand the highest randomness possible. When programming games, we can take it easy.

Every programming language has its own function to generate random numbers, and that's enough for game development.

There are a lot of routines to shuffle an array, but we are using a modern variant of the **Fisher–Yates shuffle algorithm** because it's very similar to randomly picking cards from a deck one after another until there are no more left.

A real world representation modern Fisher-Yates shuffle algorithm works this way:

1. Align all tiles from left-to-right.
2. Place a coin on the rightmost tile.
3. Swap the tile with the coin with a random tile chosen among the ones to its left, but the coin doesn't move.
4. Move the coin one card left.
5. Repeat from step 3 until the coin is on the leftmost card.

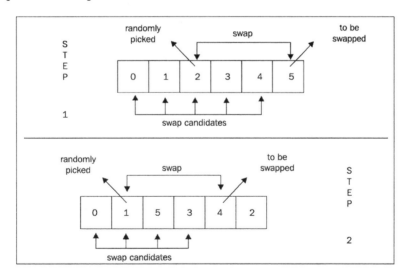

Hopefully you get the idea that the tiles are array elements and the coin is array index:

Just after `// end of tiles creation loop` add the following code:

```
// shuffling loop
var swap,tmp:uint;
for (i=NUMBER_OF_TILES-1; i>0; i--) {
  swap=Math.floor(Math.random()*i);
  tmp=tiles[i];
  tiles[i]=tiles[swap];
  tiles[swap]=tmp;
}
trace("My shuffled tiles: "+tiles);
// end of shuffling loop
```

Now test the movie and you will get:

My tiles: 0,0,1,1,2,2,3,3,4,4,5,5,6,6,7,7,8,8,9,9

My shuffled tiles: 1,6,2,5,7,3,0,8,3,2,0,9,9,8,4,7,6,4,1,5

The second sequence of numbers will change every time you execute the script because it's the representation of the shuffled array.

Let's see how we got this result:

```
var swap,tmp:uint;
```

We need two more variables, both of them unsigned integers. Notice you can declare more variables of the same type in a single line. This time the variables don't have an initial value, because they'll get their values during the script. I also said generally it's good to give explanatory names to variables, but here, as we're only using them very locally we can give them nice and short names that are easy to type and quick to read.

```
for (i=NUMBER_OF_TILES-1; i>0; i--) { ... }
```

This is another `for` loop. Do you see some differences between this loop and the one used to create the tiles? Let's compare them. This was the previous loop:

```
for (var i:uint=0; i<NUMBER_OF_TILES; i++) { ... } // previous loop
```

In the second loop we don't need to declare the `i` variable because it has already been declared in the first one. So we are just using `i=value` instead of `var i:type=value`.

Another difference is that the first loop increases the variable at every iteration, while the second one decreases it.

Double check your `for` loops to ensure they will end after a finite number of iterations. This is a correct `for` loop `for(i=0;i<1000000;i++) {` `... }` because it will end after a million iterations, and this is a wrong loop `for(i=0;i>=0;i++) { ... }` because it will never end. A loop that never ends is called an **infinite loop** and will crash your application.

```
swap=Math.floor(Math.random()*i);
```

We already know what `Math.floor()` method does. It's time to meet another Math method. `Math.random()` method returns a random number between 0 and 1 with 1 excluded.

This is likely to be a number with many decimal places, like 0.4567443452 so we can use it to get random numbers for high values as well. For example, if you want a random number between 0 (included) and 5 (excluded) you can just call `Math.random()*5`. If you want a random number between 5 (included) and 10 (excluded) you will call `Math.random*5+5`. In our loop we want an integer number between 0 (included) and `i` (excluded), so `Math.floor(Math.random()*i)` is exactly what we need.

At this time, `swap` contains an integer number between 0 (included) and `i` (excluded). It's time to apply Fisher-Yates shuffle algorithm and swap the content of the `i-th` element of the array with the `swap-th` one.

To do this we need a temporary variable (called `tmp`) to save the content of the `i-th` array element before overwriting it with the content of the `swap-th` element. Then we can overwrite the content of the `swap-th` element with the value we just saved.

You can think of this as like swapping apples between hands. As you cannot hold two apples in one hand to do the swap you need the help of a third hand (your `tmp` variable) to hold one of the apples while you swap hands for the first.

Back to our script, the swapping process can be described with this picture:

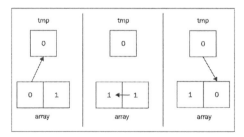

At the end of the `for` loop, your array will be shuffled according to the Fisher-Yates algorithm.

The Concentration core is ready. You've just managed to:

- Declare and use variables and constants.
- Handle arrays to store information.
- Use loops to reiterate sequences of code.
- Work with numbers using mathematical functions.

Take a short break, in a moment your graphics skills will be proven.

Placing the tiles on stage

Until now, we just have a numeric representation of the shuffled tiles. There is nothing the player can see or interact with. We need to draw the tiles.

Stop working (at the moment) at `Main.as` and select `concentration.fla` file from the upper left tabs (you should see the blank stage) and create a new symbol (**Insert | New Symbol...**). You will be taken to **Create New Symbol** window.

Fill the fields in this way:

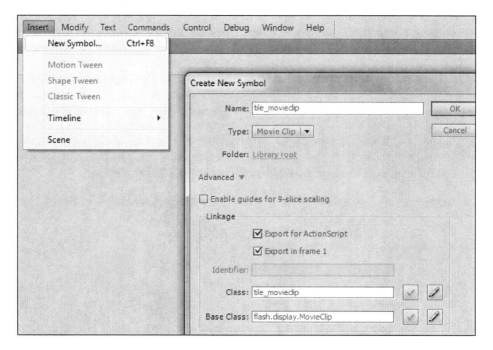

- Name (the name you want to give to the object): **tile_movieclip**.
- Type (it can be Movie Clip, Button, or Graphic): Movie Clip (it should be the default value).
- Folder: Library root (it should be the default value).
- Export for ActionScript (defines if the symbol can be dynamically created using ActionScript or not): checked.
- Export in frame 1 (used to automatically export the symbol if you don't place it on the Stage): checked (it should automatically be checked when you check Export for Actionscript).
- Class (symbol's class): **tile_movieclip** (it should be prefilled using the name you gave the symbol).
- Base Class (the class your symbol will extend): **flash.display.MovieClip** (it should automatically appear when you check Export for Actionscript).

Press **OK**.

You'll probably get the same warning as before. Ignore it. I said "probably" because you could have removed alerts or changed default values.

If you do not provide a class for your exported symbol, Flash will create the class for you with this content:

```
package {
  import flash.display.MovieClip;
  public class movieclip_name extends MovieClip {
    public function movieclip_name() {
    }
  }
}
```

That is a class doing nothing. When you create a new symbol, Flash just warns you it will create this basic class if you won't make your own.

To create the tiles, draw 10 distinct shapes in the first 10 frames of your symbol, and the back of the tile in the 11th frame. You are free to draw them as you want, but I suggest you make them as 90 pixels squares with registration point (starting x and y position) at 0, because these are the properties of the tiles used in this chapter's examples. At least, they should all be the same size.

Also notice the first frame is 1 while the first tile value is 0. You will need to remember this when you make tiles flip.

You should be familiar with Flash timeline and drawing tools. If you have not been using Flash for a long time, don't worry. Basic drawing and timeline management haven't changed that much since the very first Flash version. If you don't know how to draw objects in Flash, refer to the official documentation.

Once you are satisfied, it's time to place the tiles on the stage: change the block of code delimited by comment `//variables and constants` this way:

```
// variables and constants
const NUMBER_OF_TILES:uint=20;
const TILES_PER_ROW:uint=5;
var tiles:Array=new Array();
var tile:tile_movieclip;
// end of variables and constants
```

Here we need a new constant called `TILES_PER_ROW`. It will store the number of tiles to be displayed in a row. Setting it to 5 means we want four rows of five tiles. If we set it to 4, we will have five rows made of four tiles. This way you can modify the game layout by simply changing a value.

`tile` is a variable of `tile_movieclip` type.

Now we have to use the new variable and constant to place tiles on the stage, so add after`// end of shuffling loop` comment a new `for` loop (with a couple of new comments):

```
// tile placing loop
for (i=0; i<NUMBER_OF_TILES; i++) {
  tile=new tile_movieclip();
  addChild(tile);
  tile.cardType=tiles[i];
  tile.x=5+(tile.width+5)*(i%TILES_PER_ROW);
  tile.y=5+(tile.height+5)*(Math.floor(i/TILES_PER_ROW));
  tile.gotoAndStop(NUMBER_OF_TILES/2+1);
}
// end of tile placing loop
```

Test the movie and you'll see something like this:

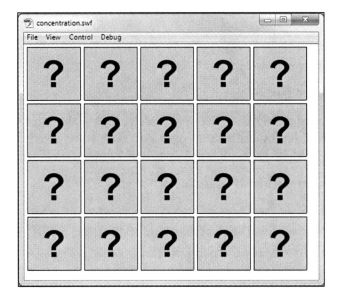

The gray square with a "?" is the 11th frame of the `tile_movieclip` symbol.

Let's see how we made it possible:

At every `for` loop iteration the script places a tile on the stage.

```
tile=new tile_movieclip();
```

Creates a new `tile_movieclip` object.

```
addChild(tile);
```

`addChild()` adds an object to the **Display List**. It's the list that contains all visible Flash content. To make an object capable of appearing on the stage, it must be inserted in the Display List. A Display List object is called **DisplayObject**.

 Although Display List contains all visible objects, you may not be able to see some of them, for instance if they are outside the stage, or if they are behind other objects, or even because they have been told to hide.

```
tile.cardType=tiles[i];
```

Once a tile is added, you have to store somewhere its real value. We made it just by adding a property called `cardType` which contains the value of `tiles` array `i-th` element.

```
tile.x=5+(tile.width+5)*(i%TILES_PER_ROW);
tile.y=5+(tile.height+5)*(Math.floor(i/TILES_PER_ROW));
```

Just place the tile to be part of a grid.

Notice the presence of the modulo (`%`) operator. Modulo calculates the remainder of the first operator divided by the second operator. So 5%3 will give 2, because 2 is the remainder of 5 divided by 3.

Also notice the properties involved in this process:

- `x`: x coordinate of the DisplayObject, in pixels from the left edge of the stage
- `y`: y coordinate of the DisplayObject, in pixels from the top edge of the stage
- `width`: the width of the DisplayObject, in pixels
- `height`: the height of the DisplayObject, in pixels

In our example, tile number zero is the upper left one, followed by tile number one at its right, then tile number two, and so on until tile number twenty, at the bottom-right of the stage.

The recurring `5` number is the spacing between tiles. Why don't you try to define it as a constant? It would be a good exercise at this time.

```
tile.gotoAndStop(NUMBER_OF_TILES/2+1);
```

As we said, the last frame of `tile_movieclip` object contains the tile graphics when facing down. `gotoAndStop(n)` tells tile DisplayObject to go to `n-th` frame and stop. In our case, it's showing the 20/2+1 = 11th frame, that is the tile facing down.

Picking tiles

We said we are going to pick tiles with a mouse click. To manage mouse events such as clicks, movements, and rollovers, AS3 provides a dedicated class called `MouseEvent`. The first thing we need to do is to import this new class.

Import it before main class declaration, in the code delimited by `// importing classes` just like you imported `Sprite` class:

```
// importing classes
import flash.display.Sprite;
import flash.events.MouseEvent;
// end of importing classes
```

`MouseEvent` class is contained in the `flash.events` package, that's why I had to import another package.

Now you are ready to handle mouse events. Modify the tile placing loop (the code between `// tile placing loop` and `// end of tile placing loop`) this way:

```
// tile placing loop
for (i:uint=0; i<NUMBER_OF_TILES; i++) {
  tile = new tile_movieclip();
  addChild(tile);
  tile.cardType=tiles[i];
  tile.x=5+(tile.width+5)*(i%TILES_PER_ROW);
  tile.y=5+(tile.height+5)*(Math.floor(i/TILES_PER_ROW));
  tile.gotoAndStop(NUMBER_OF_TILES/2+1);
  tile.buttonMode = true;
  tile.addEventListener(MouseEvent.CLICK,onTileClicked);
}
// end of tile placing loop
```

If you remember the previous example, you will see when you hover a tile there isn't anything that lets you know you can click on it. People are used to seeing a hand cursor when over some content they can click.

```
tile.buttonMode = true;
```

Setting `buttonMode` property to `true` will make the tile behave like a button, showing the hand pointer when the mouse is over it.

```
tile.addEventListener(MouseEvent.CLICK,onTileClicked);
```

A tile has to wait for the player to click on it. That's why we are using an event listener. An event is an occurrence of any type, and a listener may be described as a duty given to an entity, that patiently waits for the event to happen. Once it happens, the entity will do an assigned task.

 In the real world, imagine a light bulb (the entity) to have its own life. Its duty is to wait (listening) for someone to turn on the switch button. Once such an event occurs, the bulb does the assigned task: making electric current pass through its filament, heating it until it produces the light.

Back to our Concentration game, each tile waits for the mouse to click over it, and once it happens, executes the `onTileClicked` function. In this function, we will code everything that must happen when the player clicked on a tile.

Add this function inside the `Main` class but outside `Main` function, this way:

```
package {
  // importing classes
  import flash.display.Sprite;
  import flash.events.MouseEvent;
  // end of importing classes
  public class Main extends Sprite {
    public function Main(){
      ...
    }
    private function onTileClicked(e:MouseEvent) {
      trace("you picked a "+e.currentTarget.cardType);
      e.currentTarget.gotoAndStop(e.currentTarget.cardType+1);
    }
  }
}
```

First, notice function name `onTileClicked` is the same as the second parameter in the event listener. We also have a `MouseEvent` argument called e which will give us useful information about the entity that generated the event. In this case we'll use it to know which tile triggered the click event.

`onTileClicked` function is declared as `private` because it's meant to be used only by `Main` class.

 Fully explaining the difference between public and private functions is beyond the scope of this book, anyway keep in mind you will use **public** when you want the function to be called from classes outside the class in which it has been declared, and **private** when you want the function to be used only by the class in which it has been declared.

`currentTarget` property returns us the object that is actively processing the event. In our case, the tile the player just clicked.

Do you remember `cardType` property you set for each tile? You can access it through `e.currentTarget.cardType`. Not only do you know the hidden value that lies in the front of the card, but you can flip the card showing its content.

A simple `gotoAndStop(e.currentTarget.cardType+1)` method tells the tile to show the `cardType+1-th` frame. The `+1` should remind you that the frames start from 1 while tile values start from 0.

Test the movie and try to pick various tiles. You can pick all tiles and see their content both in the game and in the debug window.

The "graphic engine" is ready. At this time, you discovered how to:

Add and manage DisplayObjects on the stage on the fly.

Handle mouse click events.

That's everything the player is supposed to do: picking tiles.

Checking for matching tiles

It's time to let the player know whether he picked two matching tiles or not. Let's think about Concentration like a turn-based game; at every turn the player can pick no more than two cards before knowing if he has got a matching pick.

So we are going to add the following features:

- Don't let the player pick the same tile twice in a turn.
- Once he picked the second tile, check if selected tiles match.
- If they match, remove them from stage.
- If they do not match, turn them back again.

The idea is quite simple as we'll be using an array to store picked tiles. Once the array contains two elements (two picked tiles), we'll see if tile values match.

So we need to declare a new array to be available in all main class functions and make the NUMBER_OF_TILES constant available too. We'll be using both variables in onTileClicked function, so we need to make them available throughout the entire class.

 If a variable is declared inside a function, it's called **function level variable** or **local variable** and it's available only inside the function. If a variable is declared in the class, then it is called **class level variable** or **instance variable** and it will be available in the whole class, all functions included.

Modify class variable declaration and variables and constants block this way:

```
package {
    // importing classes
    import flash.display.Sprite;
    import flash.events.MouseEvent;
    // end of importing classes
    public class Main extends Sprite {
    private var pickedTiles:Array = new Array();
```

```
    private const NUMBER_OF_TILES:uint=20;
      public function Main() {
        // variables and constants
    // no more NUMBER_OF_TILES here
        const TILES_PER_ROW:uint=5;
        var tiles:Array=new Array();
        var tile:tile_movieclip;
        // end of variables and constants
        ...
      }
    }
  }
```

Nothing special as you can see, just remember to remove NUMBER_OF_TILES declaration from Main function or you will get an error as you can only define a variable once.

Now NUMBER_OF_TILES can be accessed throughout the whole class. As with onTileClicked function, we need to decide if we want to make it available to all classes that try to retrieve its value, or only by the class in which it has been defined (Main).

We want the latter case, so we set it to private. If we wanted the first case, we should have used public.

Now let's heavily rewrite onTileClicked function. Delete the existing one and write:

```
    private function onTileClicked(e:MouseEvent) {
      var picked:tile_movieclip=e.currentTarget as tile_movieclip;
      trace("you picked a "+e.currentTarget.cardType);
      // checking if the current tile has already been picked
      if (pickedTiles.indexOf(picked)==-1) {
        pickedTiles.push(picked);
        picked.gotoAndStop(picked.cardType+1);
      }
      // end checking if the current tile has already been picked
      // checking if we picked 2 tiles
      if (pickedTiles.length==2) {
        if (pickedTiles[0].cardType==pickedTiles[1].cardType) {
          // tiles match!!
          trace("tiles match!!!!");
          pickedTiles[0].removeEventListener(MouseEvent.
            CLICK,onTileClicked);
```

```
        pickedTiles[1].removeEventListener(MouseEvent.
CLICK,onTileClicked);
        removeChild(pickedTiles[0]);
        removeChild(pickedTiles[1]);
      } else {
        // tiles do not match
        trace("tiles do not match");
        pickedTiles[0].gotoAndStop(NUMBER_OF_TILES/2+1);
        pickedTiles[1].gotoAndStop(NUMBER_OF_TILES/2+1);
      }
      pickedTiles = new Array();
    }
    // end checking if we picked 2 tiles
}
```

First, we store the current picked tile in a variable called `picked`. Then we need to know if the current tile is the one the player just clicked.

```
if (pickedTiles.indexOf(picked)==-1) { ... }
```

`pickedTiles` is the array designed to store all picked tiles. So we need to check if the current tile (`picked`) is already in the array.

Remember I am using the three points (. . .) to indicate the block of code inside braces isn't changed or relevant at this time.

`indexOf` method searches for an item in an array and returns the index position of the item, or -1 if the item does not exist. So to ensure the picked tile is not the one the player just picked, we need to check if `indexOf(picked)` method of `pickedTiles` array is equal to `-1`.

The `if` statement allows execution of a block of code if a certain condition is true, and optionally can execute another block of code if the condition is false.

```
if (condition){
  // execute if condition is true
}
else {
  // execute if condition is false
}
```

Once we checked it's a new tile, we store it in `pickedTiles` array and show the tile's content.

We still don't know if this was the first or the second picked tile.

```
if (pickedTiles.length==2) {...}
```

This line counts the number of elements (picked tiles) in `pickedTiles` array thanks to `length` property that returns the number of elements in the array, and compares it with two.

Notice the difference between = and ==. The former assigns a value, the latter tests two expressions for equality.

If the condition is true, it means the player just picked the second tile and it's time to check if selected tiles match. If `pickedTiles` has two elements, the first will have index = 0 and the second index = 1, so to check if the content of picked tiles is the same, it is just necessary to add another `if` statement:

```
if (pickedTiles[0].cardType==pickedTiles[1].cardType) { ... }
```

that simply compares the `cardType` attribute of both array elements.

If they match, it's time to remove the tiles for good. Before doing it, we have to tell picked tiles not to listen anymore for mouse clicks. All in all, they are about to be removed so why make them do useless tasks?

```
pickedTiles[0].removeEventListener(MouseEvent.CLICK,onTileClicked);
pickedTiles[1].removeEventListener(MouseEvent.CLICK,onTileClicked);
```

Remove the mouse click listener. Notice it has the same syntax as `addEventListener`: same event, same function to be executed.

> Removing listeners when they are no longer needed is not just a good habit, but an imperative thing to do when working with complex scripts that could slow down the execution if a lot of listeners are waiting to be triggered.

As both click listeners have been removed, it's time to remove tiles object themselves.

```
removeChild(pickedTiles[0]);
removeChild(pickedTiles[1]);
```

`removeChild()` removes the DisplayObject from the Display List in the same way `addChild()` added it.

And the operations to do in case of success are over.

Now it's time to see what to do when selected tiles do not match.

```
pickedTiles[0].gotoAndStop(NUMBER_OF_TILES/2+1);
pickedTiles[1].gotoAndStop(NUMBER_OF_TILES/2+1);
```

That's why we had to define NUMBER_OF_TILES as a class level variable. It must be accessible from onTileClicked function.

```
pickedTiles = new Array();
```

The last thing to do, whether the tiles match or not, is to clear the pickedTiles array to let the player pick two more tiles. Constructing it again will make you have a brand new empty array.

Test the game and you won't be able to see the second tile. But if you look at trace() outputs you will see that it works. When it says tiles match, they are removed. When it says they don't match, they turn covered. So what's wrong with the second tile?

Do you remember a game is like a movie? Everything behind the stage works correctly, but there is still to work at what players will see.

Let's suppose we have a bullet time mode, the Concentration game would look like this:

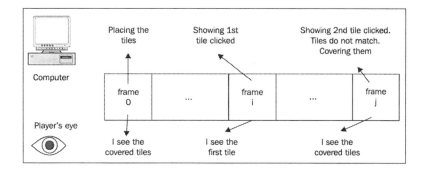

The player is not able to see everything the script is doing. At frame 0 the script places the tiles, and the player is able to view the tiles. At frame i, the script uncovers a tile and the player is able to view the uncovered tile. At frame j, the script uncovers a tile, then sees picked tiles do not match, and covers them again. The player now just sees all covered tiles. Obviously it's not just the player, but what Flash shows to the screen.

Making the player see what happened

To get a playable game you just need to wait a second after the player picked the second tile before removing/covering them.

This can be done by adding a timer in the game. Timer class included in flash.utils package will let us use timers, and TimerEvent class included in flash.events handles timer events.

Let's start importing the classes and declaring a new variable. Change your script until `Main` function looks like this:

```
package {
  // importing classes
  import flash.display.Sprite;
  import flash.events.MouseEvent;
  import flash.events.TimerEvent;
  import flash.utils.Timer;
  // end of importing classes
  public class Main extends Sprite {
    private var pickedTiles:Array = new Array();
    private const NUMBER_OF_TILES:uint=20;
    private var pauseGame:Timer;
    public function Main() {
      ...
    }
  }
}
```

We just imported the two time-related classes in our package and created a new `Timer` variable called `pauseGame`. It will come into play when the player selects the second tile, so modify the block that checks if we picked two tiles this way:

```
// checking if we picked 2 tiles
if (pickedTiles.length==2) {
  pauseGame=new Timer(1000,1);
  pauseGame.start();
  if (pickedTiles[0].cardType==pickedTiles[1].cardType) {
    // tiles match!!
    trace("tiles match!!!!");
    pauseGame.addEventListener(TimerEvent.TIMER_COMPLETE,removeTiles);
  } else {
    // tiles do not match
    trace("tiles do not match");
    pauseGame.addEventListener(TimerEvent.TIMER_COMPLETE,resetTiles);
  }
  // no more pickedTiles = new Array();
}
// end checking if we picked 2 tiles
```

Once we know the player just picked the second tile, it's time to wait for one second.

```
pauseGame=new Timer(1000,1);
```

Let's initialize the timer with the constructor, which is the function that generates it. The first parameter defines the delay between timer events, in milliseconds, while the second one specifies the number of repetitions. In this case, `pauseGame` will wait for 1 second only once.

Again, you can use a constant, to store the number of milliseconds. I am not using it because it should be clear how to use variables and constants and I want to focus on new features.

```
pauseGame.start();
```

To make the timer start, use `start()` method.

When the timer reaches 1 second, it will dispatch a `TimerEvent.TIMER_COMPLETE` event. So we have to make `pauseGame` listen for such an event.

```
pauseGame.addEventListener(TimerEvent.TIMER_COMPLETE,removeTiles);
```

and

```
pauseGame.addEventListener(TimerEvent.TIMER_COMPLETE,resetTiles);
```

Will make the program wait for the `Timer` object to complete its delay (one second) and then call `removeTiles` or `resetTiles` function.

These functions will just handle the removing and the resetting of tiles in the same way we did before. Add the functions inside `Main` class but outside `Main` function, just as you did with `onTileClicked` function:

```
private function removeTiles(e:TimerEvent) {
  pauseGame.removeEventListener(TimerEvent.
    TIMER_COMPLETE,removeTiles);
  pickedTiles[0].removeEventListener(MouseEvent.CLICK,onTileClicked);
  pickedTiles[1].removeEventListener(MouseEvent.CLICK,onTileClicked);
  removeChild(pickedTiles[0]);
  removeChild(pickedTiles[1]);
  pickedTiles = new Array();
}
```

As you can see the function just removes the listeners and the tiles, just as before.

```
private function resetTiles(e:TimerEvent) {
  pauseGame.removeEventListener(TimerEvent.TIMER_COMPLETE,resetTiles);
  pickedTiles[0].gotoAndStop(NUMBER_OF_TILES/2+1);
  pickedTiles[1].gotoAndStop(NUMBER_OF_TILES/2+1);
  pickedTiles = new Array();
}
```

and this one just covers the tiles again.

Notice how both functions remove `TimerEvent` listener and clear `pickedTiles` array by initializing it again. Also, such array is no longer cleared in the block where we checked if we picked 2 tiles block. Why not? Because it would clear the picked tiles array before the script knows which tiles to remove/cover, as it happens after a second.

Run the program: it works! You can see the second tile for 1 second before the script decides what to do. Your Concentration game is finished!

No, it's not.

Try to quickly pick three or four tiles. You can, because nobody told the script to ignore clicks when it's waiting the second necessary to show you the tile you just picked. So you can quickly take a look at more than two cards during a single turn. That's cheating.

We can see more than two tiles if we quickly select a bunch of them.

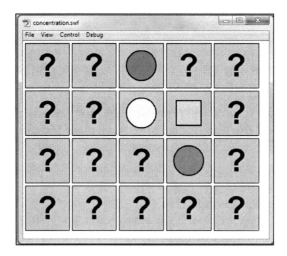

Believe it or not, although the game is not finished yet, you have learned everything you need to create a basic Concentration prototype. You just saw how to:

- Execute different blocks of code according to a specific condition
- Remove DisplayObject from the stage
- Use timers to make the game wait

Let's make life impossible for those die hard cheaters!

Preventing the player from cheating

Players will always try to cheat. When making a game, don't expect people to respect any policy of playing.

We must prevent the player from continuing to pick tiles when the script is waiting to let him see the second tile he picked.

We need another instance variable, of a new type. Change class level variables and constants by coding this way:

```
// class level variables and constants
private var pickedTiles:Array = new Array();
private const NUMBER_OF_TILES:uint=20;
private var pauseGame:Timer;
private var canPick:Boolean=true;
// end of class level variables and constants
```

Boolean variables can only have a `true` or `false` value. `canPick` variable will decide whether the player can pick another tile or not. Initially, it's `true` because the player can pick a tile when the game begins.

Now change the `onTileClicked` function this way:

```
private function onTileClicked(e:MouseEvent) {
  if(canPick){
    var picked:tile_movieclip=e.currentTarget as tile_movieclip;
    trace("you picked a "+e.currentTarget.cardType);
    // checking if the current tile has already been picked
    if (pickedTiles.indexOf(picked)==-1) {
      pickedTiles.push(picked);
      picked.gotoAndStop(picked.cardType+1);
    }
    // end checking if the current tile has already been picked
    // checking if we picked 2 tiles
    if (pickedTiles.length==2) {
      canPick=false;
      pauseGame=new Timer(1000,1);
      pauseGame.start();
      if (pickedTiles[0].cardType==pickedTiles[1].cardType) {
        // tiles match!!
        trace("tiles match!!!!");
      pauseGame.addEventListener(TimerEvent.
        TIMER_COMPLETE,removeTiles);
      } else {
        // tiles do not match
```

```
        trace("tiles do not match");
        pauseGame.addEventListener(TimerEvent.
          TIMER_COMPLETE,resetTiles);
      }
      // no more pickedTiles = new Array();
    }
    // end checking if we picked 2 tiles
  }
}
```

The entire function is executed only if the player can pick a tile. And that's right. When the player picked the second tile, simply set canPick value to false and you're done. The player cannot pick anymore.

The last thing to complete the game is letting the player be able to pick tiles again once the game has covered/removed the tiles.

Change removeTiles function this way:

```
private function removeTiles(e:TimerEvent) {
pauseGame.removeEventListener(TimerEvent.TIMER_COMPLETE,removeTiles);
pickedTiles[0].removeEventListener(MouseEvent.CLICK,onTileClicked);
pickedTiles[1].removeEventListener(MouseEvent.CLICK,onTileClicked);
  removeChild(pickedTiles[0]);
  removeChild(pickedTiles[1]);
  pickedTiles = new Array();
  canPick = true;
}
```

And do the same with resetTiles function:

```
private function resetTiles(e:TimerEvent) {
  pauseGame.removeEventListener(TimerEvent.TIMER_COMPLETE,resetTiles);
  pickedTiles[0].gotoAndStop(NUMBER_OF_TILES/2+1);
  pickedTiles[1].gotoAndStop(NUMBER_OF_TILES/2+1);
  pickedTiles = new Array();
  canPick = true;
}
```

Simply set canPick value to false and again enable the player to pick tiles.

Test the movie. No more cheating!

Now we could just sit and play, but we want more.

Fine-tuning the game: adding educational content

At the beginning of this chapter I said this was going to be an educational game. It's time to fine-tune the game and add educational content.

 Polishing your game is a critical process, as it makes the difference between a great game and "just another game". Once you have a playable prototype like our Concentration game, it's time to fuel up your creativity and try to distinguish it from the masses.

What if there were no more duplicate tiles with the same shape but, for instance, a tile with a green circle and a tile with a "Green Circle" text? Children would need to remember both tiles' positions and their meaning.

How can we add this feature without rewriting too much code? In two simple steps:

1. Create 20 distinct tiles with values from 0 to 19.

2. Let the script know matching tiles are 0 and 1, 2 and 3, 4 and 5, and so on.

This is the final code, stripped of all comments and `trace()` outputs. There isn't any new concept, so you should be able to understand what it does by yourself.

`Main` function:

```
public function Main() {
  const TILES_PER_ROW:uint=5;
  var tiles:Array=new Array();
  var tile:tile_movieclip;
  for (var i:uint=0; i<NUMBER_OF_TILES; i++) {
    tiles.push(i);
  }
  var swap,tmp:uint;
  for (i=NUMBER_OF_TILES-1; i>0; i--) {
    swap=Math.floor(Math.random()*i);
    tmp=tiles[i];
    tiles[i]=tiles[swap];
    tiles[swap]=tmp;
  }
  for (i=0; i<NUMBER_OF_TILES; i++) {
    tile=new tile_movieclip();
    addChild(tile);
    tile.cardType=tiles[i];
    tile.x=5+(tile.width+5)*(i%TILES_PER_ROW);
    tile.y=5+(tile.height+5)*(Math.floor(i/TILES_PER_ROW));
```

```
        tile.gotoAndStop(NUMBER_OF_TILES+1);
        tile.buttonMode=true;
        tile.addEventListener(MouseEvent.CLICK,onTileClicked);
    }
}
```

This is `onTileClicked` function

```
private function onTileClicked(e:MouseEvent) {
  if(canPick){
    var picked:tile_movieclip=e.currentTarget as tile_movieclip;
    if (pickedTiles.indexOf(picked)==-1) {
      pickedTiles.push(picked);
      picked.gotoAndStop(picked.cardType+1);
    }
    if (pickedTiles.length==2) {
      canPick=false;
      pauseGame=new Timer(1000,1);
      pauseGame.start();
      if (Math.floor(pickedTiles[0].cardType/2)==
        Math.floor(pickedTiles[1].cardType/2)) {
      pauseGame.addEventListener(TimerEvent.
        TIMER_COMPLETE,removeTiles);
      } else {
      pauseGame.addEventListener(TimerEvent.
        TIMER_COMPLETE,resetTiles);
      }
    }
  }
}
```

and this is `resetTiles` function

```
private function resetTiles(e:TimerEvent) {
  pauseGame.removeEventListener(TimerEvent.TIMER_COMPLETE,resetTiles);
  pickedTiles[0].gotoAndStop(NUMBER_OF_TILES+1);
  pickedTiles[1].gotoAndStop(NUMBER_OF_TILES+1);
  pickedTiles = new Array();
  canPick = true;
}
```

The other functions and declarations remain unchanged.

And this is an example of a matching pair:

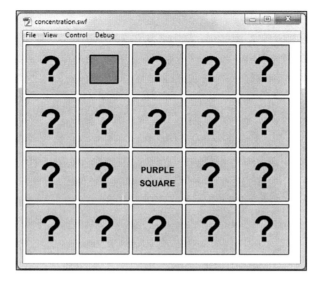

Purple square picture is tile 18 and "purple square" text is tile 19. They match.

Your Concentration game is now complete and ready to be played.

Summary

Concentration, while being an easy game to make and play, opened the path to the world of programming games. Now you are able to set up a Flash project to make a game, work with DisplayObjects, interact with basic data types such as variables and arrays and manage mouse and timer listeners.

Where to go now

Test your AS3 skills adding new features to the game. I am giving you two suggestions:

1. Detect when the player completed the game. You can easily do it by creating a new instance variable that counts the successful matches and checks if they are equal to the total number of tiles / 2.

2. Count how many tries the player is making using another instance variable that you'll increment every time the player picks the second tile. Print these values in the Output window.

2
Minesweeper

Minesweeper is a single player turn-based game whose goal is to clear a mine field without being killed by a mine. The mine field is represented by a grid of covered tiles, some of them hiding a mine. Grid size and number of mined tiles vary according to difficulty level. At each turn, the player must pick a tile with a mouse click. If he clicks on a tile without a mine, a digit with the amount of adjacent tiles containing a mine will appear. Using logic, the player must click all free tiles. If he hits a mine, the game is over. With a right-click on the tile, the player can "flag" that tile, to help him remember where he thinks there is a mine. In some versions, the player must flag all mines.

In this chapter you will learn how to make a complete Minesweeper game, using these main techniques:

- Multidimensional arrays
- Loops with an unknown (yet not infinite) number of iterations
- Functions with return values
- Logical AND and OR operators
- Recursive functions
- Dynamic text fields
- DisplayObjects hierarchy and DisplayObjectContainers
- Adding custom variables to objects

Moreover, you will discover new AS3 features that will help you in the making of the game.

Defining game design

Although there have been many variants of the game since it first appeared in the early 1980s, the game is best known for being included in every Windows OS release. The beginner version has a 9x9 tiles mine field with 10 mines in it, and is the one we are going to create.

There are also a couple of major features I want you to develop:

- Flash movies have a reserved use of right mouse button, so to flag a tile we will use *Shift*+click.
- It can be frustrating when you start a game and you first click on a mine, causing a "sudden death", so we'll make sure the first click is always on an empty tile.

But first let's create a working prototype.

Creating the empty field

The very first step in the development of a Minesweeper game is the creation of the empty field where mines will be placed.

The idea: As seen in the Concentration game, an array is the best way to represent a set of elements such as cards or tiles, so we'll be using an array. At this time, we have two options. Look at the picture (using a 4x4 field for the sake of simplicity):

0	1	2	3
4	5	6	7
8	9	10	11
12	13	14	15

0,0	0,1	0,2	0,3
1,0	1,1	1,2	1,3
2,0	2,1	2,2	2,3
3,0	3,1	3,2	3,3

On the left, a representation of the field as an array of tiles, just like the one used in the Concentration game. Each tile is represented by an index from 0 to 15. On the right, it's the same field represented by an array in which each row is an array of tiles. Think about it as an array of lines, and each line is an array of tiles. This kind of array is called **multi-dimensional** array.

Unlike single dimensional arrays, with just one index representing a linear set of data, multi-dimensional arrays allow you to nest arrays into arrays.

A two-dimensional array intuitively manages information that in the real world is represented in two dimensions, such as a chessboard or the mine field we are about to create. That is, it's a lot easier to figure out the second tile of that the third line is at index 2,1 (remember an array index starts with zero) rather than at index 9. Even accessing elements is more intuitive, while in the case of the first example to access the second tile of the third line you have to do something like:

```
myElement = myArray[2*tilesPerRow+1]
```

with a multi-dimensional array you can simply access with something like:

```
myElement = myArray[2][1]
```

Moreover, we already used a single dimensional array in Concentration, so it's time to meet multi-dimensional arrays.

Since the entire mine field will be represented by an array, we have to decide how to code the various statuses a tile can have. We will use a two-dimensional array in which every element can have one of these values:

- 0 if represents a tile with no mines in it and no mines in its adjacent tiles
- 1-8 if represents a tile with no mines in it and with 1 to 8 mines in its adjacent tiles
- 9 if represents a tile with a mine in it. You can even define a constant called something like HAS_MINE to store this value

The flag won't be represented by a numeric value since it does not affect the game, it's just a marker.

So at first let's create a two-dimensional array completely filled by zeros.

The development: Create a new file (**File | New**) then from **New Document** window select **Actionscript 3.0.** Set its properties as width to 550 px, height to 400 px, background color to #FFFFFF (white), and frame rate to 24. Also define the Document Class as Main and save the file as minesweeper.fla.

Without closing minesweeper.fla, create a new file and from **New Document** window select **ActionScript 3.0 Class.** Save this file as Main.as in the same path you saved minesweeper.fla. It's the same process described during the creation of the Concentration game, so if you have some troubles refer to *Chapter 1, Concentration.*

Now in `Main.as` file write:

```
package {
  // importing classes
  import flash.display.Sprite;
  import flash.events.MouseEvent;
  import flash.events.TimerEvent;
  import flash.utils.Timer;
  // end of importing classes
  public class Main extends Sprite {
    // class level variables
    private const FIELD_W:uint=9;
    private const FIELD_H:uint=9;
    private var mineField:Array=new Array();
    // end of class level variables
    public function Main() {
      // mine field creation
      for (var i:uint=0; i<FIELD_H; i++) {
        mineField[i]=new Array();
        for (var j:uint=0; j<FIELD_W; j++) {
          mineField[i].push(0);
        }
        trace("Row "+i+": "+mineField[i]);
      }
      trace("The whole mine field: "+mineField);
      // end of mine field creation
    }
  }
}
```

Test the movie and you'll see:

```
Row 0: 0,0,0,0,0,0,0,0,0
Row 1: 0,0,0,0,0,0,0,0,0
Row 2: 0,0,0,0,0,0,0,0,0
Row 3: 0,0,0,0,0,0,0,0,0
Row 4: 0,0,0,0,0,0,0,0,0
Row 5: 0,0,0,0,0,0,0,0,0
Row 6: 0,0,0,0,0,0,0,0,0
Row 7: 0,0,0,0,0,0,0,0,0
Row 8: 0,0,0,0,0,0,0,0,0
The whole mine field: 0,0,0,0,0, ... ,0,0,0,0
```

As you can see, each row is an array of numbers, and the whole mine field is an array of rows (arrays).

First, notice mouse and timer classes have already been imported. We know we are going to use mouse clicks and timers, so why not import all required classes right now? At least, I won't bother you by asking you to include them later.

FIELD_W and FIELD_H class level (instance) constants store respectively the width and the height of the mine field, while mineField variable is going to be our multi-dimensional array. At the moment, it's declared and constructed just as a normal array.

Also notice I declared them as class level variables/constants even if I am not using them outside the main function at the moment. But I know I'll do it later. Going through a stage of game design allows you to plan where to use critical variables, and speeds up declaration since there is no cut/paste of variable declarations here and there.

```
for (var i:uint=0; i<FIELD_H; i++) { ... }
```

Looping through all mine field rows. Obviously the height of the mine field represents the number of rows while the width represents the number of columns.

```
mineField[i]=new Array();
```

Here we go: The i-th element of mine field array is constructed as an empty array. Congratulations. You just built your first multi-dimensional array.

```
for (var j:uint=0; j<FIELD_W; j++) {
  mineField[i].push(0);
}
```

Just fill the newborn array with as many zeros as the number of columns in the mine field.

And now the mine field is ready to be filled with mines.

Placing the mines

Once the empty mine field has been created, we need to add the mines. We just have to define how many mines we want in the game, then place them in random spots.

The idea: We know a mined tile will have 9 value, so the idea is to select a random tile, check if its value is 0, then set it to 9. You must check if its value is zero to avoid placing a mine on a tile that already contains a mine. You would end up with a number of mined tiles that's less than the one you defined.

The development: Remove all previous `traces` to clean the code and change class level variables this way:

```
// class level variables
private const FIELD_W:uint=9;
private const FIELD_H:uint=9;
private const NUM_MINES:uint=10;
private var mineField:Array=new Array();
// end of class level variables
```

`NUM_MINES` represents the number of mines we want to place in the mine field. Then after the end of mine field creation add this code:

```
// placing mines
var placedMines:uint=0;
var randomRow,randomCol:uint;
while (placedMines<NUM_MINES) {
  randomRow = Math.floor(Math.random()*FIELD_H)
  randomCol = Math.floor(Math.random()*FIELD_W);
  if (mineField[randomRow][randomCol]==0) {
    mineField[randomRow][randomCol]=9;
    placedMines++;
  }
}
trace("My dangerous mine field: "+mineField);
// end of placing mines
```

Test the movie and you'll see something like this in the output window:

My dangerous mine field: 0,0,0,0,0,0,0,0,0,0,0,0,9,0,0,0,0,0,9,0,0,0,0
,0,0,0,0,0,0,0,9,0,9,0,0,0,0,0,0,0,9,0,0,9,0,0,0,0,0,0,9,9,0,0,0,0
,0,0,0,0,0,0,0,0,0,0,9,0,0,0,0,0,0,9,0,0,0,0

Obviously this will change every time because it's randomly generated, but there will always be `NUM_MINES` values set to 9.

```
var placedMines:uint=0;
```

Declares a new variable called `placedMines` that will store the number of mines we placed so far. Obviously it starts at 0.

```
var randomRow,randomCol:uint;
```

Declares two variables used to store random numbers representing the row and column in which we want to place a mine.

```
while (placedMines<NUM_MINES) { ... }
```

while loop is really easy to understand because it just executes the block of code as long as its condition is true.

```
while(condition==true){ ... }
```

In this case everything between { and } will be executed until the condition is not true.

In a practical example, this for loop:

```
for(var i:uint=0;i<10;i++){ ... }
```

and this while loop:

```
var i:uint=0;
while(i<10){
   ...
   i++
}
```

work the same way, because both will reiterate until i is less than 10 and both increase i by 1 at the end of each iteration.

Why didn't I just use another for loop? Because while is a better loop when you don't know how many times you will need to reiterate the code. In this case, I don't know how many times I will try to place a mine because I don't know if the random tile I am going to pick already contains a mine, forcing me to choose another one.

The while loop in the code will iterate over the block between { and } until the number of mines is equal to the number of mines we want.

```
randomRow = Math.floor(Math.random()*FIELD_H);
randomCol = Math.floor(Math.random()*FIELD_W);
```

Simply generates two random integer numbers between 0 (included) and the number of rows/columns (excluded) in the mine field.

```
if (mineField[randomRow][randomCol]==0) { ... }
```

Checks if the mine field contains an empty tile in the random row and column we've just chosen. Notice how you can access multi-dimensional arrays:

```
value = multi_array[dim1_][dim_2]...[dim_n]
```

Just specify the series of indexes one after another.

```
mineField[randomRow][randomCol]=9;
```

Places a mine in the randomly chosen tile.

```
placedMines++;
```

We know we just placed a mine so we have to increment by 1 the number of placed mines, to see if `while` loop should reiterate again.

At the end of the code, the mine field will contain exactly NUM_MINES mines, no matter how many times you tried to place a mine in a tile already containing a mine.

Adding the digits

Now the array is filled with empty tiles and mines, so it's time to complete it with the digits representing the amount of adjacent mines to every empty tile.

The idea: There are two strategies to determine the number of mines around a tile: We can locate all mines and for every mine increase by one the value of all adjacent tiles that do not contain a mine, or we can locate all empty tiles, and for each tile count the number of mines in its adjacent tiles. It's just a matter of speed, and since in traditional Minesweeper games there are less mines than empty tiles, we can reasonably think the first method is the fastest.

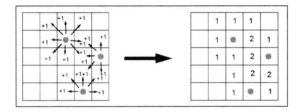

This is how it works: every mine increases by one the value of its adjacent tiles to give the complete mapping of the tile's adjacent mines.

The development: Remove all previous `traces` to clean unnecessary code and add after `// end of placing mines`:

```
// placing digits
for (i=0; i<FIELD_H; i++) {
  for (j=0; j<FIELD_W; j++) {
    if (mineField[i][j]==9) {
      // to the left
      if (j!=0&&mine_field[i][j-1]!=9) {
        mineField[i][j-1]++;
      }
      // to the right
```

```
      if (j!=FIELD_W-1&&mineField[i][j+1]!=9) {
        mineField[i][j+1]++;
      }
      // up
      if (i!=0&&mineField[i-1][j]!=9) {
        mineField[i-1][j]++;
      }
      // down
      if (i!=FIELD_H-1&&mineField[i+1][j]!=9) {
        mineField[i+1][j]++;
      }
      // up left
      if (i!=0&&j!=0&&mineField[i-1][j-1]!=9) {
        mineField[i-1][j-1]++;
      }
      // up right
      if (i!=0&&j!=FIELD_W-1&&mineField[i-1][j+1]!=9) {
        mineField[i-1][j+1]++;
      }
      // down left
      if (i!=FIELD_H-1&&j!=0&&mineField[i+1][j-1]!=9) {
        mineField[i+1][j-1]++;
      }
      // down right
      if (i!=FIELD_H-1&&j!=FIELD_W-1&&mineField[i+1][j+1]!=9) {
        mineField[i+1][j+1]++;
      }
    }
  }
}
var debugString:String;
trace("My complete and formatted mine field: ");
for (i=0; i<FIELD_H; i++) {
   debugString="";
  for (j=0; j<FIELD_W; j++) {
    debugString+=mineField[i][j]+" ";
  }
  trace(debugString);
}
// end of placing digits
```

Yes, it's a lot of code but don't worry: there is room for optimization.

Test the movie and look at your output window:

```
My complete and formatted mine field:

0  0  1  9  2  9  1  0  0

0  0  1  1  2  2  2  1  0

0  0  0  0  0  2  9  2  0

0  0  0  0  1  4  9  3  0

1  1  1  0  1  9  9  2  0

2  9  2  0  1  2  3  2  1

2  9  2  0  0  0  1  9  2

1  1  1  0  0  0  1  2  9

0  0  0  0  0  0  0  1  1
```

As usual your result will be different, but it will represent a Minesweeper level.

I used the same couple of `for` loops that were used before to scan the entire array.

```
if (mineField[i][j]==9) { ... }
```

This entire block is executed only if the tile I am currently checking contains a mine.

The rest of the code simply checks if adjacent tiles exist and do not contain a mine. In this case, their value is increased.

```
// to the left
if (j!=0&&mineField[i][j-1]!=9) {
    mineField[i][j-1]++;
}
```

When checking for the tile on the left, first we must know if we aren't already on the first column: in this case there can't be any tile on the left.

 != is the inequality operator and acts as the opposite of the equality operator (==) testing two expressions for inequality.

Be careful when accessing array elements. Trying to access array elements that do not exist will cause errors in the code.

If we aren't on the first column (j value is different than 0) and the tile on the left does not contain a mine, then we can increase by one the value of the tile on the left.

The && is the logical AND operator. The and operator returns `true` if both expressions are true, in this case if `j` is different than zero AND `mineField[i][j-1]` is different than nine.

```
// to the right
if (j!=FIELD_W-1&&mineField[i][j+1]!=9) {
  mineField[i][j+1]++;
}
```

Same concept applied to the tile on the right. First we must check if the current tile is not on the last column (`j` value is different than the field width minus one, or `FIELD_W-1`), then we check if the tile on the right contains a mine, and increase by one the value of the tile on the right if it doesn't.

This concept is repeated for all eight possible directions. At the end of the couple of `for` loops, I just made another quick loop to display the finished mine field in a readable way. This will help you to check everything works fine when you test the complete game.

Optimization needed

As you probably noticed, writing the code for the digits was extremely boring. You had to repeat eight similar controls to check for tile values. Not to mention that you had to verify you were working on existing tiles.

When you realize you are writing pieces of code that look similar and do similar operations, it's time to optimize the code.

Let's start with the `if` checking for tile existence and value. Wouldn't it be good if there was a unique instruction to determine if the tile exists and in that case to retrieve its value?

Well, it exists, it's called `tileValue` and you are about to make it.

Add this new function to your class:

```
private function tileValue(row,col:uint):int {
  if(mineField[row]==undefined || mineField[row][col]==undefined){
    return -1
  } else {
    return mineField[row][col];
  }
}
```

You've already seen functions and how to add them to your class when you added the mouse click and timer listeners during the making of the Concentration game. Now it's time to create custom functions to make our life easier.

```
private function tileValue(row,col:uint):int { ... }
```

This is the way you specify the function that requires two unsigned integer arguments and returns an integer. A function does not just execute a code, like the ones you met during the making of the Concentration game, but can give a value as a result.

Just think about a function like a mad witch. You give her some strange stuff such as bat wings and lizard tails, and after making something mysterious she gives you a potion to turn someone into a frog. The great thing is once you've made your functions (witch) you don't need to know how they do the magic anymore.

Back to Minesweeper, you give `tileValue` function two unsigned integers, the row and the column number of the tile you want to know the value of, and it returns you an integer: the value of the tile in the selected row and column, or `-1` if the tile does not exist.

The core of the function lies here:

```
if(mineField[row]==undefined||mineField[row][col]==undefined){ ... }
```

this is the line that checks if the tile exists. Accessing an array index that does not exist, returns `undefined`. We can look for `undefined` to check if an array element exists.

 The `||` is the logical OR operator. The logical OR returns `true` if either or both expressions are true, in this case if `mineField[row]` is equal to `undefined` or `mineField[row][col]` is equal to `undefined`.

Also, checking for the second dimension index `mineField[row][col]` after checking for the first one `mineField[row]` has its meaning: performing a logical OR, the condition is true as soon as `mineField[row]` is undefined, so `mineField[row][col]` won't be checked unless `mineField[row]` is not undefined. This will present us a warning because trying to access a two-dimensional index when the first dimensional index is `undefined` throws a warning message.

```
return -1
```

This is how you can return a result from a function: `return value` or `return(value)` will make function return `value` when called.

We could return any value that is not used already (0-9) such as 10 or 99, but it is a standard to return -1 to indicate an error when programming.

Now we have a custom function doing the dirty job for us, but there is still room for optimization: finding the value of surrounding tiles.

i-1,j-1	i-1,j	i-1,j+1
i,j-1	i,j	i,j+1
i+1,j-1	i+1,j	i+1,j+1

i and j being the starting indexes, values range from i-1 to i+1 and from j-1 to j+1. Why not include them in another couple of `for` loops?

That's what the couple of `for` loops to place digits becomes:

```
for (i=0; i<FIELD_H; i++) {
  for (j=0; j<FIELD_W; j++) {
    if (mineField[i][j]==9) {
      for (var ii:int =-1; ii<=1; ii++) {
        for (var jj:int =-1; jj<=1; jj++) {
          if (ii!=0||jj!=0) {
            if (tileValue(i+ii,j+jj)!=9&&tileValue(i+ii,j+jj)!=-1) {
              mineField[i+ii][j+jj]++;
            }
          }
        }
      }
    }
  }
}
```

As you can see, I added another couple of `for` loops counting from -1 to +1. The new variables used in the loops are `ii` and `jj`.

```
if (ii!=0||jj!=0) { ... }
```

You have to check if `ii` or `jj` are different than `0`, because if both `ii` and `jj` are `0`, this means I am on the tile itself and not on a surrounding one.

```
if (tileValue(i+ii,j+jj)!=9&&tileValue(i+ii,j+jj)!=-1) { ... }
```

This is how I use `tileValue` function to check if the surrounding tile is not a mine (different than 9) and exists (different than -1).

```
mineField[i+ii][j+jj]++;
```

Incrementing the surrounding tile the same way as before optimization.

At the end of this process, the entire mine field is ready.

Placing tiles on stage

It's time to make the player see something, so prepare yourself to design some cute tiles.

The idea: The simplest way to place tiles on stage is to create a movie clip with a frame for each tile state, then add it on the stage.

The development: In `minesweeper.fla`, create a new Movie Clip symbol called `tile_movieclip` and set it as exportable for ActionScript making sure the export name is also `tile_movieclip`. Leave all other settings at their default values, just like you did during the making of Concentration game.

Now you need to draw four types of tiles, one for each frame.

- frame 1: the covered tile
- frame 2: the clicked tile with the digit
- frame 3: the tile you don't want to see: the mine.
- frame 4: the flagged tile

I know in Windows Minesweeper there is the question mark tile too, but we're not going to be adding this feature in our version, since solving a 9x9 game is more a matter of speed.

Try to draw tiles in a way that a complete 9x9 field fits well in the stage, so don't make them too big or too small. Also make sure they're all exactly the same size on each frame. The ones I made are squares with a 20 pixels side, with registration point at (0,0).

Here they are:

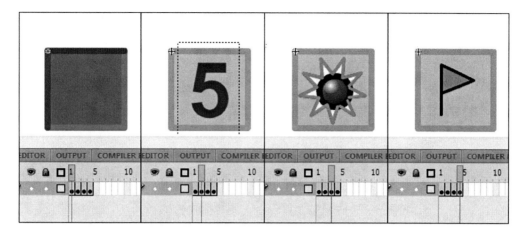

As said during the making of Concentration, you should be familiar with timeline and drawing, but I want to focus on the text field you have to draw.

As you can see in the picture, I inserted a text field with a 5 in it, but its content will vary from nothing (an empty string) to represent a safe tile with no mines around it, to any integer number between 1 and 8, to represent a safe tile with some mines around it.

I could have made you draw nine tiles, one for each number from 1 to 8 plus a tile with no numbers, but it would have been a malpractice. We will use a Dynamic Text to change text field's value on the fly.

To turn a text field in a Dynamic Text, just select **Dynamic Text** in Text type and give it a name in the **Instance name** field. This name, in our case `tile_text`, will be the way we'll access the text field in the script.

Also, make sure Selectable is unchecked or the player will be able to select the text and the cursor will change as if you were over a text in an HTML page.

Finally, click on **Embed...** and check **Numerals [0..9]** because that's the characters we are going to use.

The previous settings should look like this:

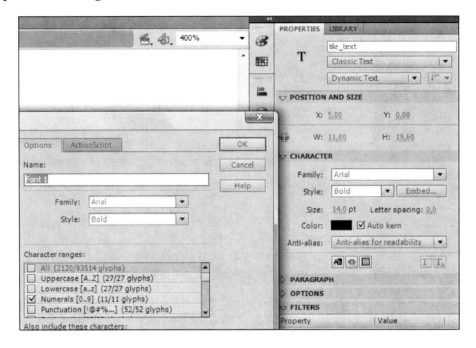

If you create a dynamic text field without embedding any font, once executed the game looks for that font on the user's computer. If it does not find it, the font is replaced with a default one. To prevent this you can use common fonts such as Arial or Verdana, or embed the fonts you are using in your game.

Embedding brings a lot of benefits, such as anti-aliasing, transparency, and the complete freedom of using the font you prefer.

The cost of this technique is an embedded font increases the file size of your game. That's why we must carefully select the characters we want to embed.

Once the tile movieclip has been created, it's time to turn back editing `Main.as` file. First we need two more class level variables:

```
// class level variables
private const FIELD_W:uint=9;
private const FIELD_H:uint=9;
private const NUM_MINES:uint=10;
private var mineField:Array=new Array();
private var game_container:Sprite=new Sprite();
private var tile:tile_movieclip;
// end of class level variables
```

We will use `tile` variable to create `tile_movieclip` instances, following the same concept already explained during the making of Concentration.

The interesting line anyway is the creation of a new sprite called `game_container` which may seem useless. You already have a tile with everything you need, why should you create another Sprite?

It's time to deeply dive into Display List I quickly introduced during the creation of Concentration game.

You know the Display List is the list that contains all visible Flash content, but it's not just a matter of visualization. The Display List also manages objects depth and hierarchy.

If you add two objects on the Display List, and they overlap then the second object will be placed over the first one, covering it. Same thing if you add a third objects, it will be placed over the first and the second ones, covering them, and so on. It's as if they were layered.

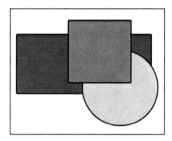

In the previous picture, here's what you see if you add to the Display List the blue rectangle, then the green circle, then the red square. Display List's depth starts from zero, so the rectangle, the circle, and the square will have respectively a depth of 0, 1, and 2.

About the hierarchy, the Display List has three types of objects:

- The stage, the father of the Display List hierarchy. Every Flash movie has one and only one stage object that contains the main class (called `Main` in our case).

- DisplayObjectContainer, an object capable of containing other DisplayObjects and DisplayObject Containers as children.

- DisplayObjects: any visual element. After a DisplayObject is created, it won't appear on screen until it's added to a DisplayObjectContainer. Sprites and MovieClips are both DisplayObjects and DisplayObjectContainers.

The entire hierarchy can be displayed as a tree, as in this picture.

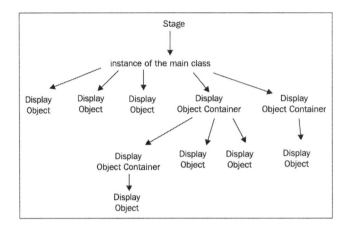

Organizing your DisplayObjects in a proper hierarchy not only will allow you to easily access and manipulate multiple DisplayObjects with a single action, but will help you to remember the role of a DisplayObject if you haven't worked on the script for a long time. It follows the same principle of giving variables and constants names that make sense.

Also remember a DisplayObject is a DisplayObjectContainer as well, and both Sprite and MovieClip are DisplayObjects.

Back to Minesweeper, `game_container` is the DisplayObjectContainer that will contain all tiles.

After `// end of placing digits` add this code:

```
// tile creation
addChild(game_container);
for (i=0; i<FIELD_H; i++) {
  for (j=0; j<FIELD_W; j++) {
    tile = new tile_movieclip();
    game_container.addChild(tile);
    tile.gotoAndStop(1);
    tile.nrow=i;
    tile.ncol=j;
    tile.buttonMode=true;
    tile.x=tile.width*j;
    tile.y=tile.height*i;
    tile.addEventListener(MouseEvent.CLICK,onTileClicked);
  }
}
// end of tile creation
```

And the function to handle mouse click is:

```
private function onTileClicked(e:MouseEvent):void {
   trace("row: "+e.currentTarget.nrow+", column: "+e.currentTarget.
ncol);
}
```

Test the movie and you'll see your mine field:

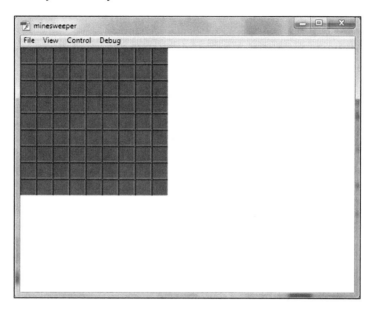

Click on some tiles and in the Output window you'll see:

```
row: 5, column: 2
```

That obviously changes according to the tile you clicked. If you aren't familiar with listeners, check *Chapter 1, Concentration*.

The way we placed tiles is not that different to the one we have already seen in Concentration game so I won't explain it, but I want you to see how to use a DisplayObjectContainer.

```
addChild(game_container);
```

The first DisplayObject to be added is `game_container` sprite.

```
game_container.addChild(tile);
```

This is how to add a DisplayObject to a DisplayObjectContainer. Just use `addChild()` method on the object to be added, just as if you were adding it on the stage.

```
tile.gotoAndStop(1);
```

Showing the first frame, the covered tile.

```
tile.nrow=i;
tile.ncol=j;
```

Saves tile row and column position in the mine field. This will allow us to know its position and retrieve its value in `mineField` array.

`nrow` and `ncol` aren't AS3 keywords, but arbitrary variable names I assigned to `tile` object. You can assign any variable you want on an object.

This is a graphical representation of our Display List at the end of the script:

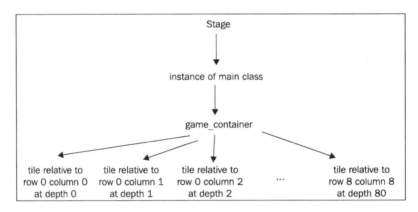

Knowing this structure and that depths in AS3 are contiguous and cannot be negative, will come in handy when continuing in the making of the game.

```
tile.buttonMode=true;
```

Makes the tile act like a button, showing the cursor hand when the mouse is over it.

```
tile.x=tile.width*j;
tile.y=tile.height*i;
```

Places the tile at its final coordinates according to its position in the array.

```
tile.addEventListener(MouseEvent.CLICK,onTileClicked);
```

Adds an event listener. At this time it just prints in the output window the coordinates of the tile you clicked, so it's time to enhance it.

Showing tile contents

Once the player clicks on a tile, no matter its type, he/she must be able to see its content.

The idea: Once the mouse click listener has been triggered, the clicked tile will react this way:

- show frame 3 if it's a mine.

- show frame 2 and change the text according to the number of surrounding mines if it's not a mine.

- show frame 2 and display no text if it's not a mine and there aren't adjacent tiles with a mine.

And, for all cases, remove the listener. A tile can be clicked only once.

The development: Rewrite `onTileClicked` function this way:

```
private function onTileClicked(e:MouseEvent):void {
  var clicked_tile:tile_movieclip=e.currentTarget as tile_movieclip;
  clicked_tile.removeEventListener(MouseEvent.CLICK,onTileClicked);
  clicked_tile.buttonMode=false;
  var clickedRow:uint=clicked_tile.nrow;
  var clickedCol:uint=clicked_tile.ncol;
  var clickedValue:uint=mineField[clickedRow][clickedCol];
  trace("row: "+clickedRow+", column: "+clickedCol+" ->
    "+clickedValue);
  // empty tile
  if (clickedValue==0) {
    clicked_tile.gotoAndStop(2);
    clicked_tile.tile_text.text="";
  }
  // end of empty tile
  // numbered tile
  if (clickedValue>0&&clickedValue<9) {
    clicked_tile.gotoAndStop(2);
    clicked_tile.tile_text.text=clickedValue.toString();
  }
  // end of numbered tile
  // mine
  if (clickedValue==9) {
    clicked_tile.gotoAndStop(3);
  }
  // end of mine
}
```

Test the movie and you will be able to click on tiles and reveal their contents.

```
var clicked_tile:tile_movieclip=e.currentTarget as tile_movieclip;
```

Creates a new `tile_movieclip` variable and assigns it the value of the tile the player just clicked. Remember `currentTarget` property returns us the object that is actively processing the event.

```
clicked_tile.removeEventListener(MouseEvent.CLICK,onTileClicked);
clicked_tile.buttonMode=false;
```

A tile can be clicked only once, so let's remove the listener for mouse click and the property to make it look like a button.

```
var clickedRow:uint=clicked_tile.nrow;
var clickedCol:uint=clicked_tile.ncol;
```

Retrieving `nrow` and `ncol` values we inserted when we created the tiles.

```
var clickedValue:uint=mineField[clickedRow][clickedCol];
```

And finally this is the real value of the tile. At this stage, the game must show the proper result.

```
// empty tile
if (clickedValue==0) {
  clicked_tile.gotoAndStop(2);
  clicked_tile.tile_text.text="";
}
// end of empty tile
```

If it's an empty tile, then you must show the second frame and set the digit to an empty string setting `text` property to `""` (nothing).

Look how I accessed the text field: `clicked_tile.tile_text`: this way you access a child of `clicked_tile` called `tile_text` that is the instance name we gave to the text field.

```
// numbered tile
if (clickedValue>0&&clickedValue<9) {
  clicked_tile.gotoAndStop(2);
  clicked_tile.tile_text.text=clickedValue.toString();
}
// end of numbered tile
```

When you find a numbered tile, a tile with a digit, the process is almost the same: show the second frame and set the digit according to tile value. Since `clickedValue` is an unsigned integer and the text to write is a string, you must convert `clickedValue` to a string using `toString()` method.

```
    // mine
    if (clickedValue==9) {
       clicked_tile.gotoAndStop(3);
    }
    // end of mine
```

Managing a mine is even easier because you only need to show the third frame.

At this time you are virtually ready to play the game, because the script generates the mine field and shows any kind of tile when you click over it. The playable prototype is over. But the hardest part is yet to come.

Auto showing adjacent empty tiles

In every respectable version of Minesweeper, if the player clicks a tile whose value is zero, the game automatically shows all its surrounding tiles, and if any of these tiles has a zero value, then its surrounding tiles are revealed too, and if one of its surrounding tiles has a zero, it continues this way.

The idea: There is a well known algorithm that can help you to do this task: it is called flood fill and it's commonly used in paint programs when you use the "bucket" fill tool. We'll apply the same principle to the game, because we have to "fill" the empty tiles as if we were painting them with a bucket tool.

This is how the flood fill works:

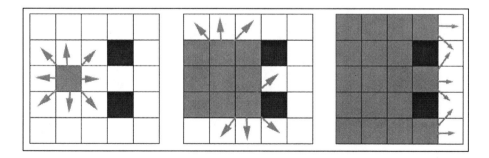

In the first step, the node (a tile, a pixel, or whatever) selected to be painted changes its color (state) and tries to change the color of all its surrounding nodes (in some versions, diagonal nodes are ignored).

Then every painted node tries to perform the flood fill to its surrounding nodes, and then again every newly painted node applies to flood fill until the entire fill-able area is processed.

The development: we'll use a custom version of the flood-fill algorithm to show adjacent empty tiles. Replace the section that manages the empty tile this way:

```
// empty tile
if (clickedValue==0) {
  floodFill(clickedRow,clickedCol);
}
// end of empty tile
```

We found an empty tile so it's time to call `floodFill` function passing tile's coordinates and arguments.

And now add a new function:

```
private function floodFill(row,col:uint):void {
  var emptyTile:tile_movieclip;
  emptyTile=game_container.getChildAt(row*FIELD_W+col) as tile_
movieclip;
  if (emptyTile.currentFrame==1) {
    emptyTile.removeEventListener(MouseEvent.CLICK,onTileClicked);
    emptyTile.buttonMode=false;
    emptyTile.gotoAndStop(2);
    if (mineField[row][col]>0) {
      emptyTile.tile_text.text=mineField[row][col].toString();
    } else {
      emptyTile.tile_text.text="";
    }
    if (mineField[row][col]==0) {
      for (var ii:int =-1; ii<=1; ii++) {
        for (var jj:int =-1; jj<=1; jj++) {
          if (ii!=0||jj!=0) {
            if (tileValue(row+ii,col+jj)!=9) {
              if (tileValue(row+ii,col+jj)!=-1) {
                floodFill(row+ii,col+jj);
              }
            }
          }
        }
      }
    }
  }
}
```

Do you notice anything new in this function? It's a function that calls itself. Functions that call themselves are called **recursive functions**.

Recursive functions are generally dealt with as more advanced programming but they are very useful for games, so we'll be looking at them early. Do you remember you use a `while` loop when you don't exactly know how many times you will need to reiterate the code? The same concept lies behind recursive functions: we use them when we don't know how many times we have to call the same function in order to accomplish a task.

```
var emptyTile:tile_movieclip;
```

Declares a new `tile_movieclip` variable. This will represent the tile on which we are starting the flood fill algorithm

```
emptyTile=game_container.getChildAt(row*FIELD_W+col) as tile_
movieclip;
```

This is how you know what tile you are on according to its row and column values. I showed you how DisplayObjects are placed at different indexes (depths). Now it's time, given a row and a column position, to retrieve DisplayObject. `getChildAt(index)` method returns the child DisplayObject instance having the specified index. So we know the third tile on the fourth row, for instance, is the `(3*9+2)`th child of `game_container` DisplayObject.

```
if (emptyTile.currentFrame==1) { ... }
```

Before applying the flood fill, we must ensure the current tile is still covered. If you don't check for it, you'll probably end with an infinite loop, with the same two tiles applying the flood fill algorithm one to each other.

The possibility of ending in an infinite loop is why recursive functions are normally left to more advanced programmers because you can end up killing your program. But don't worry because if it happens Flash will warn you after 15 seconds of being stuck.

Checking for the tile to be covered, we ensure the flood fill will be applied only once. You know a tile is covered when it's showing the first frame. `currentFrame` property returns the number of the frame the MovieClip is currently showing.

```
emptyTile.removeEventListener(MouseEvent.CLICK,onTileClicked);
emptyTile.buttonMode=false;
emptyTile.gotoAndStop(2);
```

Removing the listener and the button behavior, and showing the second frame.

```
if (mineField[row][col]>0) {
  emptyTile.tile_text.text=mineField[row][col].toString();
} else {
  emptyTile.tile_text.text="";
}
```

This simply updates the digit on the tile according to its value, as seen before.

```
if (mineField[row][col]==0) { ... }
```

If the tile is an empty tile with no adjacent mines, it's time to perform the flood fill on its surrounding tiles. That's how recursion comes into play.

```
for (var ii:int =-1; ii<=1; ii++) {
  for (var jj:int =-1; jj<=1; jj++) {
    if (ii!=0||jj!=0) {
      if (tileValue(row+ii,col+jj)!=9) {
        if (tileValue(row+ii,col+jj)!=-1) {
          floodFill(row+ii,col+jj);
        }
      }
    }
  }
}
```

This is the same couple of `for` loops used when we optimized the code, it scans all adjacent cells and if they exist (value different than `-1`) and do not contain a mine (value different than `9`), `floodFill` is recursively called on them.

You can now test the movie and play with the auto-show feature.

Flagging tiles

Now the player must be given the option to flag tiles. You can take a breath as it's quite easy.

The idea: The player can flag/unflag a tile by clicking on it while holding *Shift* key. A flagged tile cannot be uncovered until it's unflagged.

The development: Modify onTileClicked function this way:

```
private function onTileClicked(e:MouseEvent):void {
  var clicked_tile:tile_movieclip=e.currentTarget as tile_movieclip;
  var clickedRow:uint=clicked_tile.nrow;
  var clickedCol:uint=clicked_tile.ncol;
  var clickedValue:uint=mineField[clickedRow][clickedCol];
  if (e.shiftKey) {
    clicked_tile.gotoAndStop(5-clicked_tile.currentFrame);
  } else {
    if (clicked_tile.currentFrame==1) {
      clicked_tile.removeEventListener(
        MouseEvent.CLICK,onTileClicked);
      clicked_tile.buttonMode=false;
      // empty tile
      if (clickedValue==0) {
        floodFill(clickedRow,clickedCol);
      }
      // end of empty tile
      // numbered tile
      if (clickedValue>0&&clickedValue<9) {
        clicked_tile.gotoAndStop(2);
        clicked_tile.tile_text.text=clickedValue.toString();
      }
      // end of numbered tile
      // mine
      if (clickedValue==9) {
        clicked_tile.gotoAndStop(3);
      }
      // end of mine
    }
  }
}
```

Test the movie and you will be able to flag tiles.

Let's see what happened:

```
if (e.shiftKey) { ... }
```

The current block is executed only if the player presses *Shift* key when he clicks a tile. shiftKey property of a MouseEvent event returns a Boolean value that is true if the *Shift* key has been pressed or false otherwise.

```
clicked_tile.gotoAndStop(5-clicked_tile.currentFrame);
```

This is a dirty way to make the tile switch between frame 1 to frame 4 using `currentFrame` property. It's a quick dirty way to toggle between frame 1 and frame 4.

```
if (clicked_tile.currentFrame==1) { ... }
```

This is how we ensure clicked tile is not a flagged one: it must be showing the first frame.

Timer and game over

The last thing I am going to explain is the creation of a toolbar to show various information such as a timer and the game over message.

The idea: We need to create a dynamic text in which we'll display various messages according to game events. Also, a timer is needed.

The development: Create a new Movie Clip symbol called `toolbar_mc` and set it as exportable for ActionScript. Leave all other settings at their default values, just as you are used to. Draw anything you want, just remember to place a dynamic text called `message_text` and embed Uppercase, Lowercase, Numerals, and Punctuation. You can also use "Basic Latin", but try to embed as few characters as possible while being able to write anything you want. This is the one I made, 550 pixels wide, as wide as the stage, starting at 0,0.

Now change class level variables this way:

```
// class level variables
private const FIELD_W:uint=9;
private const FIELD_H:uint=9;
private const NUM_MINES:uint=10;
private var mineField:Array=new Array();
private var game_container:Sprite=new Sprite();
private var tile:tile_movieclip;
private var timer:Timer=new Timer(1000);
private var toolbar:toolbar_mc;
private var gameOver:Boolean=false;
// end of class level variables
```

we need three more variables: a timer, that will tick every 1,000 milliseconds as you can see from the constructor. Then we need the toolbar itself, and a Boolean variable called gameOver that will be checked to see if the game is over. At the beginning, it's set to false because the game has yet to start, so it cannot be over.

Now in main function after // end of tile creation add:

```
// time management and game over
toolbar = new toolbar_mc();
addChild(toolbar);
toolbar.y=stage.stageHeight-toolbar.height;
timer.start();
timer.addEventListener(TimerEvent.TIMER,onTick);
// end of time management and game over
```

Here we add the toolbar to the Display List. To place it at the bottom of the stage I used:

```
toolbar.y=stage.stageHeight-toolbar.height;
```

stageHeight stage property returns the current height of the stage, in pixels.

The last two lines are used to start the timer and add a listener, as seen during the making of the Concentration game.

Here it is the onTick function that will be called each time the timer event listener is triggered (every second):

```
Private function onTick(e:TimerEvent):void {
   toolbar.message_text.text="Elapsed time: "+e.target.
currentCount+"s";
}
```

As you can see, the function just updates the message text in the toolbar with the number of elapsed seconds. currentCount property returns the number of times the timer event has been triggered, that in our case is the number of elapsed seconds.

The last thing to do is stopping the game when the player hits a mine and eventually write a message in the toolbar.

Modify the onTileClicked function this way:

```
function onTileClicked(e:MouseEvent) {
   if (! gameOver) { ... }
}
```

Now the content of the entire function will be executed only if `gameOver` value is `false`. Since it's defined as `false`, it will always be executed until something sets `gameOver` to `true`. Here is how we are doing it: in `onTileClicked` function change the mine management this way:

```
// mine
if (clickedValue==9) {
  clicked_tile.gotoAndStop(3);
  timer.removeEventListener(TimerEvent.TIMER,onTick);
  toolbar.message_text.text="BOOOOOOOM!!!";
  gameOver=true;
}
// end of mine
```

First, we remove the timer event listener, then we write a message in the toolbar saying it's game over, and finally we set `gameOver` to `true`. At this time, the player won't be able to click any other mine.

Test the movie and play with all these new features.

No sudden death

There is still the "sudden death" issue, that happens when the player makes their first click on a mine. This must be prevented.

The idea: Avoiding sudden death is simple: just create the mine field after the player clicked on the first tile, setting such a tile as an empty one.

The development: The development of this feature does not introduce anything new, so you should be able to figure out by yourself how it works. I just cut/pasted some code from `main` to `onTileClicked` function.

This is how class level variables block changes:

```
// class level variables
...
private var firstClick:Boolean=true;
// end of class level variables
```

`Main` function now does not fill `mineField` array with mines and digits:

```
public function Main() {
  // mine field creation
  ...
  // end of mine field creation
```

```
    // look! No more placing mines and placing digits!
    // tile creation
    ...
    // end of tile creation
    // time management and game over
    ...
    // end of time management and game over
}
```

Mines and digits creation are delegates to `onTileClicked` function:

```
private function onTileClicked(e:MouseEvent):void {
  if (! gameOver) {
    var clicked_tile:tile_movieclip=e.currentTarget as tile_movieclip;
    var clickedRow:uint=clicked_tile.nrow;
    var clickedCol:uint=clicked_tile.ncol;
    if (firstClick) {
      firstClick=false;
      // placing mines
      var placedMines:uint=0;
      var randomRow,randomCol:uint;
      while (placedMines<NUM_MINES) {
        randomRow=Math.floor(Math.random()*FIELD_H);
        randomCol=Math.floor(Math.random()*FIELD_W);
        if (mineField[randomRow][randomCol]==0) {
          if (randomRow!=clickedRow||randomCol!=clickedCol) {
            mineField[randomRow][randomCol]=9;
            placedMines++;
          }
        }
      }
      // end of placing mines
      // placing digits
      for (var i:uint=0; i<FIELD_H; i++) {
        for (var j:uint=0; j<FIELD_W; j++) {
          ...
        }
      }
      ...
      // end of placing digits
    }
    ...
  }
}
```

Just notice how the blocks to place mines and digits are inserted in the function and are executed only once, when `firstClick` is `true`. Then, it's set to `false`.

Also, this `if`:

```
if (randomRow!=clickedRow||randomCol!=clickedCol) { ... }
```

Prevents the mine being placed on the first tile the player clicked. Remember to declare `i` and `j` in your loops since they are function level variables that have not been declared yet in `onTileClicked` function.

Enjoy your Minesweeper.

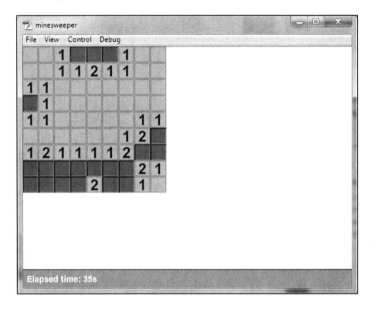

It was almost easier to code than to play.

Summary

The most important thing you learned in this chapter is the DisplayObjects hierarchy. Also, dealing with recursive functions at such an early stage will help you master a feature that will help you in the creation of countless games.

Where to go now

Although the prototype is completed, there are a couple of things you should do to complete your training:

1. Organize the frames to show using constants. Define four constants called something like COVERED_TILE, UNCOVERED_TILE, MINE_TILE and FLAG_TILE, then call gotoAndStop(FLAG_TILE) rather than gotoAndStop(4).

2. Print an "end game" message when the player solves the game. You could count the uncovered tiles, and when they are FIELD_W*FIELD_H-NUMBER_OF_MINES, the game is solved.

3
Connect Four

Connect Four is a two player turn-based game played on a vertical six row–seven column grid. At the beginning of the game, the grid is empty and each player has 21 discs of the same color, normally red or yellow. At each turn a player drops a disc from the top of the grid in a column of his choice, making it fall straight down and occupying the lowest available space in the column. Then it's the other player's turn to move. The aim of the game is connecting four discs of the same color next to each other horizontally, vertically or diagonally. The first player to connect four discs wins. If the board is filled without there being any winning matches then the game is a draw.

Through this chapter, you will create a fully working Connect Four prototype, learning among other techniques, these principles:

- Creating smooth animations
- Splitting the script into little functions to improve code readability and reusability
- Animating DisplayObjects with AS3, without using the timeline
- Triggering events related to stage and frames
- Creating sub classes to manage DisplayObjects
- Forcing a loop to stop using break
- Accessing parents of DisplayObjects
- Basic artificial intelligence to make the computer play the game

Also, recursive functions and DisplayObject hierarchy introduced during the making of Minesweeper will be carried on.

Defining game design

You are making a game people played as a real board game during their childhood, so they reasonably expect the overall look and feel to be the same. Apart from board and discs colors, the most important feature is the gravity. When a player places one of his discs, it must fall down as in the real board game.

A brief list of game characteristics can be described as:

- Single player game against CPU.
- Player will use red discs. CPU will use yellow discs.
- The game randomly chooses which color will move first.
- Discs falls down as if they were governed by gravity.
- Some kind of artificial intelligence to make CPU player competitive.

You also should draw the graphics a way which reminds the original game, with a blue board filled by red and yellow discs.

The game field

As usual, the first thing we have to do is defining and setting up the game field.

The idea: Just like Minesweeper game, the best solution is a two-dimensional array representing the six rows and seven columns. The first index determines the row, and the second index determines the column.

Then, any element can have these values:

- 0: an empty cell.
- 1: a cell occupied by player one.
- 2: a cell occupied by player two.

Look at this picture with a typical Connect Four situation:

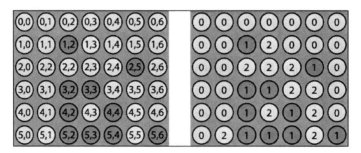

On the left, array indexes for each cell. On the right, array values to represent board's situation.

When the game starts, all cells are empty, so the entire array must be filled with zeros.

The development: Create a new file (**File | New**) then from **New Document** window select **Actionscript 3.0.** Set its properties as width to 640 px, height to 480 px, background color to #FFFFFF (white), and frame rate to 30. Also define the Document Class as Main and save the file as connect4.fla.

Showing smooth animations

There's a difference between previous game settings and this one. Apart from the size, that's larger than what we saw in previous chapters for an aesthetic choice, I set the frame rate to 30 frames per second.

Unlike games as Concentration and Minesweeper, Connect Four will include animations. The average human eye will see the individual frames on an animation (or a movie) if the frame rate is lower than a certain amount of frames per second (fps). In films, using 24fps along with motion blur, eyes get tricked and they won't be able to see individual frames anymore, as if they were looking at a smooth animation. Without motion blur, some people are able to see individual frames up to 30 fps and more, according to the complexity of the scene. On the other hand, a frame rate that's too fast will negatively affect the performance, if games aren't played on high end computers.

A good choice if you have to show animations is 30fps, as they are a good compromise between smoothness and performance. Anyway if you want eye proof animations, I suggest you use 60fps, keeping an eye on performances.

Without closing connect4.fla, create a new file and from **New Document** window select **ActionScript 3.0 Class**. Save this file as Main.as in the same path you saved connect4.fla.

Now in Main.as file write:

```
package {
  import flash.display.Sprite;
  public class Main extends Sprite {
    private var gameField:Array;
    public function Main() {
      prepareField();
    }
    private function prepareField():void {
```

```
        gameField=new Array();
        for (var i:uint=0; i<6; i++) {
          gameField[i]=new Array();
          for (var j:uint=0; j<7; j++) {
            gameField[i].push(0););
          }
        }
        trace("the field: "+gameField);
      }
    }
  }
```

Test the movie and in the output window you will see:

the field: 0,0,0,0,0,0,0,0,0,0,0,0,0,0,0,0,0,0,0,0,0,0,0,0,0,0,0,0,0,0
,0,0,0,0,0,0,0,0,0,0,0,0

That's what you've already seen when you created a new array filled with zeros during Concentration or Minesweeper development.

You should be familiar with this code as there is nothing new. At the end of the script, gameField array will be a two-dimensional 6x7 array filled with zeros.

But I want you to notice the content of Main function:

```
prepareField();
```

There's nothing more than a call to prepareField function which manages gameField array. Why use a function just to execute only once a block of code we always inserted into Main class until now?

Splitting the code

There are three reasons why you should always split the code: first, this practice improves script readability. Remember that script readability is everything when you aren't working on your projects for a while. It's easier to see what this script is supposed to do:

```
connectToServer();
displaySplashScreen();
startTheMusic();
```

rather than this one:

```
// connecting to server
...
... // big set of instructions to connect to the server
```

```
...
// display splash screen
...
... // big set of instructions to display the splash screen
...
// starting the music
...
... // big set of instructions to start the music
...
```

With the first method, the one you'll be using from now on, you can easily see what the script does just looking at the first three lines. You don't have to read anything more unless you want to check how the functions connect to the server, display splash screen or start the music. The second script is not as intuitive, although there are comments, especially if a lot of lines of code are required to connect to the server, display splash screen, and so on.

Second, in large scripts you will find yourself cutting and pasting code from one position to another. It's a normal practice because as the script grows and includes more features, you may want to execute some branches of code in a different order, or under different conditions. Cutting and pasting an one-line function call is much simpler than selecting a large block of code and moving it here and there. There are good chances you will end leaving some lines in the wrong place, causing you a big headache when it's time to debug.

The third, and most important reason, is splitting the code into little functions will allow you to easily reuse your code for future projects. You may not want to make just one game in your career, so quickly locating and editing existing and already tested functions will speed up development.

Back to Connect Four, once the array representing the board has been created, it's time to draw the board itself.

Adding the board

The first thing we will place on the stage is the game board.

The idea: We just need to draw a game board that looks like the one in the original board game. A rectangle with a series of holes will fit our needs.

The development: In `connect4.fla`, create a new Movie Clip symbol called `board_movieclip` and set it as exportable for ActionScript. Leave all other settings at their default values, just like you did in previous chapters. Then draw a rectangle with registration point at 0,0 and create the holes, doing something like this:

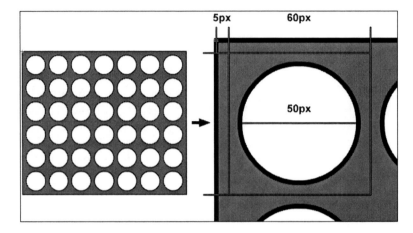

From the picture you can easily determine the size of the board, in pixels:

- width: 60 pixels * 7 columns + 5 pixels * 2 = 430 pixels
- height: 60 pixels * 6 rows + 5 pixels * 2 = 370 pixels

You are free to give your board the size and shape you want, but during this chapter I will refer to these sizes, so if you are an absolute beginner I suggest you draw the board the same way I did.

Placing the board to stage

Once the board is completed, you have to add it to the stage. First, you need to declare a variable to construct the board and add it to Display List.

Change your class level variables this way:

```
private var gameField:Array;
private var board:board_movieclip;
```

`board` is the variable name and `board_movieclip` is the type.

Let's add it to Display List. Add a new line to `Main` function:

```
public function Main() {
  prepareField();
  placeBoard();
}
```

Following the rule to split the code, we delegate to `placeBoard` function the dirty job and keep clean `Main` function.

This is `placeBoard` function:

```
private function placeBoard():void {
  board=new board_movieclip();
  addChild(board);
  board.x=105;
  board.y=100;
}
```

The function(s) just creates a `board_movieclip` instance and adds it to Display List, just like you made a dozen times' to 'you've done a dozen times.

Just notice this time I set `x` and `y` position manually (directly inserting values) rather than using DisplayObject's `width` property like I did during the creation of Minesweeper and Concentration.

If you don't plan to change assets' size in the future, inserting numerical values is quicker because you don't have to deal with a lot of constants.

In this case it only happens once, but I am showing you the basic principle. While in games like Minesweeper and Concentration I may want to increase/decrease the number of elements in the game to make gameplay easier or harder, Connect Four will be always played on a 7x6 board, so I preferred to position the board using numerical values.

Anyway, this line:

```
board.x=105;
```

and this one:

```
board.x=(stage.stageWidth-board.width)/2;
```

Would have placed the board in the same place since `(640-430)/2=105`.

Test the movie: you will see your board horizontally centered on the stage.

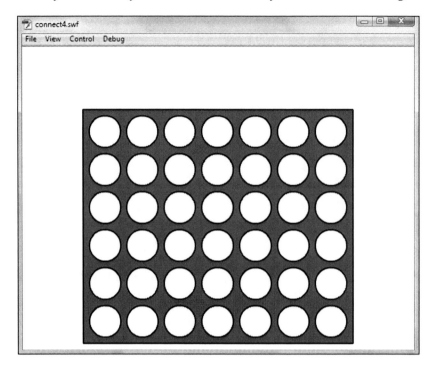

But it's time to make another improvement to the code.

Creating more classes

Do you remember the creation of the Concentration game, when I told you to ignore the alert saying "A definition for the document class could not be found in the classpath, so one will be automatically generated in the SWF file upon export."?

You can keep ignoring it, but this time you will create the famous "definition for the document class", that is a file like `Main.as`, with the class relative to `board_movieclip`.

Delete these two lines from `placeBoard` function, as we will position `board` object in its own class.

```
board.x=105;
board.y=100;
```

Test the movie and you will see the board aligned with the upper-left corner of the stage. That's ok because you just removed x and y properties.

Without closing `connect4.fla`, create a new file and from **New Document** window select **ActionScript 3.0 Class**. Save this file as `board_movieclip.as` in the same path you saved `connect4.fla` and `Main.as`.

Then enter this code:

```
package {
  import flash.display.Sprite;
  public class board_movieclip extends Sprite {
    public function board_movieclip() {
      x=105;
      y=100;
    }
  }
}
```

Test the movie and you will see the board correctly placed again in the stage.

What happened? As you can see, the script has the same structure as `Main.as`. There's the package definition, there are imported packages/classes, class and constructor function names are the same as the filename, and so on.

The main difference, and this is the core concept, is that this class is the definition of a `board_movieclip` object. In other words, every time a new `board_movieclip` instance is created, the content of `board_movieclip` function is executed.

In this case, we are only talking about a couple of properties, but during this book you will see how important it is to create a custom class for every actor you will place in the game.

Also notice how properties are directly assigned with:

```
x=105;
y=100;
```

while in `Main` class to achieve the same result you had to write:

```
board.x=105;
board.y=100;
```

This is because you are working directly with `board_movieclip` class, so every property directly refers to it.

Now that you have learned how to create custom classes, you will see how easy and quick it is to manage objects this way.

Placing the disc

Once the board has been created, it's time to draw the discs.

The idea: There are two types of disc, a red one and a yellow one. We will create a Movie Clip symbol with two frames, one for each color of disc and each player.

The development: In `connect4.fla`, create a new Movie Clip symbol called `disc_movieclip` and set it as exportable for ActionScript.

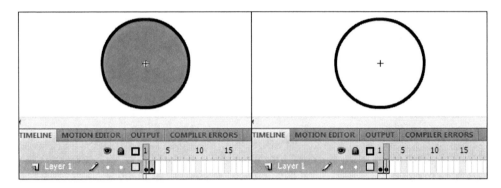

Timeline contains:

- frame 1: a red disc, used by player one (the human)
- frame 2: a yellow disc, used by player two (the computer)

Both discs have a 60 pixel diameter and registration point at 0,0.

To use them in the game, modify `Main.as` class level variables this way:

```
private var gameField:Array;
private var board:board_movieclip;
private var disc_container:Sprite = new Sprite();
private var disc:disc_movieclip;
```

`disc_container` is the DisplayObject that will contain all discs, while `disc` is a `disc_movieclip` instance. We want to create a container to place all discs behind the board although they are added once the board is already on stage, and without any container they will overlap it.

Change `Main` function:

```
public function Main() {
  prepareField();
  placeBoard();
  placeDisc(Math.floor(Math.random()*2)+1);
}
```

There is a call to a new function called `placeDisc` with an argument. If you remember random numbers generation, you should see such argument can be `1` or `2`. That's the number of the player who will begin the game.

Then it's time to modify `placeBoard` function to add discs container. It forms part of the board, since it will keep all discs behind `board` DisplayObject.

```
private function placeBoard():void {
  board=new board_movieclip();
  addChild(disc_container);
  disc_container.x=board.x;
  disc_container.y=board.y;
  addChild(board);
}
```

The interesting thing of new lines isn't their content, but their sequence. In these few lines you will find the magic of Display List hierarchy:

```
board=new board_movieclip();
```

First, a new instance of `board_movieclip` is created. At this time, `board_movieclip` function in `board_movieclip.as` file is executed, setting its x and y properties respectively to `105` and `100`.

```
addChild(disc_container);
disc_container.x=board.x;
disc_container.y=board.y;
```

Then `board_movieclip` is added to Display List, and is moved in the same position as the board, simply setting x and y properties at the same values the board has.

```
addChild(board);
```

Only at this point, the board is added to Display List. This way, it will be placed in front of the disc container, at the same coordinates. Refer to the creation of Minesweeper game if you're unfamiliar with Display List depths and hierarchy.

Obviously disc_container's x and y properties could have been manually set to 105 and 100 respectively as we did with the board but I wanted you to see what happens when an instance of a DisplayObject is created and what happens when such object is added to Display List.

placeDisc function wants one unsigned integer and does not return anything. If you don't need a function to return anything, just make it return a type of void.

```
private function placeDisc(player:uint):void {
    disc=new disc_movieclip(player);
    disc_container.addChild(disc);
}
```

This function simply creates a new disc_movieclip instance and adds it to Display List as a child of disc_container. This way the disc will be placed behind the board.

Notice how player value is passed as an argument to the instance. There's nothing strange as we are just passing an argument to a function, no matter if it is a simple function or a constructor.

Just like you created board_movieclip.as, create disc_movieclip.as and write:

```
package {
    import flash.display.MovieClip;
    public class disc_movieclip extends MovieClip {
        public function disc_movieclip(player:uint) {
            gotoAndStop(player);
        }
    }
}
```

This time the main function disc_movieclip wants an argument, the aforementioned player number we created in Main function. At the moment, the function just displays frame 1 or 2 according to player value.

But there's something new. Did you notice it? This package imports MovieClip class and disc_movieclip class extends MovieClip. All classes we've seen until now imported and extended Sprite class. Why does this one use MovieClip?

Because MovieClip DisplayObject can have any number of frames in its timeline, while Sprite has no timeline. That is, Sprite can be meant as a MovieClip with just one frame.

So, when the timeline of the main function of your DisplayObject contains more than one frame, use it to extend MovieClip. If it contains only one frame, use it to extend Sprite.

In this case, `board_movieclip` extends a Sprite because it has only one frame, while `disc_movieclip` extends a MovieClip because it has two frames.

Obviously you have to take care of the number of frames only if you are creating a specific class for a DisplayObject.

Test the movie and you will see something like this:

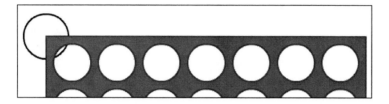

The disc can be red or yellow, according to `Math.floor(Math.random()*2)+1` result.

The disc is placed on `disc_container` DisplayObject so that the board overlaps it even if the disc was added after the board. Also, notice how the disc has its origin placed at the origin of `disc_container`, that has the same origin of the board.

This demonstrates how DisplayObject children inherit, among other things, the position of their father.

> You can access a DisplayObject when it's instantiated even if it's not added to Display List yet.
>
> Extend Sprite class when you deal with DisplayObjects with only one frame in their timeline or with no timeline at all.
>
> Extend MovieClip class when you deal with DisplayObjects with more than a frame in their timeline.
>
> DisplayObject children inherit the position from their parents.

Now you will need to let the player choose in which column he wants to place the disc.

Moving the disc

There are lots of ways to let the player choose which column to play, but to preserve the look and feel of the original board game you should make him select the column moving the disc over it. Obviously you can't allow the player to freely move the disc, but you will have to lock y coordinate and let the player move the disc horizontally with the mouse.

The idea: Let the player move the disc with the mouse along x-axis to select the column where the disc should be dropped. It looks simple, but leads to two problems:

- What happens when the player moves the disc outside the game board?
- What happens when the player moves the disc inside the game board, but in a position unclear to determine which column he's choosing?

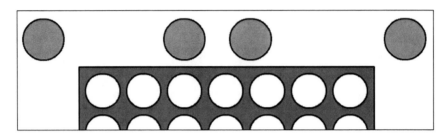

This picture resumes the possible disc positions:

From left to right:

- An illegal place: too far on the left
- A legal place: perfectly aligned over a column
- An illegal place: not perfectly aligned with any column
- An illegal place: too far on the right

You must make the player have a clear idea of the column he is about to pick, so while he/she will be able to move the mouse anywhere, the disc will move only in legal positions.

So you must check whether the disc is on a legal place or not, and in this case, adjust its position to the closest legal place.

The problem is the player can move the mouse at any time, updating the disc position and forcing us to make the check.

We need a way to continuously check for mouse and disc position. To our help here comes a new listener that will do the task: Event.ENTER_FRAME.

ENTER_FRAME is triggered continuously in conjunction with the frame rate, at every new frame. It will become the most used listener because it will help you to manage animations and to make necessary operations that need to be executed at every frame.

Just for your information, there is a specific listener that triggers mouse movements called `MouseEvent.MOUSE_MOVE` but I prefer you to familiarize yourself with `ENTER_FRAME` first, showing the former event later in the book.

The development: The disc must have an enter frame event listener that will manage the horizontal position at every frame. We also need to save the current column position in a class level variable to make it available through the entire class, when we'll manage clicks, animations, and more features.

Change `disc_movieclip.as` this way:

```
package {
  import flash.display.MovieClip;
  import flash.events.Event;
  public class disc_movieclip extends MovieClip {
    private var currentColumn:int;
    public function disc_movieclip(player:uint) {
      gotoAndStop(player);
      addEventListener(Event.ENTER_FRAME,onEnterFrame);
    }
    private function onEnterFrame(e:Event) {
      moveHorizontally();
    }
    private function moveHorizontally():void {
      currentColumn=Math.floor((stage.mouseX-this.parent.x)/60);
      if (currentColumn<0) {
        currentColumn=0;
      }
      if (currentColumn>6) {
        currentColumn=6;
      }
      x=35+60*currentColumn;
      y=-40;
    }
  }
}
```

Test the movie, and move the mouse around the screen. You will see the disc placing only in legal places.

Let's see how we managed disc movement:

```
import flash.events.Event;
```

Importing `Event` class. This class contains the listener we are looking for.

```
private var currentColumn:int;
```

A class level variable to store the value of the current column the disc is on.

```
addEventListener(Event.ENTER_FRAME,onEnterFrame);
```

`Event.ENTER_FRAME` is the listener that will be triggered in conjunction with the frame rate, added as usual with `addEventListener`. Once triggered, it calls `onEnterFrame` function. It's like telling the script to execute `onEnterFrame` function at every frame. This is exactly what we needed.

```
private function onEnterFrame(e:Event) {
  moveHorizontally();
}
```

This is the `onEnterFrame` function. There's only a call to another function, `moveHorizontally`. Although this may seem redundant, we are just at an early stage of the game, so obviously `onEnterFrame` function will do a lot more things once the game is completed.

```
currentColumn=Math.floor((stage.mouseX-this.parent.x)/60);
```

This is the core line of the function, that determines the current column position according to mouse x-coordinate this way:

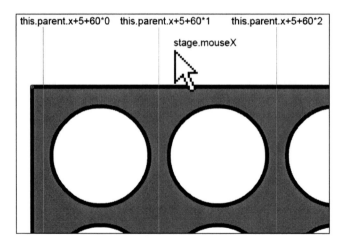

We exactly know the x-boundary between a column and the next one, so with a simple formula we can determine which column the mouse is hovering over.

Also notice how you can directly access the stage with `stage` keyword and how you can access the father of a DisplayObject using `parent` keyword.

```
if (currentColumn<0) {
  currentColumn=0;
}
```

Since the stage is wider than the mouse, `currentColumn` may have negative values if the mouse is on the far left of the board. We want to prevent this happening, so if the column would be negative, we set it to zero.

```
if (currentColumn>6) {
  currentColumn=6;
}
```

This is the same concept applied when the mouse is on the far right.

```
x=35+60*currentColumn;
y=-40;
```

Finally, the disc is centered over the selected column.

Test the movie and you will be able to move the disc exactly over one of the seven columns, while you can move the mouse anywhere you want.

Applying game rules

Rules define legal player moves and make the game balanced. You have to ensure players cannot break the rules or they might be able to cheat.

Unlike some other "put some symbols in a row" games like Tic Tac Toe that let you place your move in every empty spot, in Connect Four you can't place discs everywhere.

In the real world, discs fall down to occupy the lowest available space in each column. Moreover, players can't place a disc on a completely filled column.

Unfortunately, the program does not know we are playing on a vertical board where discs fall, and that a disc is a solid entity that does not physically fit in a fully completed column. The whole game field is just an array, a bunch of indexed numbers.

So these are the two golden rules you need to apply:

1. If a column is already fully occupied, you can't place a disc in it.
2. If the column has some free spaces, your disc will be placed on the lowest one.

Look at this picture:

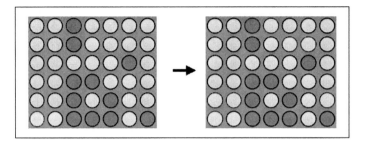

In the previous picture, on the left there is a typical Connect Four situation. On the right, green discs represent the possible moves. No discs can be placed on the third column.

The idea: Once a player selects a column to drop the disc, the script must check whether it's a legal move or not.

The development: It's easier than it may seem. A column is a legal move when it has at least one space available. Since columns are filled from bottom to top, we can say a free column must have the highest row empty.

Checking for possible columns

Before we can determine how long a disc will fall down a column, we have to know in which columns we can make a move.

In your `Main.as` file, add this function:

```
public function possibleColumns():Array {
  var moves_array = new Array();
  for (var i:uint=0; i<7; i++) {
    if (gameField[0][i]==0) {
      moves_array.push(i);
    }
  }
  return moves_array;
}
```

`possibleColumns` returns an array with all the columns a player can place the disc in.

Also I want you to notice that this is the first function different to the one with the same name of the class that is declared as `public`. That's because the program will need to access this function from within `disc_movieclip` class.

```
var moves_array = new Array();
```

Constructing a new array called `moves_array`, that will store all possible column indexes.

```
for (var i:uint=0; i<7; i++) { ... }
```

`for` loop to go through all seven columns.

```
if (gameField[0][i]==0) { ... }
```

This is the core of the function: checking if the upper row of the `i-th` column is empty. That's all you need to know to say whether a column is playable or not.

```
moves_array.push(i);
```

If we found the `i-th` column to be playable, then add it to the array.

```
return moves_array;
```

And finally return the array with all possible columns.

It's raining discs

Then add the other function: this function has two arguments: the column where we are going to place the disc, and the player who is placing it.

The function will be executed only after checking the column is a legal one, so we assume we will find at least an empty space.

It updates the game field and returns the row where the disc is going to be placed.

```
public function firstFreeRow(column:uint,player:uint):int {
  for (var i:uint=0; i<6; i++) {
    if (gameField[i][column]!=0) {
      break;
    }
  }
  gameField[i-1][column]=player;
  return i-1;
}
```

While `possibleColumns` scans all columns, `firstFreeRow` scans all rows

```
for (var i:uint=0; i<6; i++) { ... }
```

`for` loop to go through all six rows, from top to bottom.

```
if (gameField[i][column]!=0) { ... }
```

The core of the function: checking if the `i-th` row of a given column is occupied

```
break;
```

If you find an occupied row in a playable column, you don't need to reiterate the loop anymore because you already found what you were looking for. `break` stops processing a loop.

```
gameField[i-1][column]=player;
```

If the `i-th` row of a playable column is occupied, then the `(i-1)th` row is the first free row, from bottom to top. That's where the player placed the disc, so we assign `player` value to `gameField[i-1][column]`. Now the array is updated at the latest move.

```
return i-1;
```

Returns `i-1`, that is the index of the first free row.

Determining a cell value (if any)

We are working behind the scenes, so we need to add a function to return the value of a cell, or `-1` if it does not exist, just like we did during the creation of Minesweeper.

```
private function cellValue(row:uint,col:uint):int {
  if (gameField[row]==undefined||gameField[row][col]==undefined) {
    return -1;
  } else {
    return gameField[row][col];
  }
}
```

It will come in hand later, moreover it was developed at no cost since it has already been created and tested during the making of Minesweeper. Do you understand the importance of having little functions to use again and again?

public functions can be accessed by all classes which attempt to use them.

break stops processing a loop.

Now you have everything you need to determine whether a move is valid, and when the disc will stop once dropped in a valid column.

Making your move

Everything is ready to let the player drop his/her disc. You can check whether each column represents a legal move or not, and you know which row will occupy a falling disc, given a column.

The idea: When the player clicks the mouse, we check if the column he picked is a legal one, in this case we place the disc in the proper row and let the other player move. At the moment, there isn't a computer-controlled opponent yet, so you will have to play both with red and yellow discs.

The development: To make the player drop the disc with a mouse click, you have to import MouseEvent class in disc_movieclip.as to use your old friend MouseEvent. CLICK listener.

```
import flash.display.MovieClip;
import flash.events.Event;
import flash.events.MouseEvent;
```

You also need to know which player is playing through all classes, so add a new variable to class level variables.

```
private var currentColumn:int;
private var currentPlayer:uint;
private var par:Main;
```

currentPlayer will store the number of the currently moving player.

par variable is called this way because it is a shortcut of parent that's a reserved name. It will be used to access Main class (as its type suggests) to execute the function to check for a valid move.

Waiting for the disc to be added to stage

We said the player drops the disc with a mouse click. Unfortunately, we cannot place a mouse click listener to the disc itself as it would trigger only if the player clicks on the disc. It's not that intuitive, as the player expects to place the disc with the mouse and release it by clicking anywhere.

We can solve this issue by adding a mouse click listener on the stage, and once triggered, check if it's a possible move and eventually place the disc in its place and pass the turn to the other player.

Unfortunately, a programmer's life is never easy, and it's not possible for DisplayObjects access the stage if they aren't on the Display List yet.

AS3 comes to our help with `Event.ADDED_TO_STAGE` that triggers when a DisplayObject is added to the Display List, both directly and as a child of an object added to the Display List.

With this in mind, it's easy to rewrite `disc_movieclip` function:

```
public function disc_movieclip(player:uint) {
  currentPlayer=player
  addEventListener(Event.ADDED_TO_STAGE,onAdded);
}
```

First, the content of `player` argument is stored in class level variable `currentPlayer` to make it available through the entire class.

Then, it's time to add the listener:

```
addEventListener(Event.ADDED_TO_STAGE,onAdded);
```

to execute `onAdded` function when the disc is added to the stage.

`onAdded` function will manage all listeners including the one to look for a mouse click on the stage.

```
private function onAdded(e:Event) {
  par=this.parent.parent as Main;
  gotoAndStop(currentPlayer);
  addEventListener(Event.ENTER_FRAME,onEnterFrame);
  stage.addEventListener(MouseEvent.CLICK,onMouseClick);
}
```

Let's see the core lines:

```
par=this.parent.parent as Main;
```

now par can access all Main functions.

```
stage.addEventListener(MouseEvent.CLICK,onMouseClick);
```

The previous line of code adds the mouse click event listener to the stage. It's possible because we are sure the disc has been already added to the stage, thanks to Event.ADDED_TO_STAGE listener.

At each click, the listener calls onMouseClick function:

```
private function onMouseClick(e:MouseEvent) {
  if (par.possibleColumns().indexOf(currentColumn)!=-1) {
    dropDisc();
  }
}
```

This function checks if the current column is a legal move by searching into the array of possible columns the value of currentColumn with indexOf method as you've already seen during the creation of Concentration game.

If it's a legal move, then dropDisc function is executed.

```
private function dropDisc():void {
  y=35+par.firstFreeRow(currentColumn,currentPlayer)*60;
  removeEventListener(Event.ENTER_FRAME,onEnterFrame);
  stage.removeEventListener(MouseEvent.CLICK,onMouseClick);
  par.placeDisc(3-currentPlayer);
}
```

This function just places the disc in the first available place and removes the listeners as this disc won't be moved anymore.

Then this line:

```
par.placeDisc(3-currentPlayer);
```

passes the hand to the other player

Test the movie and nothing will happen, except this message in the Compiler Errors window.

1195: Attempted access of inaccessible method placeDisc through a reference with static type Main.

This is the error you get when you try to call a private function (in this case placeDisc) you don't have the permission to access.

To make the script work, simply replace `private` with `public`.

```
public function placeDisc(player:uint):void {
  disc=new disc_movieclip(player);
  disc_container.addChild(disc);
}
```

Test the movie again and everything will work fine.

Checking for victory

Applying rules to correctly place discs is not enough: you have to check if a player's move makes him win the game. You know a player wins the game when he connects four (or more) discs next to each other horizontally, vertically, or diagonally.

So we need to check for victory.

The idea: A very cheap way to check for a victory would be scanning the entire field at every turn, disc after disc, until you find four discs in a row. I don't want you to use brute force to check for victory, so let's have a deeper look at game mechanics.

According to Connect Four rules, we can say:

- A player can win, but cannot lose during his turn. There's no way a player can end the game during his turn, unless he wins. This means when red plays, only red can win. So only red discs can form a winning streak.
- When a player wins, the winning move is always the latest disc he played. So the latest disc is part of the winning streak.

With these two concepts in mind, we only need to check whether the latest dropped disc is part of a winning combination of the same color.

What does this mean? That when a player drops a disc, we must look for contiguous discs of the same color at its left and right and see if they form a horizontal winning streak.

If not, we will check for the discs of the same color below the latest disc, and if they don't form a vertical winning streak, repeat the same thing with the diagonals.

Look at this picture:

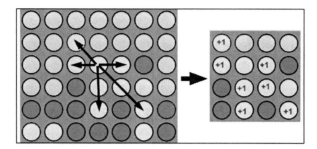

Once the disc in the middle column has been dropped, we check in seven directions (all possible eight directions minus the top vertical one, because the latest dropped disc can't have another disc above it) and we stop when we find an empty space or a disc with another color.

It's easy to see we have a winning move when the sum of the number of adjacent discs in a direction is three. The fourth, winning disc is the one the player just dropped.

The development: The first thing to do is enabling the script to count how many discs of the same color we can find at a given direction.

Just like with Minesweeper flood fill, you don't know how many adjacent discs you will find in each direction, so the best thing to do is use a recursive function to do the job.

In `Main.as` file add this function:

```
private function getAdj(row:uint,col:uint,row_inc:int,col_inc:int):
uint {
  if (cellValue(row,col)==cellValue(row+row_inc,col+col_inc)) {
    return 1+getAdj(row+row_inc,col+col_inc,row_inc,col_inc);
  } else {
    return 0;
  }
}
```

it wants four arguments:

- `row` (unsigned integer): the current row position
- `col` (unsigned integer): the current column position
- `row_inc` (integer): the value to add to row to get the position of the disc to examine in the desired direction

- `col_inc` (integer): the value to add to column to get the position of the disc to examine in the desired direction

Knowing the structure of the array which represents the game field, we can make the function look in all seven directions this way:

- `row_inc = 0`, `col_inc = 1` scans for the disc on the right
- `row_inc = 0`, `col_inc = -1` scans for the disc on the left
- `row_inc = 1`, `col_inc = 0` scans for the disc on the bottom
- `row_inc = -1`, `col_inc = 1` scans for the disc on the upper-right
- `row_inc = 1`, `col_inc = -1` scans for the disc on the bottom-left
- `row_inc = 1`, `col_inc = 1` scans for the disc on the bottom-right
- `row_inc = -1`, `col_inc = -1` scans for the disc on the upper-left

We can now write a function called `checkForVictory` which given a row and a column counts all adjacent discs of the same color in the four directions and returns `true` if a direction at least contains more than two adjacent discs (that is, three adjacent discs plus the one you just dropped = four in a row!) and `false` if not.

```
public function checkForVictory(row:uint,col:uint):Boolean {
  if (getAdj(row,col,0,1)+getAdj(row,col,0,-1)>2) {
    return true;
  } else {
    if (getAdj(row,col,1,0)>2) {
      return true;
    } else {
      if (getAdj(row,col,-1,1)+getAdj(row,col,1,-1)>2) {
        return true;
      } else {
        if (getAdj(row,col,1,1)+getAdj(row,col,-1,-1)>2) {
          return true;
        } else {
          return false;
        }
      }
    }
  }
}
```

The four directions are scanned this way:

```
if (getAdj(row,col,0,1)+getAdj(row,col,0,-1)>2) { ... }
```

counts horizontal adjacent tiles

```
if (getAdj(row,col,1,0)>2) { ... }
```

counts vertical adjacent tiles. Notice I only look at the bottom

```
if (getAdj(row,col,-1,1)+getAdj(row,col,1,-1)>2) { ... }
```

counts diagonal adjacent tiles, from top-right to bottom-left

```
if (getAdj(row,col,1,1)+getAdj(row,col,-1,-1)>2) { ... }
```

counts diagonal adjacent tiles, from bottom-right to top-left.

Now we need a class level variable called `currentRow` to make the value of the row we just placed the disc in available through the entire class

```
private var currentColumn:int;
private var currentPlayer:uint;
private var par:Main;
private var currentRow:uint;
```

and in `dropDisc` function we assign `currentRow` the value of the played row, and only later we update `y` property.

```
private function dropDisc():void {
  currentRow=par.firstFreeRow(currentColumn,currentPlayer);
  y=35+currentRow*60;
  removeEventListener(Event.ENTER_FRAME,onEnterFrame);
  stage.removeEventListener(MouseEvent.CLICK,onMouseClick);
  checkForVictory();
}
```

Finally we have to check for a winning move. `checkForVictory` function will take care of it.

```
private function checkForVictory():void {
  if (! par.checkForVictory(currentRow,currentColumn)) {
    par.placeDisc(3-currentPlayer);
  } else {
    trace("Player "+currentPlayer+" wins!!!");
  }
}
```

This just sees if `checkForVictory` function returns `true` or `false`. In the first case, the game is over and a message is displayed in the output window. In the second case, the turn passes to the other player.

Animating discs

Until now, when you place a disc in the board, it jumped to its final position. As said at the beginning of this chapter, recreating the look and feel of the original board game is important, so you will need to create the animation of the falling disc.

It's nothing difficult, as we will only create a linear movement without simulating gravity and collision bounces.

The idea: When the player selects a column to play, show the disc falling down moving along its vertical axis. The other player can't play until the disc reaches its place.

The development: The main question is: how long will the disc fall?

We don't know and we don't care how long the disc will fall, because we know its final position we already used it in `dropDisc` function with this line:

```
y=35+par.firstFreeRow(currentColumn,currentPlayer)*60;
```

So we just have to move the disc along its vertical axis until it reaches the final position.

Anyway, we will need to use such position here and there around the script, so it's better to create a new class level variable to make the final position available through all classes.

```
private var currentColumn:int;
private var currentPlayer:uint;
private var par:Main;
private var currentRow:uint;
private var fallingDestination:uint=0;
```

`fallingDestination` will store the `y` position we must reach with the disc. Its starting value is zero because it's not falling yet.

We still don't know for how long the disc will fall, but for sure it will take a while. Let's say more than a single frame. So we can't remove the enter frame event listener as soon as the player drops the disc, or we won't be able to see the animation.

Remove the listener from `dropDisc` function. Also remove `checkForVictory` call as saying a player won before the disc stopped would look like a bug. I commented the code you should remove.

```
private function dropDisc():void {
  currentRow=par.firstFreeRow(currentColumn,currentPlayer);
  fallingDestination=35+currentRow*60;
```

```
    // removeEventListener(Event.ENTER_FRAME,onEnterFrame);
    stage.removeEventListener(MouseEvent.CLICK,onMouseClick);
    // checkForVictory();
}
```

Also at this time we can determine the falling destination of the disc:

```
fallingDestination=35+currentRow*60;
```

At the end of the function, you knew the final position of the disc and removed the mouse click listener. That's enough. It's easy to see when `fallingDestination` is greater than zero, then the disc must fall, because the player made his move.

Now, at every frame, you must tell the disc if it should move horizontally (the player is selecting a column to move) or vertically (the player dropped the disc). Change `onEnterFrame` function this way:

```
private function onEnterFrame(e:Event) {
    if (fallingDestination=0) {
        moveHorizontally();
    } else {
        moveVertically();
    }
}
```

This way you will keep moving the disc horizontally until `fallingDestination` is different (and obviously greater) than zero. Then, `moveVertically` function will handle the animation.

The animation itself

Animating the disc is not that hard once you know where it will end, because we already decided it's just a linear motion. So you just need to move down the disc for a certain amount of pixels until it reaches its destination. Defining such an amount is the hardest decision. Let me explain the concept.

During the game, when the disc is moving horizontally, its y position is -40. Then, it must reach 35+60*r where r is the number of the row. The total amount of pixels is 40+35+60*r = 75+60*r. To make a smooth, good looking animation, the disc must move for the same amount of pixels at every frame, so it must be a number that perfectly divides 60 and 75. The candidates in this case are 3, 5 and 15.

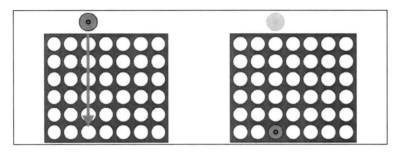

According to the amount of pixel per frame, the disc will fall at different speeds.

```
private function moveVertically():void {
    y+=15;
    if (y==fallingDestination) {
        fallingDestination=0;
        removeEventListener(Event.ENTER_FRAME,onEnterFrame);
        checkForVictory();
    }
}
```

Test the movie and you will see discs falling down as in the original board game. You are almost done with the animation, but to make things work perfectly we need to properly place the disc according to mouse position as soon as it's added to the game.

```
private function onAdded(e:Event) {
    moveHorizontally();
    par=this.parent.parent as Main;
    gotoAndStop(currentPlayer);
    addEventListener(Event.ENTER_FRAME,onEnterFrame);
    stage.addEventListener(MouseEvent.CLICK,onMouseClick);
}
```

Calling moveHorizontally function as soon as the disc is added to the stage will do the job.

Making computer play

Playing Connect Four against yourself is not the best gaming experience ever. What about making CPU play against you?

The idea: At the very beginning, the computer will randomly choose a move among the possible columns and place the disc, without caring whether it is a good move or not. This will help us to focus on the other things to fix to let the computer play. Obviously, when the computer plays, the player cannot place discs, so we have to remove some listeners when it's player two's turn.

The development: The first thing to change is `onAdded` function, because we want the player to take control over the disc only when it's player one's turn.

Rewrite the function this way:

```
private function onAdded(e:Event) {
  par=this.parent.parent as Main;
  moveHorizontally();
  if (currentPlayer==1) {
    stage.addEventListener(MouseEvent.CLICK,onMouseClick);
  } else {
    computerMove();
  }
  gotoAndStop(currentPlayer);
  addEventListener(Event.ENTER_FRAME,onEnterFrame);
}
```

There aren't many changes, just some re-arrangement of the code. The core of the function is this `if` statement:

```
if (currentPlayer==1) {
  stage.addEventListener(MouseEvent.CLICK,onMouseClick);
} else {
  computerMove();
}
```

because the mouse click listener is added only if the current player is a human, otherwise `computerMove` function is called. Since `computerMove` uses some functions defined in `Main` class, I had to place this line:

```
par=this.parent.parent as Main;
```

at the very beginning of the function, since `par` variable must be defined before `computerMove` is executed.

Also, since computer player does not use mouse click listener, you may not want to execute the line which removes the listener once the player dropped the disc.

Changing `dropDisc` function this way:

```
private function dropDisc():void {
  currentRow=par.firstFreeRow(currentColumn,currentPlayer);
  fallingDistance=35+currentRow*60;
  if (currentPlayer==1) {
    stage.removeEventListener(MouseEvent.CLICK,onMouseClick);
  }
}
```

will prevent removing the listener if the player is not human.

Everything is ready to let the computer make its move.

Unleashing CPU power

Finally it's time for the computer to make its move. At the moment it will be a random move, so you just need to check for legal columns to move, and randomly choose one of them.

The idea: Choose a random column among the possible ones and place the disc.

The development: This is `computerMove` function, to be inserted in `disc_movieclip.as`:

```
private function computerMove():void {
  var possibleMoves:Array=par.possibleColumns();
  var cpuMove:uint=Math.floor(Math.random()*possibleMoves.length)
  currentColumn=possibleMoves[cpuMove];
  x=35+60*currentColumn;
  currentRow=par.firstFreeRow(currentColumn,currentPlayer);
  fallingDestination=35+currentRow*60;
}
```

Apart from computer decision, it works as if the player was human.

```
var possibleMoves:Array=par.possibleColumns();
```

`possibleMoves` variable stores the array with all legal columns.

```
var cpuMove:uint=Math.floor(Math.random()*possibleMoves.length)
```

cpuMove is a random number between zero (included) and the number of elements in possibleMoves array (excluded).

```
currentColumn=possibleMoves[cpuMove];
```

Now currentColumn variable takes the value of the cpuMove-th element of possibleMoves array. That is, a random legal column.

The rest of the function just manages disc positioning and falling exactly in the same way the script does when dealing with a human player.

Test the movie, and you will be able to play, and almost every time win, against the computer.

Yes, even my grandmother would win. That's why artificial intelligence algorithms exist.

Playing with AI: defensive play

While the creation of an algorithm to make the computer play perfectly is beyond the scope of this book, we'll see the basics of artificial intelligence making the CPU player at least trying not to let the human player win that easily.

The idea: When it's time to choose the column, don't pick it randomly among all possible columns, but among the columns that can give the highest number of connected discs if played by the opponent. Look at this picture:

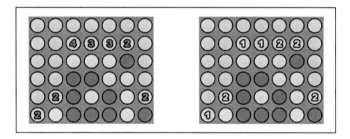

The same board configuration, on the left the possible red moves with the number of possible yellow streaks. The third column from the left is the best move, as it will prevent yellow from winning. On the right, possible yellow moves. There are four possible red moves that will make the red player have two discs in a row, so we'll randomly choose a column among the second, the fifth, the sixth and the seventh from the left.

The development: As said `computerMove` in `disc_movieclip.as` does not randomly pick the column among all possible columns anymore, so we'll delegate the choice of candidate columns to an external function. Change `computerMove` this way:

```
private function computerMove():void {
  var possibleMoves:Array=par.think();
  var cpuMove:uint=Math.floor(Math.random()*possibleMoves.length)
  currentColumn=possibleMoves[cpuMove];
  x=35+60*currentColumn;
  currentRow=par.firstFreeRow(currentColumn,currentPlayer);
  fallingDistance=35+currentRow*60;
}
```

Now `possibleMoves` array will be populated by think function, defined in `Main.as`.

Let's see how it works:

```
public function think():Array {
  var possibleMoves:Array=possibleColumns();
  var aiMoves:Array=new Array();
  var blocked:uint;
  var bestBlocked:uint=0;
  for (var i:uint=0; i<possibleMoves.length; i++) {
    for (var j:uint=0; j<6; j++) {
      if (gameField[j][possibleMoves[i]]!=0) {
        break;
      }
    }
    gameField[j-1][possibleMoves[i]]=1;
    blocked=getAdj(j-1,possibleMoves[i],0,1)+getAdj(j-
1,possibleMoves[i],0,-1);
    blocked=Math.max(blocked,getAdj(j-1,possibleMoves[i],1,0));
    blocked=Math.max(blocked,getAdj(j-1,possibleMoves[i],-
1,1)+getAdj(j-1,possibleMoves[i],1,-1));
    blocked=Math.max(blocked,getAdj(j-1,possibleMoves[i],1,1)+getAdj(j
-1,possibleMoves[i],-1,-1));
    if (blocked>=bestBlocked) {
      if (blocked>bestBlocked) {
        bestBlocked=blocked;
        aiMoves=new Array();
      }
      aiMoves.push(possibleMoves[i]);
    }
    gameField[j-1][possibleMoves[i]]=0;
  }
  return aiMoves;
}
```

This is your first step into AI world, so let me explain the function in detail:

```
var possibleMoves:Array=possibleColumns();
```

We start creating the same old array with all possible columns.

```
var aiMoves:Array=new Array();
```

`aiMoves` is the array that will contain the possible moves after being processed by computer's AI.

```
var blocked:uint;
var bestBlocked:uint=0;
```

`blocked` will track how many connected discs I am blocking for each possible column, while `bestBlocked` stores the highest number of connected discs blocked so far.

```
for (var i:uint=0; i<possibleMoves.length; i++) {
  for (var j:uint=0; j<6; j++) {
    if (gameField[j][possibleMoves[i]]!=0) {
      break;
    }
  }
}
```

These two `for` loops and the `if` statement with the `break` to force the second `for` to exit just helps you find the first free row (from bottom-to-top) for each possible column just like the `firstFreeRow` function does.

```
gameField[j-1][possibleMoves[i]]=1;
```

At this time we know a disc can be placed at row `j-1` and column `possibleMoves[i]` so we update `gameField` array as if the human player (player 1) placed a disc in it.

```
blocked=getAdj(j-1,possibleMoves[i],0,1)+getAdj(j-
1,possibleMoves[i],0,-1);
blocked=Math.max(blocked,getAdj(j-1,possibleMoves[i],1,0));
blocked=Math.max(blocked,getAdj(j-1,possibleMoves[i],-1,1)+getAdj(j-
1,possibleMoves[i],1,-1));
blocked=Math.max(blocked,getAdj(j-1,possibleMoves[i],1,1)+getAdj(j-
1,possibleMoves[i],-1,-1));
```

This is the core of the script: we are assigning `blocked` the maximum value of adjacent discs found in the four directions.

Note as `Math.max` method returns the highest among two or more expressions.

At this time we know how many discs in a row would get the human player if placing a disc at row `j-1` and column `possibleMoves[i]`.

```
if (blocked>=bestBlocked) {
  if (blocked>bestBlocked) {
    bestBlocked=blocked;
    aiMoves=new Array();
  }
  aiMoves.push(possibleMoves[i]);
}
```

This block manages the consequences of the previous check. We match `blocked` with `bestBlocked` to see if it's the best possible player move so far or not. We can have three cases:

1. `blocked` is greater than `bestBlocked`: this means placing a disc in the current column causes to stop the longest streak of connected discs found until now. It's the best move so far. We have to empty `aiMoves` array of all previously inserted columns and insert this column value. Also, we need to update `bestBlocked` value assigning it `blocked` value.

2. `blocked` is equal to `bestBlocked`: this means placing a disc in the current column causes to stop the longest streak of connected discs found until now, but there are other moves that would cause the same effect. We'll add column value to `aiMoves` array as it's a possible move.

3. `blocked` is less than `bestBlocked`: this means we already found better moves, so we are skipping it.

Finally, we have to restore `gameField` array:

```
gameField[j-1][possibleMoves[i]]=0;
```

and return the array of possible moves:

```
return aiMoves;
```

Test the movie now, and you will see the CPU playing in defensive mode. Now beating it will require more skill.

Summary

During the making of Connect Four you learned how to create smooth animations on the fly and to create a basic computer artificial intelligence. Remember in board games computer can play as an opponent, so you should always consider creating a smart CPU player.

Where to go now

You should prove yourself creating an offensive play strategy. Defensive play only tries to block the human player, without trying to beat it. It tries to draw. Try to make the computer more aggressive trying to block the human player and at the same time connecting more discs. This can be done in three steps:

1. Watch if there are winning moves. If there is a winning column, simply play that column and don't care about the human player.

2. If there aren't winning moves, and playing defensively you get only one column in `aiMoves` array, that is there's a move which will cause the most damage to a human player, play that column.

3. If there aren't winning moves and playing defensively you get more than one column in `aiMoves` array, don't pick a column randomly but choose the one that will make you get the highest number of your discs in a row.

Once the computer is able to give you a real challenge, you can be proud of your work.

4
Snake

Snake was one of the first video games to be released in arcades during the mid 1970s and it became a worldwide classic once Nokia included a version of the game in its phones.

In the game the player controls a snake, typically represented with a sequence of dots or characters, that moves in a maze and must pick up food while avoiding its own body and the walls. When the snake eats food, its body becomes longer, making it more difficult to move around the maze without hitting himself. The player can move the snake in four directions (up, down, left, and right) but cannot stop it. Once the snake hits its own body or a wall, it's game over.

In this chapter you will create a fully working Snake game, learning these concepts:

- Adding DisplayObjects at a given index using `addChildAt` method
- Calculating distance between two points in a tile-based environment
- Using `Point` class to deal with points
- Determining which DisplayObjects lie under a given point in the stage

But above all you'll learn that using arrays is not the only way to create a tile-based game.

Defining game design

There are too many snake games out there with nothing more than a bunch of dots to represent the snake, so we are going to make something with a better visual appeal. One thing we will avoid is the "where's the head" effect. Look at these screenshots:

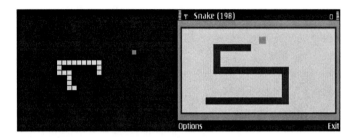

Can you tell me where the head of the snake is? You can't because there aren't any specific graphics to represent the head. Our snake will have a head. Also, notice there aren't any specific graphics to represent the snake when it turns. It's just another tile.

Also, try to play a classic snake and you will find how much a boring game it can be, if you just play running in straight lines and grabbing the fruits once in a while as in this picture:

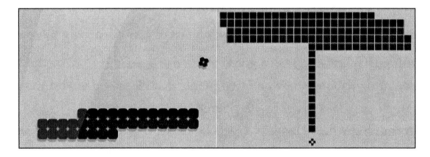

Running in straight lines and making close U-turns can make this game almost endless.

In our Snake game, the snake itself will have its own head, and for every fruit collected, a random obstacle will appear in the game field, preventing players from using the "run and U-turn" strategy and adding some challenge to the game.

Array-based games versus Movie Clip-based games

During the making of the previous games I showed how arrays can manage the game behind the scene, while Movie Clips are just actors you place here and there according to game array values.

Obviously Snake, for its tile-based game nature, can be also developed this way, but I want you to learn another way of managing tile-based games.

This time you won't use any array, and you will handle all game events directly on DisplayObjects.

Although Snake would be easier to develop using arrays, some kind of games, especially non-tile-based games, cannot be developed using arrays, so you'd better get used to DisplayObjects games management.

The entire process will be a bit more complicated but don't worry, the game is quite easy.

The basic idea is to make the script understand what's happening in the game directly looking at the various actors in the stage.

Preparing the field

Create a new file (**File | New**) then from **New Document** window select **Actionscript 3.0.** Set its properties as width to 640 px, height to 480 px, background color to #FFFFFF (white), and frame rate to 6. Also define the Document Class as Main and save the file as snake.fla. I want you to note the low frame rate, set to six. This is because we'll update snake position at every frame, without smooth animations, as it's not required in these kind of games. Anyway, you can make the game run at any number of frames per second, having a variable, with a counter, that runs the update function and resets itself at every n frames. We'll discuss this at the end of the chapter.

Drawing the graphics

Let's start drawing all the graphics. A snake prototype requires:

- A background, such as a grass field
- A "game over" overlay, used to add a dramatic effect when the game is over
- The fruit (collectible)

- The wall
- The snake

They are all very easy to draw, except for the snake. In `snake.fla`, create four new Movie Clip symbols and call them `bg_mc` for the background, `game_over_mc` for the game over overlay, `fruit_mc` for the fruit, and `obstacle_mc` for the wall. Set them all as exportable for ActionScript. Leave all other settings at their default values, just like you did in previous chapters.

These are the objects I drew:

From left to right, the background and the game over overlay (which is a bit transparent), both 640x480 pixels with registration point at 0,0. Then, the collectible fruit and the deadly wall, with registration point at 0,0 and inside an imaginary 40x40 pixels square. This is also the size of the tile the game is based on.

Drawing the snake is a bit harder because you will need 10 frames.

In `snake.fla`, create a new Movie Clip symbol called `the_snake_mc` and set it as exportable for ActionScript. Leave all other settings at their default values, just like you did in previous chapters. Then draw your snake this way:

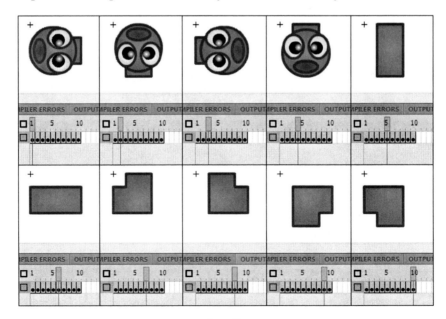

Snake's pieces are also drawn with registration point at 0,0 and inside the imaginary 40x40 tile, just like the fruit and the wall.

Every frame represents a possible snake piece:

1. Snake's head heading left
2. Snake's head heading up
3. Snake's head heading right
4. Snake's head heading down
5. Vertical snake body
6. Horizontal snake body
7. Snake body going right then turning up or going down then turning left
8. Snake body going left then turning up or going down then turning right
9. Snake body going left then turning down or going up then turning right
10. Snake body going right then turning down or going up then turning left

That's a lot of frames, but this will give our snake a respectable look.

Placing the snake

Let's start placing the snake. Without closing `snake.fla`, create a new file and from **New Document** window select **ActionScript 3.0 Class**. Save this file as `Main.as` in the same path you saved `snake.fla`. Then write:

```
package {
  import flash.display.Sprite;
  public class Main extends Sprite {
    private const FIELD_WIDTH:uint=16;
    private const FIELD_HEIGHT:uint=12;
    private const TILE_SIZE:uint=40;
    private var the_snake:the_snake_mc;
    private var snakeDirection:uint;
    private var snakeContainer:Sprite= new Sprite();
    private var bg:bg_mc=new bg_mc();
    public function Main() {
      addChild(bg);
      placeSnake();
    }
  }
}
```

You should be used to seeing the making of a game start this way: we are importing the required classes (`Sprite` in this case), defining some variables and constants, and then creating the constructor. Let's see the constants and variables defined at this stage:

- `FIELD_WIDTH`: the width of the game field, in tiles. 16 tiles multiplied by 40 pixels means 640 pixels, the whole stage.

- `FIELD_HEIGHT`: the height of the game field, in tiles.

- `TILE_SIZE`: the size of a tile, in pixels.

- `the_snake`: this variable will contain the snake itself.

- `snakeDirection`: snake's direction, using numbers from 0, 1, 2, 3 to indicate respectively left, up, right, and down.

- `snakeContainer`: the DisplayObjectContainer that will contain the snake itself.

- `bg`: the background.

As you can see, `Main` constructor just adds the background to Display List then delegates `placeSnake` function to place the snake on the game field.

The snake itself

`placeSnake` function has to place the snake in a random place of the field, facing a random direction. Add this function to `Main.as` file:

```
private function placeSnake():void {
  addChild(snakeContainer);
  var col:uint=Math.floor(Math.random()*(FIELD_WIDTH-10))+5;
  var row:uint=Math.floor(Math.random()*(FIELD_HEIGHT-10))+5;
  snakeDirection=Math.floor(Math.random()*4);
  the_snake=new the_snake_mc(col*TILE_SIZE,row*TILE_
SIZE,snakeDirection+1);
  snakeContainer.addChild(the_snake);
  switch (snakeDirection) {
    case 0 : // facing left
      trace("left");
      the_snake = new the_snake_mc((col+1)*TILE_SIZE,row*TILE_SIZE,6);
      snakeContainer.addChild(the_snake);
      the_snake = new the_snake_mc((col+2)*TILE_SIZE,row*TILE_SIZE,6);
      snakeContainer.addChild(the_snake);
      break;
    case 1 : // facing up
      trace("up");
```

```
    the_snake = new the_snake_mc(col*TILE_SIZE,(row+1)*TILE_SIZE,5);
    snakeContainer.addChild(the_snake);
    the_snake = new the_snake_mc(col*TILE_SIZE,(row+2)*TILE_SIZE,5);
    snakeContainer.addChild(the_snake);
    break;
  case 2 : // facing down
    trace("down");
    the_snake = new the_snake_mc((col-1)*TILE_SIZE,row*TILE_SIZE,6);
    snakeContainer.addChild(the_snake);
    the_snake = new the_snake_mc((col-2)*TILE_SIZE,row*TILE_SIZE,6);
    snakeContainer.addChild(the_snake);
    break;
  case 3 : // facing right
    trace("right");
    the_snake = new the_snake_mc(col*TILE_SIZE,(row-1)*TILE_SIZE,5);
    snakeContainer.addChild(the_snake);
    the_snake = new the_snake_mc(col*TILE_SIZE,(row-2)*TILE_SIZE,5);
    snakeContainer.addChild(the_snake);
    break;
  }
}
```

Let's see what's happening: first we need to add snakeContainer
DisplayObjectContainer to Display List.

```
addChild(snakeContainer);
```

Then, the snake will be placed in a random location of the game field, but at least five
tiles away from the edge. We do not want the snake to appear so close to game field
edge that the player won't be able to make it turn before it hits the edge and dies.

```
var col:uint=Math.floor(Math.random()*(FIELD_WIDTH-10))+5;
```

```
var row:uint=Math.floor(Math.random()*(FIELD_HEIGHT-10))+5;
```

Once we've decided where to place the snake, let's choose a random direction.

```
snakeDirection=Math.floor(Math.random()*4);
```

At this time, we can construct the snake itself. Look at the arguments, snake's vertical
and horizontal position, and the frame to show.

```
the_snake=new the_snake_mc(col*TILE_SIZE,row*TILE_
SIZE,snakeDirection+1);
```

Showing `snakeDirection+1` frame will show frame 1 (snake's head heading left) when direction is 0 (left), frame 2 (snake's head heading up) when direction is 1 (up), and the same concept applies to frame 3 (right), and 4 (down).

Finally the snake is added to Display List.

```
snakeContainer.addChild(the_snake);
```

Before writing `the_snake_mc` class (at this time you should know there's such class to be written), let's see what else we are doing in `placeSnake` function.

```
switch (snakeDirection) { ... }
```

We want to add two more pieces to the snake according to its direction, so we have to use a `switch` statement to see which direction the snake is facing.

Let's see what happens when the snake is facing left, the remaining cases will follow the same concept:

```
case 0 : // facing left
  trace("left");
  the_snake = new the_snake_mc((col+1)*TILE_SIZE,row*TILE_SIZE,6);
  snakeContainer.addChild(the_snake);
  the_snake = new the_snake_mc((col+2)*TILE_SIZE,row*TILE_SIZE,6);
  snakeContainer.addChild(the_snake);
  break;
```

What we do is add two more snake pieces to the right of its head (since it's heading left, pieces representing the body will be added to the right) and showing frame 6, which is the horizontal piece of the body of the snake.

The same concept is applied to all directions, showing frame 5 (the vertical piece of the body of the snake) when the snake is heading up or down.

Now it's time to create `the_snake_mc` class itself: without closing `snake.fla`, create a new file and from **New Document** window select **ActionScript 3.0 Class**. Save this file as `the_snake_mc.as` in the same path you saved `snake.fla`. Then write:

```
package {
  import flash.display.MovieClip;
  public class the_snake_mc extends MovieClip {
    public function the_snake_mc(px:uint,py:uint,frm:uint) {
      x=px;
      y=py;
      gotoAndStop(frm);
    }
  }
}
```

There is really nothing to say: the snake piece is just placed and the desired frame is shown.

Test your movie and you will see your snake somewhere in the game field. In the picture you can see the four possible directions with the snake heading left, up, right, and down.

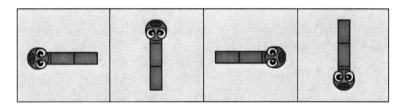

We are just creating a working code for snake placement, but there's room for simplification.

Simplifying the code

Once you get a working code, don't stop. Try to make the code more readable and maintainable, possibly reducing the number of lines.

Here's my simplified version of placeSnake function:

```
private function placeSnake():void {
  addChild(snakeContainer);
  var col:uint=Math.floor(Math.random()*(FIELD_WIDTH-10))+5;
  var row:uint=Math.floor(Math.random()*(FIELD_HEIGHT-10))+5;
  var tmpCol,tmpRow,evenDir:uint;
  snakeDirection=Math.floor(Math.random()*4);
  the_snake=new the_snake_mc(col*TILE_SIZE,
    row*TILE_SIZE,snakeDirection+1);
  snakeContainer.addChild(the_snake);
  // remove the entire switch
  for (var i:uint=1; i<=2; i++) {
    evenDir = snakeDirection%2;
    tmpCol = col+i*(1-evenDir)*(1-snakeDirection);
    tmpRow = row+i*(2-snakeDirection)*evenDir;
    the_snake = new the_snake_mc(tmpCol*TILE_SIZE,tmpRow*TILE_SIZE,
              6-evenDir);
    snakeContainer.addChild(the_snake);
  }
}
```

If you test the movie you will see it works the same way as before, but it's much shorter, as the `switch` statement has been replaced with a `for` loop.

To do it, first I added three new variables. `tmpRow` and `tmpCol` are temporary variables used to manipulate `row` and `col` variables without changing their values. `evenDir` will tell us if the snake is placed in an even direction (0 or 2, horizontal) or in an odd direction (1 or 3, vertical).

The `for` loop that replaced the `switch` statement goes from 1 to 2 as there are two snake pieces to add after its head.

```
evenDir = snakeDirection%2;
```

At this time `evenDir` will be 1 if `snakeDirection` is odd, or 0 if `snake direction` is even.

```
tmpCol = col+i*(1-evenDir)*(1-snakeDirection);
tmpRow = row+i*(2-snakeDirection)*evenDir;
```

These two lines just assign to `tmpCol` and `tmpRow` the column and row position according to `row`, `col`, and `evenDir`.

```
the_snake = new the_snake_mc(tmpCol*TILE_SIZE,tmpRow*TILE_SIZE,6-
evenDir);
```

Finally the snake piece is constructed. Notice how `evenDir` also modifies the frame to show, in the third argument.

Now that we have a simpler routine, let's make the snake move.

Letting the snake move

Snake is a simple yet fast paced game because you can't stop the snake. It will always be moving in its direction.

The idea: Make the snake move by a tile in the current direction at every frame.

The development: To move the snake at every frame, we need to import the class to handle `ENTER_FRAME` event. Add it to `Main.as`:

```
import flash.display.Sprite;
import flash.events.Event;
```

And in `Main` constructor, we need to add the listener:

```
public function Main() {
  addChild(bg);
  placeSnake();
  addEventListener(Event.ENTER_FRAME,onEnterFr);
}
```

Now I would like to introduce four Boolean functions we are going to create, called `is_up`, `is_down`, `is_left`, and `is_right`.

These functions, given two pieces of the snake called `from` and `to` passed as arguments, return `true` if `to` snake piece is up (or down, or left, or right) respect the `down` piece.

This is `is_up` function:

```
private function is_up(from:the_snake_mc,to:the_snake_mc):Boolean {
  return to.y<from.y&&from.x==to.x;
}
```

It's checking that `to`'s `y` property is less than `from`'s and that both pieces have the same `x` property. In this case, `to` piece will be above `from`.

The remaining three functions work in the same way. This is `is_down`:

```
private function is_down(from:the_snake_mc,to:the_snake_mc):Boolean {
  return to.y>from.y&&from.x==to.x;
}
```

This is `is_left`:

```
private function is_left(from:the_snake_mc,to:the_snake_mc):Boolean {
  return to.x<from.x&&from.y==to.y;
}
```

And this is `is_right`:

```
private function is_right(from:the_snake_mc,to:the_snake_mc):Boolean {
  return to.x>from.x&&from.y==to.y;
}
```

But the core of the script is in `onEnterFr` function, that will handle snake's movement.

Before you start typing, let me explain how snake movement will work. This phase can be divided into three steps:

1. Moving the head according to snake's direction.

2. At this time, there will be a gap between the head and the rest of the snake. Fill the gap with a new snake piece, connecting the head with the rest of the body.

3. The snake is longer than it should be now, so the tail is removed.

All these three steps will be performed in the same frame, so the player will only see the moving snake.

This is onEnterFr function:

```
private function onEnterFr(e:Event) {
  var the_head:the_snake_mc=snakeContainer.getChildAt(0) as the_snake_
mc;
  var new_piece:the_snake_mc=new the_snake_mc(the_head.x,the_head.
y,1);
  snakeContainer.addChildAt(new_piece,1);
  var the_body:the_snake_mc=snakeContainer.getChildAt(2) as the_snake_
mc;
  var p:uint=snakeContainer.numChildren;
  var the_tail:the_snake_mc=snakeContainer.getChildAt(p-1) as the_
snake_mc;
  var the_new_tail:the_snake_mc=snakeContainer.getChildAt(p-2) as the_
snake_mc;
  the_head.moveHead(snakeDirection,TILE_SIZE);
  // brute force
  if (is_up(new_piece,the_head)&&is_down(new_piece,the_body)) {
    new_piece.gotoAndStop(5);
  }
  if (is_down(new_piece,the_head)&&is_up(new_piece,the_body)) {
    new_piece.gotoAndStop(5);
  }
  if (is_left(new_piece,the_head)&&is_right(new_piece,the_body)) {
    new_piece.gotoAndStop(6);
  }
  if (is_right(new_piece,the_head)&&is_left(new_piece,the_body)) {
    new_piece.gotoAndStop(6);
  }
  // end of brute force
  snakeContainer.removeChild(the_tail);
}
```

Let's see how it works:

```
var the_head:the_snake_mc=snakeContainer.getChildAt(0) as the_snake_
mc;
```

You already dealt with `getChildAt` method during the making of Minesweeper. I am using this method to retrieve the DisplayObject that contains the head of the snake. Being the first DisplayObject I added to `snakeContainer` DisplayObjectContainer, using `snakeContainer.getChildAt(0)` will always make you find the head.

```
var new_piece:the_snake_mc=new the_snake_mc(the_head.x,the_head.y,1);
```

`new_piece` is the piece of the snake which will connect the head with the rest of the body. It will be placed in the same position of the head, as we are about to move the head. Note that I am telling you to show frame 1. It's an arbitrary frame as the real frame to be shown has to be decided.

```
snakeContainer.addChildAt(new_piece,1);
```

The newly created piece of the snake is now added to `snakeContainer` DisplayObjectContainer.

I want to focus on the way the new piece is being added to `snakeContainer` DisplayObjectContainer: I am not using `addChild` method, but `addChildAt` method.

What's the difference? While `addChild` adds the DisplayObject at the top of the hierarchy, overlapping previously added DisplayObjects and showing the newly added DisplayObject in front of them, with `addChildAt` I can decide the index of the DisplayObject to add. If you specify a currently occupied index, the DisplayObject that already exists at such index, as well as all other DisplayObjects existing at higher indexes will be moved up one position.

This picture will help you to understand the difference:

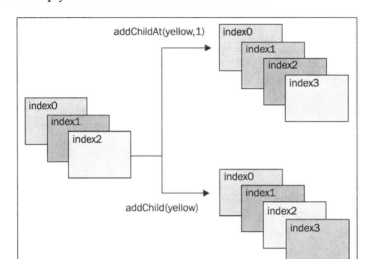

When the yellow box is added with addChildAt, you can define its index and DisplayObjects indexes are shifted to make the yellow box fit. When the yellow box is added with addChild, it's simply added in the highest index available.

At this time we have the head at index zero, and the newly added snake piece at index 1. Where can we find the rest of the snake? Obviously starting from index 2, so we will define the_body variable as the first snake piece which connects the head with the piece we should place.

```
var the_body:the_snake_mc=snakeContainer.getChildAt(2) as the_snake_
mc;
```

To know the snake's length, in pieces, you have to use numChildren property. We'll save it in a variable called p.

```
var p:uint=snakeContainer.numChildren;
```

Can you tell me where I can find the tail? Look how we can find it at index p-1.

```
var the_tail:the_snake_mc=snakeContainer.getChildAt(p-1) as the_snake_
mc;
```

At this time we defined all key snake pieces, and we can proceed with snake's movement. We'll delegate it to the moveHead function we'll define in the_snake_mc class.

```
the_head.moveHead(snakeDirection,TILE_SIZE);
```

once the head is moved, we need a bit of brute force to know which frame we have to show in the piece at index 1, the one we just added.

```
if (is_up(new_piece,the_head)&&is_down(new_piece,the_body)) {
   new_piece.gotoAndStop(5);
}
```

If the head is above the piece and the body is below the piece, then we have to show frame 5 because we are dealing with a vertical snake.

Finally, the tail is removed.

```
snakeContainer.removeChild(the_tail);
```

The rest of the code follows the same concept, while moveHead function in the_snake_mc class is made this way:

```
public function moveHead(dir:uint,pixels:uint):void {
   switch (dir) {
      case 0 :
         x-=pixels;
         break;
      case 1 :
         y-=pixels;
         break;
      case 2 :
         x+=pixels;
         break;
      case 3 :
         y+=pixels;
         break;
   }
   gotoAndStop(dir+1);
}
```

There's nothing special in it, as we are just moving the head acting on x or y properties, showing the appropriate frame.

Test the movie, and you will see the snake moving, running out of the stage. Here it is a "bullet time" of what's happening:

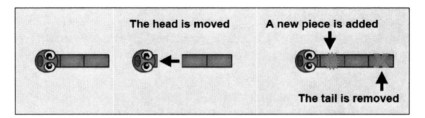

Although the snake is moved in three steps, the player won't see partial steps as everything is happening in the same frame. The same concept that caused a problem during the making of Concentration, when the player wasn't able to see two flipped cards before we inserted a timer to pause the game, this time comes to our aid.

Now, it's time to make the player control the snake.

Controlling the snake

The player will be able to control the snake with arrow keys.

The idea: As the player presses one of the arrow keys, snake's head must move in the appropriate direction.

The development: First, we need to import the class to manage keyboard events:

```
import flash.display.Sprite;
import flash.events.Event;
import flash.events.KeyboardEvent;
```

Then, in Main function, we need to place the listener:

```
public function Main() {
  addChild(bg);
  placeSnake();
  addEventListener(Event.ENTER_FRAME,onEnterFr);
  stage.addEventListener(KeyboardEvent.KEY_DOWN,onKeyD);
}
```

Now each time the player presses a key, onKeyD function is called.

We decided `snakeDirection`'s possible values are 0, 1, 2, and 3 respectively for left, up, right, and down directions, and the respective `keyCode` values are 37, 38, 39, and 40, so we can manage `snakeDirection` writing `onKeyD` function this way:

```
private function onKeyD(e:KeyboardEvent):void {
  if (e.keyCode>=37&&e.keyCode<=40) {
    snakeDirection=e.keyCode-37;
  }
}
```

`snakeDirection` will change only when `keyCode` ranges from 37 to 40, both included. Then subtracting 37 from `keyCode` will give us the correct `snakeDirection` value.

We also need to add some more `if` statements to the brute force part of code which allows us to display the correct frame according to head and rest of the body positions.

```
// brute force
...
if (is_left(new_piece,the_head)&&is_up(new_piece,the_body)) {
  new_piece.gotoAndStop(7);
}
if (is_up(new_piece,the_head)&&is_left(new_piece,the_body)) {
  new_piece.gotoAndStop(7);
}
if (is_up(new_piece,the_head)&&is_right(new_piece,the_body)) {
  new_piece.gotoAndStop(8);
}
if (is_right(new_piece,the_head)&&is_up(new_piece,the_body)) {
  new_piece.gotoAndStop(8);
}
if (is_right(new_piece,the_head)&&is_down(new_piece,the_body)) {
  new_piece.gotoAndStop(9);
}
if (is_down(new_piece,the_head)&&is_right(new_piece,the_body)) {
  new_piece.gotoAndStop(9);
}
if (is_left(new_piece,the_head)&&is_down(new_piece,the_body)) {
  new_piece.gotoAndStop(10);
}
if (is_down(new_piece,the_head)&&is_left(new_piece,the_body)) {
  new_piece.gotoAndStop(10);
}
```

There isn't that much to explain, I just included all possible combinations of head positions and rest of the body positions relative to the new piece of the snake I already added.

Test the movie and try to change the snake's direction using arrow keys.

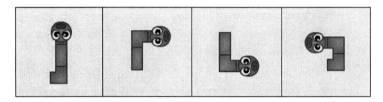

In the picture are four typical ways the snake can turn.

Also notice that if you press the arrow key at the opposite of the snake direction, that is you press LEFT when the snake is moving RIGHT, the snake will cross over itself and a little graphic glitch appears, as in this picture:

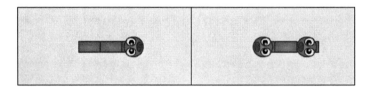

Don't worry as we won't allow it to happen, later in this chapter. But keep in mind you have to deeply test your games to prevent unwanted situations happening.

Placing fruits

Placing fruits is the hardest part of the making of this game, because you will learn some new concepts and techniques.

The idea: Placing a fruit in a random spot is not just a matter of picking a couple of random coordinates and adding the fruit.

Fruits will be placed on the game according to these two principles:

1. A fruit cannot be placed in a tile occupied by the snake
2. A fruit cannot be placed too close to the snake's head. It would be too easy, both playing and programming the game

The development: Let's divide things into steps: first, we have to define the variable to handle `fruit_mc` Movie Clip. Add this new class level variable:

```
private const FIELD_WIDTH:uint=16;
private const FIELD_HEIGHT:uint=12;
private const TILE_SIZE:uint=40;
private var the_snake:the_snake_mc;
private var snakeDirection:uint;
private var snakeContainer:Sprite= new Sprite();
private var bg:bg_mc=new bg_mc();
private var fruit:fruit_mc;
```

Then, in `Main` function, we'll call the function (yet to be written) that will place the fruit. The game must begin with a fruit on the stage, so add it immediately after you created the snake:

```
public function Main() {
   addChild(bg);
   placeSnake();
   placeStuff();
   addEventListener(Event.ENTER_FRAME,onEnterFr);
   stage.addEventListener(KeyboardEvent.KEY_DOWN,onKeyD);
}
```

Notice I called the function `placeStuff` rather than `place_fruit` because the same function will be used to place random walls.

We said we won't place fruit too close to snake's head, so we need a function to calculate the distance between the snake's head and the fruit, or between any two points. I bet you are thinking about Pythagorean Theorem, where the distance we require is the hypotenuse of the triangle built over the two points. It's certainly one solution, but it's not the one we need. Look at this picture:

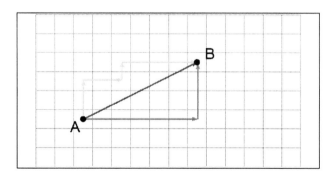

Let's say we want to calculate the distance between A and B. The blue line is the unique shortest path and it's called Euclidean distance, but it's not what we are looking for, because the snake can move only horizontally or vertically, tile by tile. So the correct distance between A and B is represented by the red or the green lines. Following both paths, you will get from A to B crossing nine tiles.

Following this concept, we can say the distance between two points is the sum of the absolute difference of their coordinates.

This way to calculate the distance between two points is called Manhattan Distance, because this way of moving from one point to another resembles the way cars move along the grid-like layout of the island of Manhattan.

With this concept in mind, let's create a function to calculate the Manhattan distance between two points:

```
private function manhattan_dist(x1:uint,x2:uint,y1:uint,y2:uint):uint
{
   return Math.abs(x1-x2)+Math.abs(y1-y2);
}
```

manhattan_dist function wants four arguments, all unsigned integers, representing the x-and y-coordinates of the points, and returns the distance as an unsigned integer.

Now, let's dive into the hard part: placeStuff function will place the fruit on the stage.

```
private function placeStuff():void {
  var the_head:the_snake_mc=snakeContainer.getChildAt(0) as
    the_snake_mc;
  var placed:Boolean=false;
  var col:uint;
  var row:uint;
  var point_to_watch:Point;
  var children:Array;
  while (!placed) {
    col=Math.floor(Math.random()*FIELD_WIDTH)*TILE_SIZE;
    row=Math.floor(Math.random()*FIELD_HEIGHT)*TILE_SIZE;
    point_to_watch=new Point(col+TILE_SIZE/2,row+TILE_SIZE/2);
    children=stage.getObjectsUnderPoint(point_to_watch);
    if (children.length<2&&manhattan_dist(the_head.x,col,
      the_head.y,row)>60) {
      placed=true;
    }
  }
```

```
    fruit =new fruit_mc();
    fruit.x=col;
    fruit.y=row;
    addChild(fruit);
    fruit.name="fruit";
}
```

As you can see, there's a couple of things you haven't seen before, so let's analyze the function line-by-line:

```
var the_head:the_snake_mc=snakeContainer.getChildAt(0) as the_snake_
mc;
```

Getting the head of the snake using `getChildAt` method. You already know the head is always at index `0`.

```
var placed:Boolean=false;
```

Boolean variable to tell us if we already placed the fruit or not. Obviously its starting value is `false` because we did not place any fruit yet.

```
var col:uint;
var row:uint;
```

A couple of unsigned integers to store row and column numbers where to place the fruit.

```
var point_to_watch:Point;
```

A `Point` variable called `point_to_watch`. `Point` represents a location in a two-dimensional coordinate system and its constructor is `Point(x,y)` where `x` represents the horizontal axis and `y` represents the vertical axis.

```
var children:Array;
```

Simply creating a new array. It's called `children` because it will contain all DisplayObjects that lie under a given point.

```
while (!placed) { ... }
```

This `while` loop repeats the code until `placed` variable becomes `true`, which means we successfully placed the fruit. The concept is similar to the one we used to place mines during the creation of Minesweeper game. We keep on trying to place fruits, or mines, until we randomly choose a legal position.

```
col=Math.floor(Math.random()*FIELD_WIDTH)*TILE_SIZE;
row=Math.floor(Math.random()*FIELD_HEIGHT)*TILE_SIZE;
```

Generating the candidate row and column where the fruit is to be placed. Notice I multiplied the result by TILE_SIZE because I am not working with arrays so I need to know the pixel where to place the fruit rather than the position in an array.

```
point_to_watch=new Point(col+TILE_SIZE/2,row+TILE_SIZE/2);
```

Constructing point_to_watch variable and assigning it the coordinate of the center of the hypothetical tile in the row-th row and the col-th column. A hypothetical tile is a square whose sides are TILE_SIZE long, so you will find its center adding TILE_SIZE/2 to the coordinates of its upper-left point.

```
children=stage.getObjectsUnderPoint(point_to_watch);
```

This is the core of the function. getObjectsUnderPoint method returns an array of objects that lie under the specified point and are children (or children of children, and so on) of the DisplayObjects Container which invoked the method.

```
if (children.length<2&&manhattan_dist(the_head.x,col,the_head.
y,row)>60) { ... }
```

This if statement checks the length of children array to be less than 2. If there is only one DisplayObjects under point_to_watch, it must be the ground, so the tile is free.

Also, the if checks for the Manhattan distance to be greater than 60 pixels.

If both conditions are true, then this line is executed:

```
placed=true;
```

this means we found a legal position where to place the fruit, so we set placed to true to exit the while loop.

The remaining lines:

```
fruit =new fruit_mc();
fruit.x=col;
fruit.y=row;
addChild(fruit);
fruit.name="fruit";
```

just construct and add the fruit to Display List, placing it in the chosen position.

Also, the fruit has a name, fruit. This will help us later.

To work with `Point` variables, we need to import a new class, so add it:

```
import flash.display.Sprite;
import flash.events.Event;
import flash.events.KeyboardEvent;
import flash.geom.Point;
```

Test the game, and a juicy fruit will appear on the stage.

Now the snake has a reason to live.

Eating fruits

Once the fruit is placed, eating is easy, let's say a piece of cake. A fruit cake, of course.

The idea: In the same way we checked for an empty tile to place the fruit in, we'll check for the tile occupied by the snake's head looking for a fruit. If we find a fruit, we have to remove it and place a new one elsewhere.

The development: Once the head has moved, we have to retrieve its middle point and see if there's a fruit under such point. Before the end of `onEnterFr` function, add this code:

```
var point_to_watch:Point=new Point(the_head.x+TILE_SIZE/2,the_head.
y+TILE_SIZE/2);
var children_in_that_point:Array=stage.getObjectsUnderPoint(point_to_
watch);
for (var i:uint=0; i<children_in_that_point.length; i++) {
  switch (children_in_that_point[i].parent.name) {
    case "fruit" :
      removeChild(fruit);
      placeStuff();
      break;
  }
}
```

Test the movie and eat a fruit: it will disappear and a new fruit will appear in another location.

In the picture, the snake eats a fruit and suddenly a new one is generated in a random position (with the principles explained before).

Let's see how it works:

```
var point_to_watch:Point=new Point(the_head.x+TILE_SIZE/2,the_head.
y+TILE_SIZE/2);
```

Creates a `Point` variable with the coordinates of the center of the snake's head.

```
var children_in_that_point:Array=stage.getObjectsUnderPoint(point_to_
watch);
```

Retrieves the children under such point with `getObjectsUnderPoint` method.

```
for (var i:uint=0; i<children_in_that_point.length; i++) { ... }
```

This `for` loop scans through the array filled with DisplayObjects that lie under `point_to_watch` point.

```
switch (children_in_that_point[i].parent.name) { ... }
```

The `switch` statement checks the name of the `i-th` DisplayObject in children's array. Notice I had to write:

```
children_in_that_point[i].parent.name
```

with `parent` rather than:

```
children_in_that_point[i].name
```

because in `children_in_that_point[i]` you'll find the shape (that is the red circle representing the fruit) that has no name. We named the DisplayObjects, which is shape's parent.

Then with this `case`:

```
case "fruit" :
```

we'll execute the following block of code if the name we found is `fruit`.

```
removeChild(fruit);
placeStuff();
break;
```

Here we remove `fruit` DisplayObject and call `placeStuff` function again, to place another fruit.

This way as soon as the snake eats a fruit, a new one is placed.

Making the snake grow

When the snake eats a fruit, it must grow. This is what makes the game increase its difficulty.

The idea: We know at every frame the snake moves its head according to its direction, a new piece is added to link the head with the rest of the body, and the tail is deleted.

To make the snake grow, we simply won't delete the tail for a given number of frames if the snake just ate a fruit. Adding a new piece without deleting anything will make the snake grow.

The development: We need a variable to know if the snake has just eaten a fruit, and eventually how many frames have passed since that moment. Add a new class level variable called `justEaten` that will start at 0 (the snake hasn't just eaten) and will contain the number of frames the snake will grow.

```
private const FIELD_WIDTH:uint=16;
private const FIELD_HEIGHT:uint=12;
private const TILE_SIZE:uint=40;
private var the_snake:the_snake_mc;
private var snakeDirection:uint;
private var snakeContainer:Sprite= new Sprite();
private var bg:bg_mc=new bg_mc();
private var fruit:fruit_mc;
private var justEaten:uint=0;
```

Now we have to modify `onEnterFr` function adding a line in the `switch` statement when the snake eats a fruit. Simply assign `justEaten` a value representing the number of frames the snake will grow. In this case, I set it to 3, but you are free to play with this number and see how it modifies the gameplay.

```
case "fruit" :
  justEaten=3;
  removeChild(fruit);
  placeStuff();
  break;
```

Finally, at the end of the brute force branch of the code, we must remove the tail only if `justEaten` is equal to 0, or decrease its value otherwise.

At the end of `onEnterFr` function, include this line:

```
snakeContainer.removeChild(the_tail);
```

into an `if` statement to execute it only if `justEaten` is equal to 0.

```
if (justEaten==0) {
  snakeContainer.removeChild(the_tail);
} else {
  justEaten--;
}
```

When `justEaten` is greater than 0, the tail is no longer removed, we only decrease `justEaten` value. The snake will grow for three frames each time it eats a fruit.

Test the game and pick up some fruit, to see your snake grow.

On the left, the snake is about to eat a fruit. On the right, the snake gets three pieces longer after it digested the fruit.

Placing walls

To make the game a little more challenging, we need to add some walls as the snake grows.

The idea: Every time a fruit is placed, a wall is added to the stage too, with the same criteria: in an empty cell, and never within a given distance. I'll refer walls as "obstacles" since they look more like square blocks rather than walls.

The development: There's not that much to explain here, as it's exactly the same concept you used to place fruits. Anyway, let's add a new class level variable called `obstacle` of `obstacle_mc` type.

```
private const FIELD_WIDTH:uint=16;
private const FIELD_HEIGHT:uint=12;
private const TILE_SIZE:uint=40;
private var the_snake:the_snake_mc;
private var snakeDirection:uint;
private var snakeContainer:Sprite= new Sprite();
private var bg:bg_mc=new bg_mc();
private var fruit:fruit_mc;
private var justEaten:uint=0;
private var obstacle:obstacle_mc;
```

Then, at the end of `placeStuff` function, copy and paste the same code you used to create the fruit, just adapting it to place an obstacle rather than the fruit.

```
private function placeStuff():void {
  . . .
  placed=false;
  while (!placed) {
    col=Math.floor(Math.random()*FIELD_WIDTH)*TILE_SIZE;
    row=Math.floor(Math.random()*FIELD_HEIGHT)*TILE_SIZE;
    point_to_watch=new Point(col+TILE_SIZE/2,row+TILE_SIZE/2);
    children=stage.getObjectsUnderPoint(point_to_watch);
    if (children.length<2&&manhattan_dist(the_head.x,col,
      the_head.y,row)>60) {
      placed=true;
    }
  }
  obstacle =new obstacle_mc();
  obstacle.x=col;
  obstacle.y=row;
  addChild(obstacle);
  obstacle.name="obstacle";
}
```

Test the movie, and your game will start with a fruit and an obstacle, and each time the snake collects a fruit, a new obstacle is added.

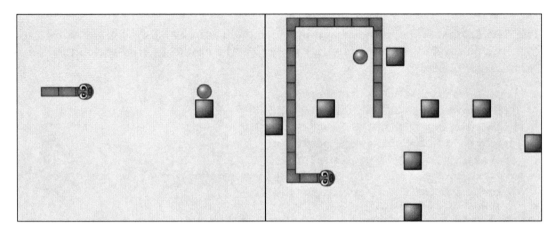

In the previous picture, on the left a typical game at the very beginning, and on the right the same game after the snake ate seven fruits. There are eight obstacles on the stage, the first one plus one for each fruit eaten.

Making the snake die

Tired of playing with "God Mode" on? Ok, let's make the snake die.

The idea: The snake will die if one of these conditions is verified:

1. The snake's head hits a wall
2. The snake's head hits any part of the snake's body
3. The snake's head leaves the stage

In some versions of the game, when the snake leaves the stage crossing through one boundary, it appears on the opposite side, but in this game the snake cannot leave the stage.

Also, the snake has only one life, so when the snake dies, it's game over.

The development: Each time the snake moves, we must check if the head is in the same tile occupied by an obstacle or by a piece of the snake's body. Also, we must check if the head is in the stage.

But first, let's see what should happen when the game is over. We have to remove all listeners as the player won't be able to interact with the keyboard and the snake won't move anymore. Also, we will finally use the game_over_mc object to give a dramatic feel to the snake's death.

This is die function that will handle snake's death:

```
private function die():void {
  removeEventListener(Event.ENTER_FRAME,onEnterFr);
  stage.removeEventListener(KeyboardEvent.KEY_DOWN,onKeyD);
  var game_over:game_over_mc = new game_over_mc();
  addChild(game_over);
}
```

As said, it removes the listeners and places game_over_mc on stage.

Now let's see when we should call such function. Add two more cases to the switch statement in onEnterFr function:

```
switch (children_in_that_point[i].parent.name) {
  case "fruit" :
    justEaten=3;
    removeChild(fruit);
    placeStuff();
    break;
  case "snake body" :
  case "obstacle" :
    die();
    break;
}
```

In this case die function will be executed when the name of the i-th children in a given point is both obstacle and snake body. Notice how name property of a DisplayObject can have spaces.

You know all obstacles have name property equal to obstacle but there aren't any children with name property equal to snake body.

You can set this property to `new_piece` variable after you declared it, in `onEnterFr` function this way:

```
private function onEnterFr(e:Event) {
  var the_head:the_snake_mc=snakeContainer.getChildAt(0) as the_snake_
mc;
  var new_piece:the_snake_mc=new the_snake_mc(the_head.x,the_head.
y,1);
  new_piece.name="snake body";
  ...
}
```

To see if snake's head left the stage, we just have to compare its `x` and `y` properties with the width and height of the stage. I know width and height are respectively `640` and `480` but I wanted to make a small recap of `stageWidth` and `stageHeight` properties you already met during the making of Connect Four.

Add this code just before `onEnterFr` function ends.

```
if (the_head.x<0) {
  die();
}
if (the_head.x>=stage.stageWidth) {
  die();
}
if (the_head.y<0) {
  die();
}
if (the_head.y>=stage.stageHeight) {
  die();
}
```

Obviously all these `if` conditions could have been placed in the same `if` statement with an `||` (logical OR) operator but I wanted to keep them separated just in case you want to upgrade your Snake game showing different game over screens according to the way the snake dies.

Anyway, let's see the meaning of each `if` statement:

```
if (the_head.x<0) { ... }
```

returns `true` if x property of `the_head` object is less than zero. This means the head left the stage to the left.

```
if (the_head.x>stage.stageWidth) { ... }
```

returns `true` if x property of `the_head` object is equal or greater than the stage width.

Why does the second `if` check for x property to be equal or greater while the first one just checked for x property to be smaller (and not to be equal)? That's because x property is `0` when the snake is on the first column so it has to be less than `0` to make you know he left the stage. When the snake is on the rightmost column, x property is `600`, so we have to wait for it to be `640` (stage's width) to say the snake is out of the screen. This happens because the head is centered into an imaginary `40x40` pixels rectangle.

The following picture will help you clarify the concept.

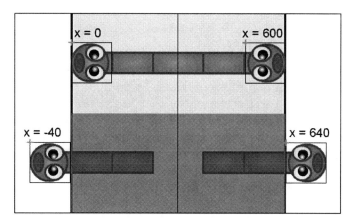

The snake is alive when x property is `0` or `600`, and it dies when x property is `-40` or `640`. There are a lot of ways to translate this concept into an `if` statement, and the one I showed you is only one of a number of possibilities.

The remaining two `if` statements apply the same concept to y property.

Test the movie and you can play with a mortal snake. No more "God Mode".

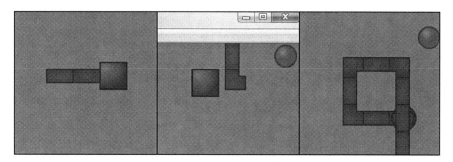

In the above picture, the three ways a snake can die: hitting a wall, leaving the stage, and hitting its own body. Also, look at the dramatic effect added by `game_over_mc` object.

Summary

In this chapter, you built a complete Snake prototype without using any array. This different approach to the creation of a tile-based game allowed you to use points and get the DisplayObjects under a point. Also, you learned how to determine the distance between two points using Manhattan distance. It will come in handy when you have to deal with distances in a tile-based game.

Where to go now

It would be great if you would allow the game to move the snake at higher speed when the player ate a certain amount of fruits. To do this, you can set the frame rate to 30 and use a counter to run the content of `onEnterFr` function only once every five frames (use modulo operator to do it). This way your snake will move at 30/5=6 frames per second, just like the one you just developed. When the player collects, let's say, 10 fruits, you will make `onEnterFr` function run its content once every four frames, updating more than six times per second the game field and consequently increasing the snake's speed and game difficulty.

5
Tetris

Tetris is a tile-based puzzle game made in the Soviet Union. It features shapes
called tetrominoes, geometric shapes composed of four squared blocks connected
orthogonally, that fall from the top of the playing field. Once a tetromino touches
the ground, it lands and cannot be moved anymore, being part of the ground itself,
and a new tetromino falls from the top of the game field, usually a 10x20 tiles vertical
rectangle. The player can move the falling tetromino horizontally and rotate by 90
degrees to create a horizontal line of blocks. When a line is created, it disappears and
any block above the deleted line falls down. If the stacked tetrominoes reach the top
of the game field, it's game over.

As you are about to experience, the making of Tetris wouldn't introduce new
programming features but it's hard enough to provide you a good challenge.
Anyway, during this chapter you will also learn the basics of drawing with AS3.

Defining game design

This time I won't talk about the game design itself, since Tetris is a well known game
and as you read this chapter you should be used to dealing with game design.

By the way, there is something really important about this game you need to know
before you start reading this chapter. You won't draw anything in the Flash IDE.
That is, you won't manually draw tetrominoes, the game field, or any other graphic
assets. Everything will be generated on the fly using AS3 drawing methods.

Tetris is the best game for learning how to draw with AS3 as it only features blocks,
blocks, and only blocks.

Moreover, although the game won't include new programming features, its
principles make Tetris the hardest game of the entire book. Survive Tetris and you
will have the skills to create the next games focusing more on new features and
techniques rather than on programming logic.

Importing classes and declaring first variables

The first thing we need to do, as usual, is set up the project and define the main class and function, as well as preparing the game field.

Create a new file (**File | New**) then from **New Document** window select **Actionscript 3.0.** Set its properties as width to 400 px, height to 480 px, background color to #333333 (a dark gray), and frame rate to 30 (quite useless anyway since there aren't animations, but you can add an animated background on your own). Also, define the Document Class as Main and save the file as tetris.fla.

Without closing tetris.fla, create a new file and from **New Document** window select **ActionScript 3.0 Class**. Save this file as Main.as in the same path you saved tetris.fla. Then write:

```
package {
  import flash.display.Sprite;
  import flash.utils.Timer;
  import flash.events.TimerEvent;
  import flash.events.KeyboardEvent;
  public class Main extends Sprite {
    private const TS:uint=24;
    private var fieldArray:Array;
    private var fieldSprite:Sprite;
    public function Main() {
      // tetris!!
    }
  }
}
```

We already know we have to interact with the keyboard to move, drop, and rotate tetrominoes and we have to deal with timers to manage falling delay, so I already imported all needed libraries.

Then, there are some declarations to do:

```
private const TS:uint=24;
```

TS is the size, in pixels, of the tiles representing the game field. It's a constant as it won't change its value during the game, and its value is 24. With 20 rows of tiles, the height of the whole game field will be 24x20 = 480 pixels, as tall as the height of our movie.

```
private var fieldArray:Array;
```

`fieldArray` is the array that will numerically represent the game field.

```
private var fieldSprite:Sprite;
```

`fieldSprite` is the DisplayObject that will graphically render the game field.

Let's use it to add some graphics.

Drawing game field background

Nobody wants to see an empty black field, so we are going to add some graphics. As said, during the making of this game we won't use any drawn Movie Clip, so every graphic asset will be generated by pure ActionScript.

The idea: Draw a set of squares to represent the game field.

The development: Add this line to `Main` function:

```
public function Main() {
    generateField();
}
```

then write `generateField` function this way:

```
private function generateField():void {
    fieldArray = new Array();
    fieldSprite=new Sprite();
    addChild(fieldSprite);
    fieldSprite.graphics.lineStyle(0,0x000000);
    for (var i:uint=0; i<20; i++) {
        fieldArray[i]=new Array();
        for (var j:uint=0; j<10; j++) {
            fieldArray[i][j]=0;
            fieldSprite.graphics.beginFill(0x444444);
            fieldSprite.graphics.drawRect(TS*j,TS*i,TS,TS);
            fieldSprite.graphics.endFill();
        }
    }
}
```

Test the movie and you will see:

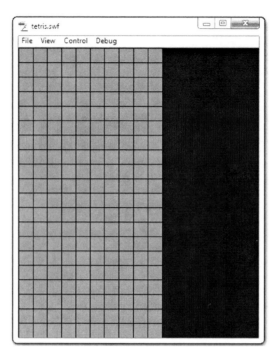

The 20x10 game field has been rendered on the stage in a lighter gray. I could have used constants to define values like 20 and 10, but I am leaving it to you at the end of the chapter.

Let's see what happened:

```
fieldArray = new Array();
fieldSprite=new Sprite();
addChild(fieldSprite);
```

These lines just construct `fieldArray` array and `fieldSprite` DisplayObject, then add it to stage as you have already seen a million times.

```
fieldSprite.graphics.lineStyle(0,0x000000);
```

This line introduces a new world called `Graphics` class. This class contains a set of methods that will allow you to draw vector shapes on Sprites.

`lineStyle` method sets a line style that you will use for your drawings. It accepts a big list of arguments, but at the moment we'll focus on the first two of them.

The first argument is the thickness of the line, in points. I set it to 0 because I wanted it as thin as a hairline, but valid values are 0 to 255.

The second argument is the hexadecimal color value of the line, in this case black.

Hexadecimal uses sixteen distinct symbols to represent numbers from 0 to 15. Numbers from zero to nine are represented with 0-9 just like the decimal numeral system, while values from ten to fifteen are represented by letters A-F. That's the way it is used in most common paint software and in the web to represent colors.

You can create hexadecimal numbers by preceding them with 0x.

Also notice that lineStyle method, like all Graphics class methods, isn't applied directly on the DisplayObject itself but as a method of the graphics property.

```
for (var i:uint=0; i<20; i++) { ... }
```

The remaining lines are made by the classical couple of for loops initializing fieldArray array in the same way you already initialized all other array-based games, and drawing the 200 (20x10) rectangles that will form the game field.

```
fieldSprite.graphics.beginFill(0x444444);
```

beginFill method is similar to lineStyle as it sets the fill color that you will use for your drawings. It accepts two arguments, the color of the fill (a dark gray in this case) and the opacity (alpha). Since I did not specify the alpha, it takes the default value of 1 (full opacity).

```
fieldSprite.graphics.drawRect(TS*j,TS*i,TS,TS);
```

With a line and a fill style, we are ready to draw some squares with drawRect method, that draws a rectangle. The four arguments represent respectively the x and y position relative to the registration point of the parent DisplayObject (fieldSprite, that happens to be currently on 0,0 in this case), the width and the height of the rectangle. All the values are to be intended in pixels.

```
fieldSprite.graphics.endFill();
```

endFill method applies a fill to everything you drew after you called beginFill method.

This way we are drawing a square with a TS pixels side for each for iteration. At the end of both loops, we'll have 200 squares on the stage, forming the game field.

Drawing a better game field background

Tetris background game fields are often represented as a checkerboard, so let's try to obtain the same result.

The idea: Once we defined two different colors, we will paint even squares with one color, and odd squares with the other color.

The development: We have to modify the way `generateField` function renders the background:

```
private function generateField():void {
  var colors:Array=new Array("0x444444","0x555555");");
  fieldArray = new Array();
  var fieldSprite:Sprite=new Sprite();
  addChild(fieldSprite);
  fieldSprite.graphics.lineStyle(0,0x000000);
  for (var i:uint=0; i<20; i++) {
    fieldArray[i]=new Array();
    for (var j:uint=0; j<10; j++) {
      fieldArray[i][j]=0;
      fieldSprite.graphics.beginFill(colors[(j%2+i%2)%2]);
      fieldSprite.graphics.drawRect(TS*j,TS*i,TS,TS);
      fieldSprite.graphics.endFill();
    }
  }
}
```

We can define an array of colors and play with modulo operator to fill the squares with alternate colors and make the game field look like a chessboard grid.

The core of the script lies in this line:

```
fieldSprite.graphics.beginFill(colors[(j%2+i%2)%2]);
```

that plays with modulo to draw a checkerboard.

Test the movie and you will see:

Now the game field looks better.

Creating the tetrominoes

The concept behind the creation of representable tetrominoes is the hardest part of the making of this game. Unlike the previous games you made, such as Snake, that will feature actors of the same width and height (in Snake the head is the same size as the tail), in Tetris every tetromino has its own width and height. Moreover, every tetromino but the square one is not symmetrical, so its size is going to change when the player rotates it.

How can we manage a tile-based game with tiles of different width and height?

The idea: Since tetrominoes are made by four squares connected orthogonally (that is, forming a right angle), we can split tetrominoes into a set of tiles and include them into an array.

The easiest way is to include each tetromino into a 4x4 array, although most of them would fit in smaller arrays, it's good to have a standard array.

Something like this:

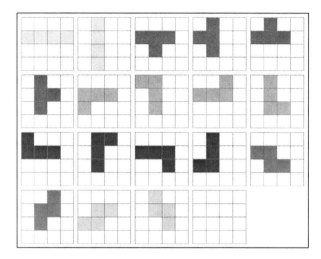

Every tetromino has its own name based on the alphabet letter it reminds, and its own color, according to The Tetris Company (TTC), the company that currently owns the trademark of the game Tetris. Just for your information, TTC sues every Tetris clone whose name somehow is similar to "Tetris", so if you are going to create and market a Tetris clone, you should call it something like "Crazy Bricks" rather than "Tetriz".

Anyway, following the previous picture, from left-to-right and from top-to-bottom, the "official" names and colors for tetrominoes are:

- I—color: cyan (0x00FFFF)
- T—color: purple (0xAA00FF)
- L—color: orange (0xFFA500)
- J—color: blue (0x0000FF)
- Z—color: red (0xFF0000)
- S—color: green (0x00FF00)
- O—color: yellow (0xFFFF00)

The development: First, add two new class level variables:

```
private const TS:uint=24;
private var fieldArray:Array;
private var fieldSprite:Sprite;
private var tetrominoes:Array = new Array();
private var colors:Array=new Array();
```

`tetrominoes` array is the four-dimensional array containing all tetrominoes information, while `colors` array will store their colors.

Now add a new function call to `Main` function:

```
public function Main() {
  generateField();
  initTetrominoes();
}
```

`initTetrominoes` function will initialize tetrominoes-related arrays.

```
private function initTetrominoes():void {
  // I
  tetrominoes[0]=[[[0,0,0,0],[1,1,1,1],[0,0,0,0],[0,0,0,0]],
  [[0,1,0,0],[0,1,0,0],[0,1,0,0],[0,1,0,0]]];
  colors[0]=0x00FFFF;
  // T
  tetrominoes[1]=[[[0,0,0,0],[1,1,1,0],[0,1,0,0],[0,0,0,0]],
   [[0,1,0,0],[1,1,0,0],[0,1,0,0],[0,0,0,0]],
   [[0,1,0,0],[1,1,1,0],[0,0,0,0],[0,0,0,0]],
   [[0,1,0,0],[0,1,1,0],[0,1,0,0],[0,0,0,0]]];
  colors[1]=0x767676;
  // L
  tetrominoes[2]=[[[0,0,0,0],[1,1,1,0],[1,0,0,0],[0,0,0,0]],
   [[1,1,0,0],[0,1,0,0],[0,1,0,0],[0,0,0,0]],
   [[0,0,1,0],[1,1,1,0],[0,0,0,0],[0,0,0,0]],
   [[0,1,0,0],[0,1,0,0],[0,1,1,0],[0,0,0,0]]];
  colors[2]=0xFFA500;
  // J
  tetrominoes[3]=[[[1,0,0,0],[1,1,1,0],[0,0,0,0],[0,0,0,0]],
   [[0,1,1,0],[0,1,0,0],[0,1,0,0],[0,0,0,0]],
   [[0,0,0,0],[1,1,1,0],[0,0,1,0],[0,0,0,0]],
   [[0,1,0,0],[0,1,0,0],[1,1,0,0],[0,0,0,0]]];
  colors[3]=0x0000FF;
  // Z
  tetrominoes[4]=[[[0,0,0,0],[1,1,0,0],[0,1,1,0],[0,0,0,0]],
   [[0,0,1,0],[0,1,1,0],[0,1,0,0],[0,0,0,0]]];
  colors[4]=0xFF0000;
  // S
  tetrominoes[5]=[[[0,0,0,0],[0,1,1,0],[1,1,0,0],[0,0,0,0]],
   [[0,1,0,0],[0,1,1,0],[0,0,1,0],[0,0,0,0]]];
  colors[5]=0x00FF00;
  // O
  tetrominoes[6]=[[[0,1,1,0],[0,1,1,0],[0,0,0,0],[0,0,0,0]]];
  colors[6]=0xFFFF00;
}
```

`colors` array is easy to understand: it's just an array with the hexadecimal value of each tetromino color.

`tetrominoes` is a four-dimensional array. It's the first time you see such a complex array, but don't worry. It's no more difficult than the two-dimensional arrays you've been dealing with since the creation of Minesweeper. Tetrominoes are coded into the array this way:

- `tetrominoes[n]` contains the arrays with all the information about the `n-th` tetromino. These arrays represent the various rotations, the four rows and the four columns.

- `tetrominoes[n][m]` contains the arrays with all the information about the `n-th` tetromino in the `m-th` rotation. These arrays represent the four rows and the four columns.

- `tetrominoes[n][m][o]` contains the array with the four elements of the `n-th` tetromino in the `m-th` rotation in the `o-th` row.

- `tetrominoes[n][m][o][p]` is the `p-th` element of the array representing the `o-th` row in the `m-th` rotation of the `n-th` tetromino. Such element can be `0` if it's an empty space or `1` if it's part of the tetromino.

There isn't much more to explain as it's just a series of data entry. Let's add our first tetromino to the field.

Placing your first tetromino

Tetrominoes always fall from the top-center of the level field, so this will be its starting position.

The idea: We need a DisplayObject to render the tetromino itself, and some variables to store which tetromino we have on stage, as well as its rotation and horizontal and vertical position.

The development: Add some new class level variables:

```
private const TS:uint=24;
private var fieldArray:Array;
private var fieldSprite:Sprite;
private var tetrominoes:Array = new Array();
private var colors:Array=new Array();
private var tetromino:Sprite;
private var currentTetromino:uint;
private var currentRotation:uint;
private var tRow:uint;
private var tCol:uint;
```

tetromino is the DisplayObject representing the tetromino itself.

currentTetromino is the number of the tetromino currently in game, and will range from 0 to 6.

currentRotation is the rotation of the tetromino and will range from 0 to 3 since a tetromino can have four distinct rotations, but for some tetrominoes such as "I", "S" and "Z" will range from 0 to 1 and it can be only 0 for the "O" one. It depends on how may distinct rotations a tetromino can have.

tRow and tCol will represent the current vertical and horizontal position of the tetromino in the game field.

Since the game starts with a tetromino in the game, let's add a new function call to Main function:

```
public function Main() {
   generateField();
   initTetrominoes();
   generateTetromino();
}
```

generateTetromino function will generate a random tetromino to be placed on the game field:

```
private function generateTetromino():void {
   currentTetromino=Math.floor(Math.random()*7);
   currentRotation=0;
   tRow=0;
   tCol=3;
   drawTetromino();
}
```

The function is very easy to understand: it generates a random integer number between 0 and 6 (the possible tetrominoes) and assigns it to currentTetromino. There is no need to generate a random starting rotation as in all Tetris versions I played, tetrominoes always start in the same position, so I assigned 0 to currentRotation, but feel free to add a random rotation if you want.

tRow (the starting row) is set to 0 to place the tetromino at the very top of the game field, and tCol is always 3 because tetrominoes are included in a 4 elements wide array, so to center it in a 10 column wide field, its origin must be at (10-4)/2 = 3.

Once the tetromino has been generated, `drawTetromino` function renders it on the screen.

```
private function drawTetromino():void {
  var ct:uint=currentTetromino;
  tetromino=new Sprite();
  addChild(tetromino);
  tetromino.graphics.lineStyle(0,0x000000);
  for (var i:int=0; i<tetrominoes[ct][currentRotation].length; i++) {
    for (var j:int=0; j<tetrominoes[ct][currentRotation][i].length;
j++) {
      if (tetrominoes[ct][currentRotation][i][j]==1) {
        tetromino.graphics.beginFill(colors[ct]);
        tetromino.graphics.drawRect(TS*j,TS*i,TS,TS);
        tetromino.graphics.endFill();
      }
    }
  }
  placeTetromino();
}
```

Actually the first line has no sense, I only needed a variable with a name shorter than `currentTetromino` or the script wouldn't have fitted on the page. That's why I created `ct` variable.

The rest of the script is quite easy to understand: first `tetromino` DisplayObject is constructed and added to Display List, then `lineStyle` method is called to prepare us to draw the tetromino.

This is the main loop:

```
for (var i:int=0; i<tetrominoes[ct][currentRotation].length; i++) {
  for (var j:int=0; j<tetrominoes[ct][currentRotation][i].length; j++)
{
    ...
  }
}
```

These two `for` loops scan through `tetrominoes` array elements relative to the current tetromino in the current rotation.

```
if (tetrominoes[ct][currentRotation][i][j]==1) { ... }
```

This is how we apply the concept explained during the creation of `tetrominoes` array.

We are looking for the `j`-th element in the `i`-th row of the `currentRotation-ct` rotation of the `ct`-th tetromino. If it's equal to `1`, we must draw a tetromino tile.

These lines:

```
tetromino.graphics.beginFill(colors[ct]);
tetromino.graphics.drawRect(TS*j,TS*i,TS,TS);
tetromino.graphics.endFill();
```

just draw a square in the same way we used to do with the field background. The combination of all squares we drew will form the tetromino.

Finally, the tetromino is placed calling `placeTetromino` function that works this way:

```
private function placeTetromino():void {
   tetromino.x=tCol*TS;
   tetromino.y=tRow*TS;
}
```

It just places the tetromino in the correct place according to `tCol` and `tRow` values. You already know these values are respectively `3` and `0` at the beginning, but this function will be useful every time you need to update a tetromino's position.

Test the movie and you will see your first tetromino placed on the game field. Test it a few more times, to display all of your tetrominoes, and you should find a glitch.

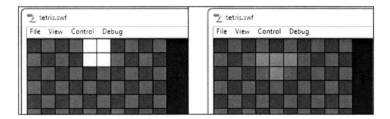

While "O" tetromino is correctly placed on the top of the game field, "T" tetromino has shifted one row down.

This happens because some tetrominoes in some rotations have the first row empty. Since all tetrominoes are embedded in a 4x4 array, when the first row is empty it looks like the tetromino is starting from the second row of the game field rather than the first one.

We should scan for the first row of a newborn tetromino and set `tRow` to `-1` rather than `0` if its first row is empty, to make it fall from the first game field row.

tRow cannot be an unsigned integer anymore as it can take a -1 value, so change the level class variables declarations:

```
private const TS:uint=24;
private var fieldArray:Array;
private var fieldSprite:Sprite;
private var tetrominoes:Array = new Array();
private var colors:Array=new Array();
private var tetromino:Sprite;
private var currentTetromino:uint;
private var currentRotation:uint;
private var tRow:int;
private var tCol:uint;
```

Then in generateTetromino function we must look for a 1 in the first row of the first rotation to make sure the current tetromino has a piece in the first row. If not, we have to set tRow to -1. Change generateTetromino function this way:

```
private function generateTetromino():void {
  currentTetromino=Math.floor(Math.random()*7);
  currentRotation=0;
  tRow=0;
  if (tetrominoes[currentTetromino][0][0].indexOf(1)==-1) {
    tRow=-1;
  }
  tCol=3;
  drawTetromino();
}
```

Then test the movie and finally every tetromino will start at the very top of the game field.

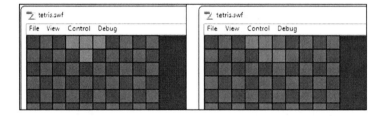

Tetrominoes won't float forever so it's time to add some interaction to the game.

Moving tetrominoes horizontally

Players should be able to move tetrominoes horizontally with arrow keys (and any other keys you want to enable, but in this chapter we'll only cover arrow keys movement).

The idea: Pressing LEFT arrow key will make the current tetromino move to the left by one tile (if allowed) and pressing RIGHT arrow key will make the current tetromino move to the right by one tile (if allowed).

The development: The first thing which comes to mind is some tetrominoes in some rotations can have the leftmost column empty, just as it happened with the first row. For this reason, it's better to declare tCol variable as an integer since it can assume negative values when you next move the tetromino to the left edge of the game field.

```
private const TS:uint=24;
private var fieldArray:Array;
private var fieldSprite:Sprite;
private var tetrominoes:Array = new Array();
private var colors:Array=new Array();
private var tetromino:Sprite;
private var currentTetromino:uint;
private var currentRotation:uint;
private var tRow:int;
private var tCol:int;
```

Now you can add the keyboard listener to make the player move the pieces. It will be added on Main function:

```
public function Main() {
  generateField();
  initTetrominoes();
  generateTetromino();
  stage.addEventListener(KeyboardEvent.KEY_DOWN,onKDown);
}
```

onKDown function will handle the keys pressed in the same old way you already know. The core of this process is the call to another function called canFit that will tell us if a tetromino can fit in its new position.

```
private function onKDown(e:KeyboardEvent):void {
  switch (e.keyCode) {
    case 37 :
      if (canFit(tRow,tCol-1)) {
        tCol--;
```

```
            placeTetromino();
        }
        break;
    case 39 :
        if (canFit(tRow,tCol+1)) {
            tCol++;
            placeTetromino();
        }
        break;
    }
}
```

If we look at what happens when the player presses LEFT arrow key (case 37) we see tCol value is decreased by 1 and the tetromino is placed in its new position using placeTetromino function only if the value returned by canFit function is true.

Also, notice its arguments: the current row (tRow) and the current column decreased by 1 (tCol-1). It should be clear canFit function checks whether the tetromino can fit in a given position or not.

So when the player presses LEFT or RIGHT keys, we check if the tetromino would fit in the new given position, and if it fits we update its tCol value and draw it in the new position.

Now we are ready to write canFit function, that wants two integer arguments for the candidate row and column, and returns true if the current tetromino fits in these coordinates, or false if it does not fit.

```
private function canFit(row:int,col:int):Boolean {
    var ct:uint=currentTetromino;
    for (var i:int=0; i<tetrominoes[ct][currentRotation].length; i++) {
        for (var j:int=0; j<tetrominoes[ct][currentRotation][i].length;
j++) {
            if (tetrominoes[ct][currentRotation][i][j]==1) {
                // out of left boundary
                if (col+j<0) {
                    return false;
                }
                // out of right boundary
                if (col+j>9) {
                    return false;
                }
            }
        }
    }
    return true;
}
```

As seen, ct variable exists for a layout purpose.

In this function we have the classical couple of `for` loops and the `if` statement to check for current tetromino's pieces:

```
for (var i:int=0; i<tetrominoes[ct][currentRotation].length; i++) {
    for (var j:int=0; j<tetrominoes[ct][currentRotation][i].length; j++)
{
        if (tetrominoes[ct][currentRotation][i][j]==1) {
            ...
        }
    }
}
```

and then the core of the function: checking for the tetromino to be completely inside the game field:

```
if (col+j<0) {
    return false;
}
```

and

```
if (col+j>9) {
    return false;
}
```

Once we found a tetromino piece at `tetrominoes[ct][currentRotation][i][j]`, we know `j` is the column value inside the tetromino and `col` is the candidate column for the tetromino.

If the sum of `col` and `j` is a number outside the boundaries of game field, then at least a piece of the tetromino is outside the game field, and the position is not legal (return `false`) and nothing is done.

If all current tetromino's pieces are inside the game field, then the position is legal (return `true`) and the position of the tetromino is updated.

Look at this picture:

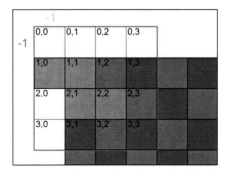

The "Z" tetromino is in an illegal position; let's see how we can spot it. The red frame indicates the tetromino's area, with black digits showing tetromino's array indexes.

The green digit represents the origin column value of the tetromino in the game field, while the blue one represents the origin row value.

When we check the tetromino piece at 1,0, we have to sum its column value (0) to the origin column value (-1). Since the result is less than zero, we can say the piece is in an illegal spot, so the entire tetromino can't be placed here.

All remaining tetromino's pieces are in legal places, because when you sum tetromino's pieces column values (1 or 2) with origin column value (-1), the result will always be greater than zero.

This concept will be applied to all game field sides.

Test the movie and you will be able to move tetrominoes horizontally.

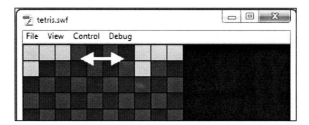

Now, let's move on to vertical movement.

Moving tetrominoes down

Moving tetrominoes down obviously applies the same concept to vertical direction.

The idea: Once the DOWN arrow key has been pressed, we should call canFit function passing as arguments the candidate row value (tRow+1 as the tetromino is moving one row down) and the current column value.

The development: modify onKDown function adding the new case:

```
private function onKDown(e:KeyboardEvent):void {
  switch (e.keyCode) {
    case 37 :
      ...
      break;
    case 39 :
      ...
```

```
        break;
    case 40 :
        if (canFit(tRow+1,tCol)) {
            tRow++;
            placeTetromino();
        }
        break;
    }
}
```

We also need to update `canFit` function to check if the tetromino would go out of the bottom boundary.

Add this new `if` statement to `canFit` function:

```
private function canFit(row:int,col:int):Boolean {
    var ct:uint=currentTetromino;
    for (var i:int=0; i<tetrominoes[ct][currentRotation].length; i++) {
        for (var j:int=0; j<tetrominoes[ct][currentRotation][i].length;
j++) {
            if (tetrominoes[ct][currentRotation][i][j]==1) {
                // out of left boundary
                if (col+j<0) {
                    return false;
                }
                // out of right boundary
                if (col+j>9) {
                    return false;
                }
                // out of bottom boundary
                if (row+i>19) {
                    return false;
                }
            }
        }
    }
    return true;
}
```

As you can see it's exactly the same concept applied to horizontal movement.

Test the movie and you will be able to move tetrominoes down.

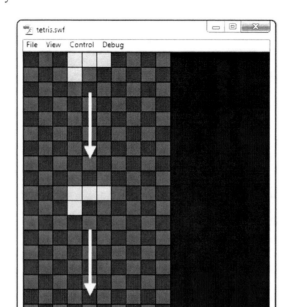

Everything is fine and easy at the moment, but you know once a tetromino touches the ground, it must stay in its position and a new tetromino should fall from the top of the field.

Managing tetrominoes landing

The first thing to determine is: when should a tetromino be considered as landed? When it should move down but it can't. That's it. Easier than you supposed, I guess.

The idea: When it's time to move the tetromino down a row (case 40 in onKDown function), when you can't move it down (canFit function returns false), it's time to make it land and generate a new tetromino.

The development: Modify onKDown function this way:

```
private function onKDown(e:KeyboardEvent) {
  switch (e.keyCode) {
    case 37 :
      ...
      break;
```

```
    case 39 :
      ...
      break;
    case 40 :
      if (canFit(tRow+1,tCol)) {
        tRow++;
        placeTetromino();
      } else {
        landTetromino();
        generateTetromino();
      }
      break;
  }
}
```

When you can't move down a tetromino, landTetromino function is called to
manage its landing and a new tetromino is generated with generateTetromino
function.

This is landTetromino function:

```
private function landTetromino():void {
  var ct:uint=currentTetromino;
  var landed:Sprite;
  for (var i:int=0; i<tetrominoes[ct][currentRotation].length; i++) {
    for (var j:int=0; j<tetrominoes[ct][currentRotation][i].length;
j++) {
      if (tetrominoes[ct][currentRotation][i][j]==1) {
        landed = new Sprite();
        addChild(landed);
        landed.graphics.lineStyle(0,0x000000);
        landed.graphics.beginFill(colors[currentTetromino]);
        landed.graphics.drawRect(TS*(tCol+j),TS*(tRow+i),TS,TS);
        landed.graphics.endFill();
        fieldArray[tRow+i][tCol+j]=1;
      }
    }
  }
  removeChild(tetromino);
}
```

It works creating four new DisplayObjects, one for each tetromino's piece, and
adding them to the Display List. At the same time, fieldArray array is updated.

Let's see this process in detail:

```
var ct:uint=currentTetromino;
```

This is the variable I created for layout purpose.

```
var landed:Sprite;
```

`landed` is the DisplayObject we'll use to render each tetromino piece.

```
for (var i:int=0; i<tetrominoes[ct][currentRotation].length; i++) {
  for (var j:int=0; j<tetrominoes[ct][currentRotation][i].length; j++)
{
    if (tetrominoes[ct][currentRotation][i][j]==1) {
      . . .
    }
  }
}
```

This is the loop to scan for pieces into the tetromino. Once it finds a piece, here comes the core of the function:

```
landed = new Sprite();
addChild(landed);
```

`landed` DisplayObject is added to Display List.

```
landed.graphics.lineStyle(0,0x000000);
landed.graphics.beginFill(colors[currentTetromino]);
landed.graphics.drawRect(TS*(tCol+j),TS*(tRow+i),TS,TS);
landed.graphics.endFill();
```

Draws a square where the tetromino piece should lie. It's very similar to what you've seen in `drawTetromino` function.

```
fieldArray[tRow+i][tCol+j]=1;
```

Updating `fieldArray` array setting the proper element to 1 (occupied).

```
removeChild(tetromino);
```

At the end of the function, the old tetromino is removed. A new one is about to come from the upper side of the game.

Test the movie and move down a tetromino until it reaches, then try to move it down again to see it land on the ground and a new tetromino appear from the top.

Everything will work fine until you try to make a tetromino fall over another tetromino.

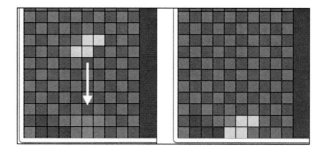

This happens because we haven't already managed the collision between the active tetromino and the landed ones.

Managing tetrominoes collisions

Do you remember once a tetromino touches the ground we updated `fieldArray` array? Now the array contains the mapping of all game field cells occupied by a tetromino piece.

The idea: To check for a collision between tetrominoes we just need to add another `if` statement to `canFit` function to see if in the candidate position of the current tetromino there is a cell of the game field already occupied by a previously landed tetromino, that is the `fieldArray` array element is equal to 1.

The development: It's just necessary to add these three lines to `canFit` function:

```
private function canFit(row:int,col:int):Boolean {
  var ct:uint=currentTetromino;
  for (var i:int=0; i<tetrominoes[ct][currentRotation].length; i++) {
    for (var j:int=0; j<tetrominoes[ct][currentRotation][i].length;
j++) {
      if (tetrominoes[ct][currentRotation][i][j]==1) {
        // out of left boundary
        if (col+j<0) {
          return false;
        }
        // out of right boundary
        if (col+j>9) {
          return false;
        }
        // out of bottom boundary
        if (row+i>19) {
          return false;
        }
```

```
        // over another tetromino
        if (fieldArray[row+i][col+j]==1) {
          return false;
        }
      }
    }
  }
  return true;
}
```

Test the movie and see how tetrominoes stack correctly.

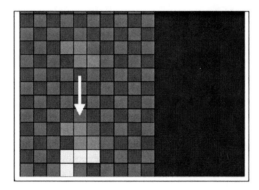

By the way, making lines is not easy if you can't rotate tetrominoes.

Rotating tetrominoes

The concept behind a tetromino rotation is not that different than the one behind its movement.

The idea: We have to see if the tetromino in the candidate rotation fits in the game field, and eventually apply the rotation.

The development: The first thing to do is to change `canFit` function to let it accept a third argument, the candidate rotation. Change it this way:

```
private function canFit(row:int,col:int,side:uint):Boolean {
  var ct:uint=currentTetromino;
  for (var i:int=0; i<tetrominoes[ct][side].length; i++) {
    for (var j:int=0; j<tetrominoes[ct][side][i].length; j++) {
      if (tetrominoes[ct][side][i][j]==1) {
        ...
      }
```

```
        }
    }
    return true;
}
```

As you can see there's nothing difficult in it: I just added a third argument called `side` that will contain the candidate rotation of the tetromino.

Then obviously any call to class level variable `currentRotation` has to be replaced with `side` argument.

Every existing call to `canFit` function in `onKDown` function must be updated passing the new argument, usually `currentRotation`, except when the player tries to rotate the tetromino (case 38):

```
private function onKDown(e:KeyboardEvent):void {
    switch (e.keyCode) {
        case 37 :
            if (canFit(tRow,tCol-1,currentRotation)) {
                ...
            }
            break;
        case 38 :
            var ct:uint=currentRotation;
            var rot:uint=(ct+1)%tetrominoes[currentTetromino].length;
            if (canFit(tRow,tCol,rot)) {
                currentRotation=rot;
                removeChild(tetromino);
                drawTetromino();
                placeTetromino();
            }
            break;
        case 39 :
            if (canFit(tRow,tCol+1,currentRotation)) {
                ...
            }
            break;
        case 40 :
            if (canFit(tRow+1,tCol,currentRotation)) {
                ...
            }
            break;
    }
}
```

Now let's see what happens when the player presses UP arrow key:

```
var ct:uint=currentRotation;
```

`ct` variable is used only for a layout purpose, to have `currentRotation` value in a variable with a shorter name.

```
var rot:uint=(ct+1)%tetrominoes[currentTetromino].length;
```

`rot` variable will take the value of the candidate rotation. It's determined by adding 1 to current rotation and applying a modulo with the number of possible rotations of the current tetromino, that's determined by `tetrominoes[currentTetromino].length`.

```
if (canFit(tRow,tCol,rot)) { ... }
```

Calls `canFit` function passing the current row, the current column, and the candidate rotation as parameters. If `canFit` returns `true`, then these lines are executed:

```
currentRotation=rot;
```

`currentRotation` variable takes the value of the candidate rotation.

```
removeChild(tetromino);
```

The current tetromino is removed.

```
drawTetromino();
placeTetromino();
```

A new tetromino is created and placed on stage. You may wonder why I delete and redraw the tetromino rather than simply rotating the DisplayObject representing the current tetromino. That's because tetrominoes' rotations aren't symmetrical to their centers, as you can see looking at their array values.

Test the movie and press UP arrow key to rotate the current tetromino.

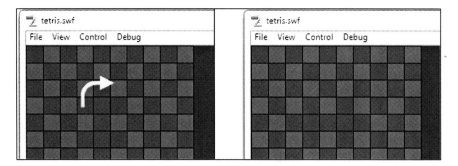

You will notice you can't rotate some tetrominoes when they are close to the first or last row or column. In some Tetris versions, when you try to rotate a tetromino next to game field edges, it's automatically shifted horizontally by one position (if possible) to let it rotate anyway.

In this prototype, I did not add this feature because there's nothing interesting from a programming point of view so I preferred to focus more in detail on other features rather than writing just a couple of lines about everything.

Anyway, if you want to try it by yourself, here's how it should work:

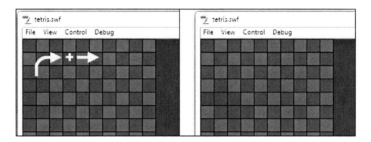

When a tetromino can't be rotated as one of its piece would go out of the game field, along with the rotation the tetromino is shifted in a safe area, if possible.

Finally, you can make lines! Let's see how to manage them.

Removing completed lines

According to game mechanics, a line can be completed only after a tetromino is landed.

The idea: Once the falling tetromino lands on the ground or over another tetromino, we'll check if there is any completed line. A line is completed when it's entirely filled by tetrominoes pieces.

The development: At the end of `landTetromino` function you should check for completed lines and eventually remove them. Change `landTetromino` this way:

```
private function landTetromino():void {
  var ct:uint=currentTetromino;
  var landed:Sprite;
  for (var i:int=0; i<tetrominoes[ct][currentRotation].length; i++) {
    for (var j:int=0; j<tetrominoes[ct][currentRotation][i].length;
j++) {
      if (tetrominoes[ct][currentRotation][i][j]==1) {
        landed = new Sprite();
```

```
                    addChild(landed);
                    landed.graphics.lineStyle(0,0x000000);
                    landed.graphics.beginFill(colors[currentTetromino]);
                    landed.graphics.drawRect(TS*(tCol+j),TS*(tRow+i),TS,TS);
                    landed.graphics.endFill();
                    landed.name="r"+(tRow+i)+"c"+(tCol+j);
                    fieldArray[tRow+i][tCol+j]=1;
                }
            }
        }
        removeChild(tetromino);
        checkForLines();
    }
```

As said, the last line calls `checkForLines` function that will check for completed lines. But before doing it, take a look at how I am giving a name to each piece of any landed tetromino. The name is meant to be easily recognizable by its row and column, so for instance the piece at the fifth column of the third row would be `r3c5`. Naming pieces this way will help us when it's time to remove them. We will be able to find them easily with the `getChildByName` method you should have already mastered.

Add `checkForLines` function:

```
    private function checkForLines():void {
        for (var i:int=0; i<20; i++) {
            if (fieldArray[i].indexOf(0)==-1) {
                for (var j:int=0; j<10; j++) {
                    fieldArray[i][j]=0;
                    removeChild(getChildByName("r"+i+"c"+j));
                }
            }
        }
    }
```

Test the movie and you will be able to remove complete lines.

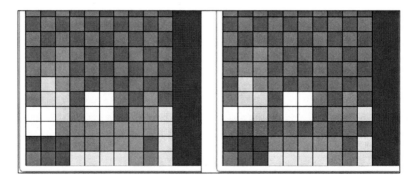

Let's see how `checkForLines` function works:

```
for (var i:int=0; i<20; i++) { ... }
```

`for` loop iterating through all 20 lines in the game field

```
if (fieldArray[i].indexOf(0)==-1) { ... }
```

Since a line must be completely filled with tetrominoes pieces to be considered as completed, the array must be filled by 1, that is, there can't be any 0. That's what this `if` statement is checking on the i-th line.

```
for (var j:int=0; j<10; j++) { ... }
```

If a line is completed, then we iterate through all its ten columns to remove it.

```
fieldArray[i][j]=0;
```

This clears the game field bringing back `fieldArray[i][j]` element at 0.

```
removeChild(getChildByName("r"+i+"c"+j));
```

And this removes the corresponding DisplayObject, easily located by its name.

Now, we have to manage "floating" lines.

Managing remaining lines

When a line is removed, probably there are some tetrominoes above it, just like in the previous picture. Obviously you can't leave the game field as is, but you have to make the above pieces fall down to fill the removed lines.

The idea: Check all pieces above the removed line and move them down to fill the gap left by the removed line.

The development: We can do it by simply moving down one tile, all tetrominoes pieces above the line we just deleted, and updating `fieldArray` array consequently.

Change `checkForLines` function this way:

```
private function checkForLines():void {
  for (var i:int=0; i<20; i++) {
    if (fieldArray[i].indexOf(0)==-1) {
      for (var j:int=0; j<10; j++) {
        fieldArray[i][j]=0;
        removeChild(getChildByName("r"+i+"c"+j));
      }
      for (j=i; j>=0; j--) {
```

```
        for (var k:int=0; k<10; k++) {
          if (fieldArray[j][k]==1) {
            fieldArray[j][k]=0;
            fieldArray[j+1][k]=1;
            getChildByName("r"+j+"c"+k).y+=TS;
            getChildByName("r"+j+"c"+k).name="r"+(j+1)+"c"+k;
          }
        }
      }
    }
  }
}
```

Let's see what we are going to do:

```
for (j=i; j>=0; j--) { ... }
```

This is the most important loop. It ranges from i (the row we just cleared) back to zero. In other words, we are scanning all rows above the row we just cleared, including it.

```
for (var k:int=0; k<10; k++) { ... }
```

This for loop iterates trough all 10 elements in the j-th row.

```
if (fieldArray[j][k]==1) { ... }
```

Checks if there is a tetromino piece in the k-th column of the j-th row.

```
fieldArray[j][k]=0;
```

Sets the k-th column of the j-th row to 0.

```
fieldArray[j+1][k]=1;
```

Sets the k-th column of the (j+1)-th row to 1. This way we are shifting down an entire line.

```
getChildByName("r"+j+"c"+k).y+=TS;
```

Moves down the corresponding DisplayObject by TS pixels.

```
getChildByName("r"+j+"c"+k).name="r"+(j+1)+"c"+k;
```

Changes the corresponding DisplayObject name according to its new position.

Test the game and try to remove one or more lines. Everything will work properly.

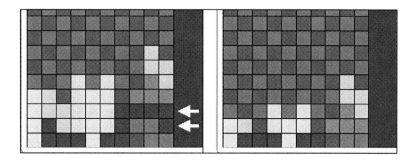

Now, to make the player's life harder, we can make tetrominoes fall down by themselves.

Making tetrominoes fall

One major feature still lacking in this prototype is the gravity that makes tetrominoes fall down at a given interval of time. With the main engine already developed and working, it's just a matter of adding a timer listener and doing the same thing as the player presses DOWN arrow key.

The idea: After a given amount of time, make the tetromino controlled by the player move down by one line.

The development: First, add a new class level variable.

```
private const TS:uint=24;
private var fieldArray:Array;
private var fieldSprite:Sprite;
private var tetrominoes:Array = new Array();
private var colors:Array=new Array();
private var tetromino:Sprite;
private var currentTetromino:uint;
private var currentRotation:uint;
private var tRow:int;
private var tCol:int;
private var timeCount:Timer=new Timer(500);
```

timeCount is the variable that will trigger the event listener every 500 milliseconds.

The timer listener will be added once a new tetromino is generated.

Modify `generateTetromino` function this way:

```
private function generateTetromino():void {
    ...
    timeCount.addEventListener(TimerEvent.TIMER, onTime);
    timeCount.start();
}
```

You already know how this listener works so this was easy, and writing `onTime` function will be even easier as it's just a copy/paste of the code to execute when the player presses DOWN arrow key (`case 40`).

```
private function onTime(e:TimerEvent):void {
    if (canFit(tRow+1,tCol,currentRotation)) {
        tRow++;
        placeTetromino();
    } else {
        landTetromino();
        generateTetromino();
    }
}
```

The listener also needs to be removed once the tetromino lands, to let the script create a brand new one when a new tetromino is placed on the game field.

Remove it in `landTetromino` function this way:

```
private function landTetromino():void {
    var ct:uint=currentTetromino;
    var landed:Sprite;
    for (var i:int=0; i<tetrominoes[ct][currentRotation].length; i++) {
        ...
    }
    removeChild(tetromino);
    timeCount.removeEventListener(TimerEvent.TIMER, onTime);
    timeCount.stop();
    checkForLines();
}
```

Test the movie, and tetrominoes will fall down one row every 500 milliseconds.

Now you have to think quickly, or you'll stack tetrominoes until you reach the top of the game field.

Checking for game over

Finally it's time to tell the player the game is over.

The idea: If the tetromino that just appeared on the top of the game field collides with tetrominoes pieces, the game is over.

The development: First we need a new class level variable:

```
private const TS:uint=24;
private var fieldArray:Array;
private var fieldSprite:Sprite;
private var tetrominoes:Array = new Array();
private var colors:Array=new Array();
private var tetromino:Sprite;
private var currentTetromino:uint;
private var currentRotation:uint;
private var tRow:int;
private var tCol:int;
private var timeCount:Timer=new Timer(500);
private var gameOver:Boolean=false;
```

gameOver variable will tell us if the game is over (true) or not (false). At the beginning obviously, the game is not over.

What should happen when the game is over? First, the player shouldn't be able to move the current tetromino, so change onKDown function this way:

```
private function onKDown(e:KeyboardEvent):void {
  if (! gameOver) {
    ...
  }
}
```

Then, no more tetrominoes should be generated. Change generateTetromino function this way:

```
private function generateTetromino():void {
  if (! gameOver) {
    currentTetromino=Math.floor(Math.random()*7);
    currentRotation=0;
    tRow=0;
    if (tetrominoes[currentTetromino][0][0].indexOf(1)==-1) {
      tRow=-1;
    }
    tCol=3;
    drawTetromino();
```

```
      if (canFit(tRow,tCol,currentRotation)) {
        timeCount.addEventListener(TimerEvent.TIMER, onTime);
        timeCount.start();
      } else {
        gameOver=true;
      }
    }
  }
```

The first `if` statement:

```
    if (! gameOver) { ... }
```

executes the whole function only if `gameOver` variable is `false`.

Then the event listener is added only if `canFit` function applied to the tetromino in its starting position returns `true`. If not, this means the tetromino cannot fit even in its starting position, so the game is over, and `gameOver` variable is set to `true`.

Test the movie and try to stack tetrominoes until you reach the top of the game field, and the game will stop.

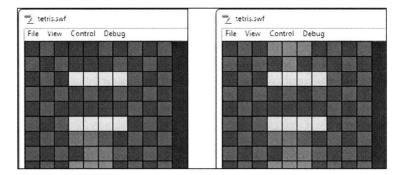

In the previous picture, when the "T" tetromino is added, it's game over.

Last but not least, we must show which tetromino will appear when the player lands the current one.

Showing NEXT tetromino

To add strategy to the game, we need to show the next tetromino that will fall after the current one has landed.

The idea: Don't random generate the current tetromino, but the next one. When the current tetromino lands, you already know which tetromino will fall from the top because the next tetromino becomes the current one, and you will generate a new random next tetromino.

The development: We need a new class level variable where the value of the next falling tetromino is stored.

```
private const TS:uint=24;
private var fieldArray:Array;
private var fieldSprite:Sprite;
private var tetrominoes:Array = new Array();
private var colors:Array=new Array();
private var tetromino:Sprite;
private var currentTetromino:uint;
private var nextTetromino:uint;
private var currentRotation:uint;
private var tRow:int;
private var tCol:int;
private var timeCount:Timer=new Timer(500);
private var gameOver:Boolean=false;
```

At this point, the logic is to generate the random value of the next tetromino first, even before generating the current one. Moreover, forget completely the current tetromino generation. Change `Main` function to generate the next tetromino this way:

```
public function Main() {
  generateField();
  initTetrominoes();
  nextTetromino=Math.floor(Math.random()*7);
  generateTetromino();
  stage.addEventListener(KeyboardEvent.KEY_DOWN,onKDown);
}
```

And the trick is done. Now when it's time to generate the current tetromino, assign it the value of the next one and generate the next random tetromino this way:

```
private function generateTetromino():void {
  if (! gameOver) {
    currentTetromino = nextTetromino;
    nextTetromino=Math.floor(Math.random()*7);
    drawNext();
    ...
  }
}
```

As you can see, you are only randomly generating the next tetromino, while the current one only takes its value.

`drawNext` function just draws the next tetromino in the same way `drawTetromino` does, just in another place.

```
private function drawNext():void {
  if (getChildByName("next")!=null) {
    removeChild(getChildByName("next"));
  }
  var next_t:Sprite=new Sprite();
  next_t.x=300;
  next_t.name="next";
  addChild(next_t);
  next_t.graphics.lineStyle(0,0x000000);
  for (var i:int=0; i<tetrominoes[nextTetromino][0].length; i++) {
    for (var j:int=0; j<tetrominoes[nextTetromino][0][i].length; j++)
  {
      if (tetrominoes[nextTetromino][0][i][j]==1) {
        next_t.graphics.beginFill(colors[nextTetromino]);
        next_t.graphics.drawRect(TS*j,TS*i,TS,TS);
        next_t.graphics.endFill();
      }
    }
  }
}
```

Test the movie, and here it is, your next tetromino.

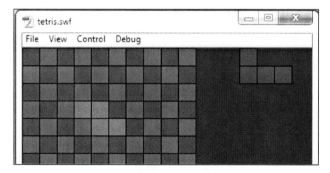

Now you can play the fully functional Tetris prototype.

Summary

You went through the creation of a complete Tetris game, and this alone would be enough. Moreover, you also managed to draw basic shapes with AS3.

Where to go now

To improve your skills, you could clean the code a bit, using constants where required. This is not mandatory, but using FIELD_WIDTH and FIELD_HEIGHT rather than 10 and 20 here and there could improve code readability. It would also be nice if you decrease the timer that controls tetrominoes' falling speed every, let's say, ten completed lines.

You can create two new class level variables called completedLines (starting at zero and increasing every time the player completes a line) and fallingTimer (to be set at 500 and used rather than new Timer(500)). Then every time completedLines is a multiple of ten (use modulo), stop the timer using stop method just like you made it start with start method, remove the listener, decrease fallingTimer by, let's say, 25, and create and start a new timer with a new listener.

6
Astro-PANIC!

No doubt Astro-PANIC! is the least known game covered in this book. It was released as an all machine language Commodore 64 game to be typed in the February 1984 issue of COMPUTE!'s Gazette magazine. At that time there wasn't any blog with source codes to download or copy/paste into your projects, so the only way to learn from other programmers was buying computer magazines and typing the example codes on your computer.

The objective is to destroy all enemy spaceships whose number and speed increases as the player progresses through levels. Since I suppose you never played this game, I would recommend you play it a bit on `http://www.freewebarcade.com/game/astro-panic/`. It's a simple and addictive game that will allow me to explain some important new concepts such as:

- Trigonometry
- Storing data in Vectors
- Filters to dynamically add effects to your DisplayObjects
- Saving data on your local computer using SharedObjects

And above all, being an almost unknown game, we'll make a complete game design.

Defining game design

Here are the rules to design our Astro-PANIC! prototype:

- The player controls a spaceship with the mouse, being able to move it horizontally on the bottom of the screen.
- At each level, a given number of enemy spaceships appear and roam around the stage at a constant speed in a constant direction.

- Enemies cannot leave the stage, and they will bounce inside it as they touch stage edges.

- Enemies don't shoot, and the only way they will kill the player is by touching the spaceship.

- The player can only have one bullet on stage at any time, and hitting an enemy with the bullet will destroy it.

- Destroying all enemies means passing the level, and at each level the number of enemies and their speed increases.

These are the basic rules. We'll add some minor improvements during the design of the game itself, but before we start drawing the graphics, keep in mind we'll design something with the look and feel of old coin operator monitors, with bright glowing graphics.

Creating the game and drawing the graphics

Create a new file (**File | New**) then from **New Document** window select **Actionscript 3.0.** Set its properties as width to 640 px, height to 480 px, background color to #000000 (black) and frame rate to 60. Also define the Document Class as Main and save the file as astro-panic.fla.

During the making of Concentration I told you 30 frames per second is the ideal choice for smooth animations, anyway we are going to use 60 frames per second this time to create a very fast paced game.

There are three actors in this game: the player-controlled spaceship, the bullet and the enemy. In astro-panic.fla, create three new Movie Clip symbols and call them spaceship_mc for the spaceship, bullet_mc for the bullet, and enemy_mc for the enemy. Set them all as exportable for ActionScript. Leave all other settings at their default values, just like you did in previous chapters.

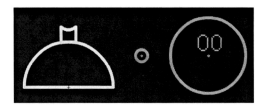

From left to right: The spaceship (spaceship_mc), the bullet (bullet_mc), and the enemy (enemy_mc).

I made all assets with the shape of a circle. The spaceship is half a circle with a radius of 30 pixels, the bullet is a circle with a 4 pixels radius, and the enemy is a circle with a radius of 25 pixels. All of them have the registration point in their centers, and `enemy_mc` has a dynamic text field in it called `level`. You've already met dynamic text fields during the making of Minesweeper so it won't be a problem to add it. At the moment I am writing a couple of zeros to test how the dynamic text field fits in the enemy shape.

Now we are ready to code.

Adding and controlling the spaceship

As usual we know we are going to use classes to manage both enter frame and mouse click events, so we'll import all the required classes immediately.

The spaceship is controlled with the mouse, but can only move along x-axis.

Without closing `astro_panic.fla`, create a new file and from **New Document** window select **ActionScript 3.0 Class**. Save this file as `Main.as` in the same path you saved `astro_panic.fla`. Then write:

```
package {
  import flash.display.Sprite;
  import flash.events.Event;
  import flash.events.MouseEvent;
  public class Main extends Sprite {
    private var spaceship:spaceship_mc;
    public function Main() {
      placeSpaceship();
      addEventListener(Event.ENTER_FRAME,onEnterFrm);
    }
    private function placeSpaceship():void {
      spaceship=new spaceship_mc();
      addChild(spaceship);
      spaceship.y=479;
    }
    private function onEnterFrm(e:Event):void {
      spaceship.x=mouseX;
      if (spaceship.x<30) {
        spaceship.x=30;
      }
      if (spaceship.x>610) {
        spaceship.x=610;
      }
    }
  }
}
```

At this time you should know everything about the concept behind this script. `placeSpaceship` is the function which constructs, adds to Display List and places the `spaceship_mc` DisplayObject called `spaceship`.

In `enter_frame` function we just move the spaceship in the same position of the x-axis of the mouse. We don't want the spaceship to hide in a corner, so it won't be able to follow the axis of the mouse if it gets too close to stage edges.

Test the movie, and move the mouse. Your spaceship will follow it, while being bound to the ground.

Now we should give the spaceship an old arcade look.

Adding a glow filter

AS3 allows us to dynamically apply a wide range of filters to DisplayObjects on the fly. We'll add a glow filter to simulate old 'arcades' pixel luminosity.

`flash.filters.GlowFilter` class lets us apply a glow effect to DisplayObjects.

First, we need to import it.

```
import flash.display.Sprite;
import flash.events.Event;
import flash.events.MouseEvent;
import flash.filters.GlowFilter;
```

at this time, we can simply create a new variable to construct a `GlowFilter` object. Change `placeSpaceship` this way:

```
private function placeSpaceship():void {
    ...
    var glow:GlowFilter=new GlowFilter(0x00FFFF,1,6,6,2,2);
    spaceship.filters=new Array(glow);
}
```

In the constructor I specified the color (`0x00FFFF` = the same cyan I used to draw the spaceship), the alpha (1 = full opacity), and the amount of horizontal and vertical blur (both 6).

I want you to notice that I used 6 for horizontal and vertical blur because I like the effect I achieve with such value. If you are planning to use a lot of filters, remember values that are a power of 2 (such as 4 and 8, but not 6) render more quickly than other values.

The remaining two arguments are the strength, that determines the spread of the filter (if you use Photoshop, it's something like spread and size of the glow filter you can apply on layers) and the quality.

Quality can range from 1 to 15 but values higher than 3 may affect performances and the same final effect can be set playing with blur.

Finally the filter is added

```
spaceship.filters=new Array(glow);
```

`filters` DisplayObject's property wants an array with all the filters you want to associate to the DisplayObject. In our case, we are adding only one filter but we have to include it in the array anyway.

Test the movie and you will see your spaceship glow.

In the previous picture, you can see the difference between the spaceship without and with the glow effect applied.

Now your spaceship is ready to fire.

Making spaceship fire

Nobody would face an alien invasion with a harmless spaceship, so we are going to make it fire.

We need to create a variable to manage `bullet_mc` DisplayObject and I have said the spaceship can fire only one bullet at a time, so we need another variable to tell us if the spaceship is already firing. If it's firing, it cannot fire. If it's not firing, it can fire.

Add two new class level variables:

```
private var spaceship:spaceship_mc;
private var isFiring:Boolean=false;
private var bullet:bullet_mc;
```

`isFiring` is the Boolean variable that we'll use to determine if the spaceship is firing. `false` means it's not firing.

`bullet` will represent the bullet itself.

The player will be able to fire with mouse click, so a listener is needed in `Main` function:

```
public function Main() {
  placeSpaceship();
  addEventListener(Event.ENTER_FRAME,onEnterFrm);
  stage.addEventListener(MouseEvent.CLICK,onMouseCk);
}
```

Now every time the player clicks the mouse, `onMouseCk` function is called.

This is the function:

```
private function onMouseCk(e:MouseEvent):void {
  if (! isFiring) {
    placeBullet();
    isFiring=true;
  }
}
```

It's very easy: if `isFiring` is `false` (the spaceship isn't already firing), `placeBullet` function is called to physically place a bullet then `isFiring` is set to `true` because now the spaceship is firing.

The same `placeBullet` function isn't complex:

```
private function placeBullet():void {
  bullet=new bullet_mc();
  addChild(bullet);
  bullet.x=spaceship.x;
  bullet.y=430;
  var glow:GlowFilter=new GlowFilter(0xFF0000,1,6,6,2,2);
  bullet.filters=new Array(glow);
}
```

It's very similar to `placeSpaceship` function, the bullet is created, added to Display List, placed on screen, and a red glow effect is added.

The only thing I would explain is the concept behind x and y properties:

```
bullet.x=spaceship.x;
```

Setting bullet's x property equal to spaceship's x property will place the bullet exactly where the spaceship is at the moment of firing.

```
bullet.y=430;
```

430 is a good y value to make the bullet seem as it were just fired from the turret.

Test the movie, and you will be able to fire a bullet with a mouse click.

The bullet at the moment remains static in the point where we fired it.

Making the bullet fly

To make the bullet fly, we have to define its speed and move it upwards. Then we'll remove it once it leaves the stage and reset isFiring to false to let the player fire again.

Add a constant to class level variables:

```
private const BULLET_SPEED:uint=5;
private var spaceship:spaceship_mc;
private var isFiring:Boolean=false;
private var bullet:bullet_mc;
```

BULLET_SPEED is the amount of pixels the bullet will fly at each frame. We won't manage upgrades or power-ups, so we can say its value will never change. That's why it's defined as a constant.

To manage bullet movement, we need to add some lines at the end of onEnterFrm function.

You may wonder why we are managing both the spaceship and the bullet inside the same class rather than creating a separate class for each one. You'll discover it when you manage enemies' movement, later in this chapter.

Meanwhile, add this code to `onEnterFrm` function.

```
private function onEnterFrm(e:Event):void {
  ...
  if (isFiring) {
    bullet.y-=BULLET_SPEED;
    if (bullet.y<0) {
      removeChild(bullet);
      bullet=null;
      isFiring=false;
    }
  }
}
```

The new code is executed only if `isFiring` is `true`. We are sure we have a bullet on stage when `isFiring` is `true`.

```
bullet.y-=BULLET_SPEED;
```

Moves the bullet upward by `BULLET_SPEED` pixels.

```
if (bullet.y<0) { ... }
```

This `if` statement checks if `y` property is less than `0`. This means the bullet flew off the screen. In this case we physically remove the bullet from the game with

```
removeChild(bullet);
bullet=null;
```

and we give the player the capability of firing again with

```
isFiring=false;
```

Test the movie and fire, now your bullets will fly until they reach the top of the stage. Then you will be able to fire again.

Since nobody wants to fire for the sake of firing, we'll add some enemies to shoot down.

Adding enemies

We want a battle with more and more enemies as the player progresses through levels, so we have to define a variable to tell us which level is currently being played and a variable to manage the enemy DisplayObject. Add these two class level variables:

```
private const BULLET_SPEED:uint=5;
private var spaceship:spaceship_mc;
private var isFiring:Boolean=false;
private var bullet:bullet_mc;
private var enemy=enemy_mc;
private var level:uint=1;
```

`level` is the current level, that starts from 1.

As the game starts, we have to place enemies on the screen according to level number. Add these lines to `Main` function:

```
public function Main() {
  placeSpaceship();
  for (var i:uint=1; i<level+3; i++) {
    placeEnemy(i);
  }
  addEventListener(Event.ENTER_FRAME,onEnterFrm);
  stage.addEventListener(MouseEvent.CLICK,onMouseCk);
}
```

The `for` loop will call `placeEnemy` function (which obviously places an enemy) for `level+2` times, so we'll have 3 enemies at level one, 4 enemies on level two, and so on.

Notice how an argument with the current enemy count is passed: knowing the cardinality of an enemy will come in hand later.

As you can imagine, `placeEnemy` function at the moment is not that much more than a copy/paste of `placeBullet` function, we are just placing enemies in a random position, not too close to the edges of the stage, and not too close to the player.

```
private function placeEnemy(enemy_level:uint):void {
  enemy=new enemy_mc();
  enemy.x=Math.random()*500+70;
  enemy.y=Math.random()*200+50;
  var glow:GlowFilter=new GlowFilter(0xFF00FF,1,6,6,2,2);
  enemy.filters=new Array(glow);
  addChild(enemy);
}
```

Test the game and you will see three enemies appear in random positions.

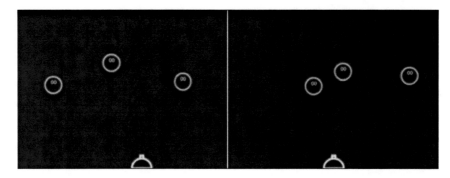

Don't worry if in some cases they overlap: the game won't deal with collisions among enemies so it does not matter.

Moving enemies

As a static enemy won't scare anyone, let's make enemies move.

With the knowledge you have at the moment, you would suggest creating `spaceship_mc` class and using an enter frame listener to update each enemy position. Most scripts relies on `Event.ENTER_FRAME` event is simultaneously dispatched to all DisplayObjects listening for it, so you don't have to synchronize animations.

That's true, but with many DisplayObjects to be updated, this technique although being the most correct from a programming point of view can dramatically increase the work of the Flash player.

In this game we won't deal with such an huge number of moving DisplayObjects to represent a risk for your CPU, anyway it's time to learn something new.

Add this new class level variable:

```
private const BULLET_SPEED:uint=5;
private var spaceship:spaceship_mc;
private var isFiring:Boolean=false;
private var bullet:bullet_mc;
private var enemy=enemy_mc;
private var level:uint=1;
private var enemyVector:Vector.<enemy_mc>=new Vector.<enemy_mc>();
```

You just defined your first Vector.

A Vector is an array with elements of the same predefined type. Such type is defined as "base type", and can be any kind of type, including custom classes like I've done.

The base type must be specified when the Vector is created or when an instance is created using the class constructor.

So to declare a Vector of `enemy_mc` class we'll use:

```
private var enemyVector:Vector.<enemy_mc>
```

Notice how the base type is declared using a dot (.) then writing the class name between angle brackets (< and >).

Then you would construct it declaring base type again, this way:

```
enemyVector=new Vector.<enemy_mc>();
```

Now the question is: when should you use a Vector rather than an Array? You should use a Vector every time you are dealing with collections of data of the same type, as Vector management has been proved to be faster than Array management.

Again, the increased performance in this game would be unnoticeable since the data we manage isn't that big, anyway it's important you know how to use vectors.

Back to our enemies, we have to make them move in a random direction at a constant speed, but we said tougher enemies will move faster, so it's time to learn some trigonometry basics. Look at this picture:

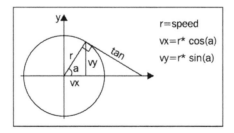

We have a circle, and a radius that we know has the same length no matter its angle. The radius represents the constant enemy speed, to be split into horizontal and vertical speed, called vx and vy.

Thanks to trigonometry, we can determine vx by multiplying the radius by the cosine of the angle formed by the radius and the horizontal axis, and vy multiplying the radius by the sine of such angle.

This concept can be translated into AS3 adding these lines at the end of placeEnemy function:

```
private function placeEnemy(enemy_level:uint):void {
  ...
  var dir:Number = Math.random()*Math.PI*2;
  enemy.xspeed=enemy_level*Math.cos(dir);
  enemy.yspeed=enemy_level*Math.sin(dir);
  enemyVector.push(enemy);
}
```

Let's see how we can choose a random direction:

```
var dir:Number = Math.random()*Math.PI*2;
```

dir is the variable which stores the random direction. It's a random number between 0 and 360 degrees, just expressed in radians. The radian is the standard unit of angular measure, and describes the plane angle subtended by a circular arc as the length of the arc divided by the radius of the arc.

Math.PI returns the value of PI, 3.141592653589793

```
enemy.xspeed=enemy_level*Math.cos(dir);
enemy.yspeed=enemy_level*Math.sin(dir);
```

Once we know enemy direction, it's easy to determine its horizontal and vertical speed thanks to the trigonometry formulas you just learned. Just notice how speed is multiplied by enemy_level argument. This way the latest enemies to be added are the faster and consequently the harder to kill.

This simple feature will allow us to have levels with increasing difficulty, with a new, fastest enemy spaceship to be added at every level.

```
enemyVector.push(enemy);
```

Finally, the enemy itself is added to enemyVector Vector with push method as if it was an array, since push works in the same way for both Arrays and Vectors.

Everything is now ready to make onEnterFrm function iterate through enemyVector Vector and update each enemy position according to its x and y speed.

Add this line to `onEnterFrm` function:

```
private function onEnterFrm(e:Event) {
  ...
  enemyVector.forEach(manageEnemy);
}
```

`forEach` method (notice the uppercase `E`) executes a function for each item in the Vector.

This means `manageEnemy` function will be executed for each `enemyVector` item, but you can't define this function as you like, because it must have some mandatory arguments.

The function has to be created with three arguments: the current Vector item, the index of such item, and the Vector itself. Also, the function won't return anything, so we will declare as `void`.

This is `manageEnemy` function:

```
private function manageEnemy(c:enemy_mc,index:int,v:Vector.<enemy_
mc>):void {
  var currentEnemy:enemy_mc = c;
  currentEnemy.x+=currentEnemy.xspeed;
  currentEnemy.y+=currentEnemy.yspeed;
  if (currentEnemy.x<25) {
    currentEnemy.x=25;
    currentEnemy.xspeed*=-1;
  }
  if (currentEnemy.x>615) {
    currentEnemy.x=615;
    currentEnemy.xspeed*=-1;
  }
  if (currentEnemy.y<25) {
    currentEnemy.y=25;
    currentEnemy.yspeed*=-1;
  }
  if (currentEnemy.y>455) {
    currentEnemy.y=455;
    currentEnemy.yspeed*=-1;
  }
}
```

let's see first how it has been declared:

```
private function manageEnemy(c:enemy_mc,index:int,v:Vector.<enemy_
mc>):void
```

As you can see, the three arguments are the current enemy, its index in the Vector and the Vector itself. All arguments are automatically passed to the function; you don't have to worry about anything when calling it in the `forEach` method.

Then in comes a line I used only for the sake of layout:

```
var currentEnemy:enemy_mc = c;
```

I was forced to call the first argument `c` to make a function declaration fit in a single row, but obviously it would have been better to call it `currentEnemy`, so I just created a variable with a more appropriate name.

```
currentEnemy.x+=currentEnemy.xspeed;
currentEnemy.y+=currentEnemy.yspeed;
```

That's how I update `currentEnemy` position according to its `xspeed` and `yspeed` properties.

Enemies cannot fly off the stage, so the remaining lines are just to make them bounce inside stage edges. I will explain only the first situation: when the enemy is about to leave the stage to the left.

```
if (currentEnemy.x<25) { ... }
```

The `if` statement checks if enemy `x` position is less than 25 (enemy's radius). This would mean the enemy is flying off the stage to the left, and we must prevent it. First we stop it at the very leftmost position it can go with:

```
currentEnemy.x=25;
```

Then, we invert its horizontal speed this way:

```
currentEnemy.x=25;
```

The remaining `if` statements check and prevent the enemies from flying off the stage respectively to right, up, and down sides.

Test the movie and you will see three enemies moving and bouncing around the stage, at a constant speed while each one has a different speed.

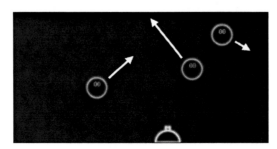

Now enemies are quite dangerous because they move around the screen, anyway nothing happens when they touch your spaceship.

Obviously hitting an enemy with the spaceship means losing the game or at least one life, so let's make enemies deadly.

Being killed by an enemy

Both enemies and the spaceship have a perfect circular shape. This will help us to determine when an enemy and the spaceship collide. Being basically two circles, we can say they collide when the distance between their centers is less than the sum of both the radius.

Let's start creating a quick function to determine the distance between two Sprites using the Pythagorean Theorem:

```
private function distance(from:Sprite,to:Sprite):Number {
   var distX:Number=from.x-to.x;
   var distY:Number=from.y-to.y;
   return distX*distX+distY*distY;
}
```

There isn't that much to explain, since we are just applying a world famous formula, but I want you to notice I am not performing any square root because it's quite CPU-expensive. It won't be a problem as long as I remember to compare the collision distance applying the power of two, which is way faster than applying a square root.

Everything is ready to check for collisions, so add these lines at the end of `manageEnemy` function:

```
private function manageEnemy(c:enemy_mc,index:int,v:Vector.<enemy_
mc>):void {
   ...
   if (distance(spaceship,currentEnemy)<3025) {
     die();
   }
}
```

Look at this statement:

```
if (distance(spaceship,currentEnemy)<3025) { ... }
```

It determines if the distance between the spaceship and the current enemy is less than `3025`, which is `25` (enemy radius) + `30` (spaceship radius) = `55` (collision distance) by the power of two. Easy and fast. Obviously you are free to store all these values in constants; I am using these raw values for a matter of speed.

Once an enemy collides with the spaceship, `die` function is called. Here it is:

```
private function die():void {
  var glow:GlowFilter=new GlowFilter(0x00FFFF,1,10,10,6,6);
  spaceship.filters=new Array(glow);
  removeEventListener(Event.ENTER_FRAME,onEnterFrm);
  stage.removeEventListener(MouseEvent.CLICK,onMouseCk);
}
```

I am sure you figured out how it works: first a new, bigger glow is applied to the spaceship, and then all the event listeners are removed. The game stops.

Test the game, and let an enemy hit the spaceship. The game will stop with the enemy hitting a greatly glowing spaceship and nothing more will happen.

That's enough at the moment, because before making something interesting happen when the spaceship dies, we must make it able to kill enemies with its bullets.

Killing an enemy

Knowing the bullet has a perfect circular shape, there's nothing easier at this time than letting the spaceship kill an enemy. We have to check if the distance between the bullet (if any) and the enemy is less than the sum of their radius, just as we made it with the spaceship.

At the end of `manageEnemy` function, add these lines:

```
private function manageEnemy(c:enemy_mc,index:int,v:Vector.<enemy_
mc>):void {
  ...
  if (isFiring) {
    if (distance(bullet,currentEnemy)<841) {
      killEnemy(currentEnemy);
    }
  }
}
```

First we check if there's a bullet flying around the game just looking at `isFiring` value. If it's `true`, then we see if the distance between the current spaceship and the bullet is less than 841, which is 25 (enemy radius) + 4 (bullet radius) = 29 (collision distance) by the power of two. In this case, `killEnemy` function is called; just like `die` function was called when the enemy and the spaceship collided. The only difference is we need to know which enemy the player killed, so we pass it as argument. Again, feel free to replace numbers with constants.

This is `killEnemy` function:

```
private function killEnemy(theEnemy:enemy_mc):void {
    var glow:GlowFilter=new GlowFilter(0xFF00FF,1,10,10,6,6);
    theEnemy.filters=new Array(glow);
    removeEventListener(Event.ENTER_FRAME,onEnterFrm);
    stage.removeEventListener(MouseEvent.CLICK,onMouseCk);
}
```

The function works absolutely the same way as `die` function does: adds a glow to the dying enemy and completely stops the game.

Test the movie and shoot to an enemy, and you will see it glow and the game will stop.

At this time all main events are defined. We can work on level progression.

Killing an enemy—for good

A level is completed when all enemies have been killed. When you kill an enemy, the game must continue rather than stop like it does now. We must flag enemies killed by the spaceship so they won't harm anymore, and let the game continue.

First, when we create a new enemy, let's set a new property called `killed`. It will be `true` if the enemy has been killed, so it starts with `false`.

```
private function placeEnemy(enemy_level:uint):void {
    enemy=new enemy_mc();
    enemy.killed=false;
    ...
}
```

Then we have to heavily recode `killEnemy` function. We won't remove listeners as we don't want the game to stop, but we'll set `killed` property to `true` and remove the bullet as if it had flown out of the stage.

```
private function killEnemy(theEnemy:enemy_mc):void {
   var glow:GlowFilter=new GlowFilter(0xFF00FF,1,10,10,6,6);
   theEnemy.filters=new Array(glow);
   // don't remove listeners
   theEnemy.killed=true;
   removeChild(bullet);
   bullet=null;
   isFiring=false;
}
```

Last but not least, we'll update enemy position and check for collision with the player or the bullet only if the enemy is still alive, that means its `killed` property is `false`.

```
private function manageEnemy(c:enemy_mc,index:int,v:Vector.<enemy_
mc>):void {
   var currentEnemy:enemy_mc=c;
   if (! currentEnemy.killed) {
      ...
   }
}
```

This way the whole function is executed only if `killed` property is `false`.

Test the movie, and you will be able to kill all enemies.

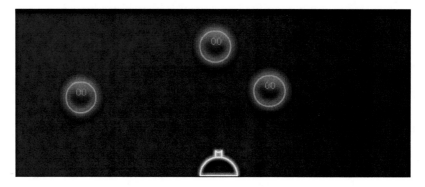

At this time the player would expect to see killed enemies removed from the screen, maybe with some kind of animation.

Killing an enemy—with style

To make something happen to the enemy when it's about to die, we could make it grow and fade out. It's a good and simple way to animate its death.

Moreover, we have to remove dead enemies from `enemyVector` Vector because there's no point in managing them as they should be removed from stage.

We know there is only one bullet at a time, so there can be only one enemy hit by a bullet in a single frame. This is precious information because it allows us to manage all deaths with a single class level variable, which we'll call `enemyToRemove`, indicating the index in `enemyVector` Vector of the enemy to remove. It starts at `-1` which means there's no enemy to remove.

```
private const BULLET_SPEED:uint=5;
private var spaceship:spaceship_mc;
private var isFiring:Boolean=false;
private var bullet:bullet_mc;
private var enemy=enemy_mc;
private var level:uint=1;
private var enemyVector:Vector.<enemy_mc>=new Vector.<enemy_mc>();
private var enemyToRemove:int=-1;
```

Once the variable is declared, we have to add a new block of code to manage dying enemies. Do you remember the whole `manageEnemy` function is executed only if `killed` property is `false`?

Now it's time to execute some code when it's `true` and the enemy has been hit by the bullet.

```
private function manageEnemy(c:enemy_mc,index:int,v:Vector.<enemy_
mc>):void {
  var currentEnemy:enemy_mc=c;
  if (! currentEnemy.killed) {
    ...
  } else {
    currentEnemy.width++;
    currentEnemy.height++;
    currentEnemy.alpha-=0.01;
    if (currentEnemy.alpha<=0) {
      removeChild(currentEnemy);
      currentEnemy=null;
      enemyToRemove=index;
    }
  }
}
```

Let's see what we are doing:

```
currentEnemy.width++;
currentEnemy.height++;
```

Increases enemy width and height to make it bigger.

```
currentEnemy.alpha-=0.01;
```

Makes it a bit less opaque decreasing its `alpha` property by `0.01`.

```
if (currentEnemy.alpha<0) { ... }
```

Checks if the `alpha` property is less than `0`. This means the enemy is completely transparent and it's time to remove it from the game.

```
removeChild(currentEnemy);
currentEnemy=null;
```

Removes the enemy from the Display List and clears its variable.

```
enemyToRemove=index;
```

Finally, setting the new `currentEnemy` variable to `index`, that represents the current index in `enemyVector` Vector.

Now in `onEnterFrm` function we can remove the corresponding item from the Vector. Doing it in a function called by `forEach` method would produce some warnings as you are making the Vector shorter while it's currently being scanned.

At the end of `onEnterFrm` function, add these lines:

```
private function onEnterFrm(e:Event):void {
  ...
  if (enemyToRemove>=0) {
    enemyVector.splice(enemyToRemove,1);
    enemyToRemove=-1;
  }
}
```

Their meaning is quite obvious: if `enemyToRemove` has a value greater than its default value `-1`, then remove the item from `enemyVector` Vector with `splice` method, then set `enemyToRemove` to `-1` again as there aren't any more enemies to remove.

splice method adds elements to and removes elements from the Vector. The same method is also available for arrays. In our case, the first parameter (enemyToRemove) is the index of the element where the deletion begins, and the second parameter (1) the number of elements to be deleted. Basically I am saying the Vector to remove one element starting from index enemyToRemove. An optional third parameter can be used to provide a list of one or more comma-separated values to insert into the Vector starting from the index specified in the first parameter. We don't need this optional third parameter in this case.

Test the movie and shoot to an enemy to see it explode.

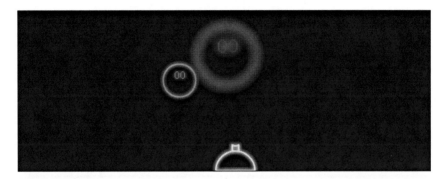

The game now starts to look good, but once you destroyed all enemies nothing happens.

Advancing levels

Once all enemies have been destroyed, the player must be able to play the next level, with more enemies moving faster.

For our convenience, we should manage level creation with a function, changing Main function removing the for loop and adding a new function called playLevel.

```
public function Main() {
  placeSpaceship();
  playLevel();
  addEventListener(Event.ENTER_FRAME,onEnterFrm);
  stage.addEventListener(MouseEvent.CLICK,onMouseCk);
}
```

This function is just a cut/paste of the `for` loop previously included in `Main` function, but this way we can call `playLevel` from elsewhere.

```
private function playLevel():void {
  for (var i:uint=1; i<level+3; i++) {
    placeEnemy(i);
  }
}
```

And in this specific case, we are calling it from `onEnterFrm` function once we removed an enemy:

```
private function onEnterFrm(e:Event) {
  ...
  if (enemyToRemove>=0) {
    enemyVector.splice(enemyToRemove,1);
    enemyToRemove=-1;
    if (enemyVector.length==0) {
      level++;
      playLevel();
    }
  }
}
```

If the length of `enemyVector` Vector is `0`, there are no enemies left, so it's time to increase `level` variable and call `playLevel` function to start a new level.

Test the movie and try to beat as many levels as you can.

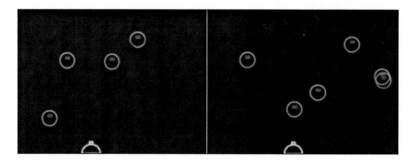

In the previous picture, level 2 with four enemies and level 4 with six enemies. The game gets harder as the player progresses through levels.

Now, something for the score maniacs.

Managing current score and high score

When playing games with a specific goal, such as saving the princess or escaping from the castle, players know exactly why they are playing: they must save the princess or escape from the castle.

In games like Astro-PANIC!, where there's no goal and you just have to survive as long as possible, the only way to have players come back to our game and play it again is giving the possibility to save their best score.

People will play again and again to achieve a better score.

At this time, we need two more class level variables: one to save the current score, which we call `score`, and another variable called `hiscore`, which will save our best score ever.

Add these two new variables:

```
private const BULLET_SPEED:uint=5;
private var spaceship:spaceship_mc;
private var isFiring:Boolean=false;
private var bullet:bullet_mc;
private var enemy=enemy_mc;
private var level:uint=1;
private var enemyVector:Vector.<enemy_mc>=new Vector.<enemy_mc>();
private var enemyToRemove:int=-1;
private var score:uint=0;
private var hiscore:uint=0;
```

Finally, it's time to make a good use of the `level` dynamic text. We'll display the number of the enemy. The higher the number, the faster the enemy, and the more points it will give once killed. This will help the player to choose which enemy to kill, making his own strategy.

```
private function placeEnemy(enemy_level:uint):void {
  enemy=new enemy_mc();
  enemy.level.text = enemy_level;
  ...
}
```

Once an enemy dies, the score is updated. Although being a very simple game, we can add complex scoring system by giving the enemy a score based on its level and its height.

The higher you kill an enemy, the more points it will give you.

```
private function killEnemy(theEnemy:enemy_mc):void {
  ...
  score+=int(theEnemy.level.text)*(4-Math.floor(theEnemy.y/100));
  trace(score);
}
```

Once you die, I want the score to be written on the output window, and eventually the high score to be updated.

```
private function die():void {
  var glow:GlowFilter=new GlowFilter(0x00FFFF,1,10,10,6,6);
  spaceship.filters=new Array(glow);
  removeEventListener(Event.ENTER_FRAME,onEnterFrm);
  stage.removeEventListener(MouseEvent.CLICK,onMouseCk);
  trace("Your score: "+score);
  trace("Current hiscore: "+hiscore);
  if (score>hiscore) {
    trace("CONGRATULATIONS!! NEW HISCORE");
    hiscore=score;
  }
}
```

There's not that much to explain in this code, as it's just a bunch of screen outputs.

Test the movie and play until you die:

You should see in the output window something like this:

```
6
9
...
56
62
66
Your score: 66
Current hiscore: 0
CONGRATULATIONS!! NEW HISCORE
```

So you are able to manage scores and high scores.

The big problem is the high score is reset to 0 every time you start a new game, making it useless. We have to find a way to save data on players' local computers.

Saving data on your local computer

AS3 provides a class, `SharedObject`, to let us save a limited amount of data on our local computer. The class does not create cookies, but something very similar called LocalSharedObjects, and the concept is the same.

It's very important to understand that LocalSharedObjects maintain local persistence. This means that you can play the game, make an high score, turn off your computer, and next time you'll play the game on the same computer, it will retrieve the high score.

Exactly what we need. Let's see how to use it. First, we need to import the `SharedObject` class:

```
import flash.display.Sprite;
import flash.events.Event;
import flash.events.MouseEvent;
import flash.filters.GlowFilter;
import flash.net.SharedObject;
```

Then we will remove `hiscore` class level variable as we won't use it anymore as it just keeps the high score when the script is running, and we will create a new variable called `sharedHiScore`, to handle with `SharedObject` class.

```
private const BULLET_SPEED:uint=5;
private var spaceship:spaceship_mc;
private var isFiring:Boolean=false;
private var bullet:bullet_mc;
private var enemy=enemy_mc;
private var level:uint=1;
private var enemyVector:Vector.<enemy_mc>=new Vector.<enemy_mc>();
private var enemyToRemove:int=-1;
private var score:uint=0;
private var hiscore:uint=0; // remove this one
private var sharedHiScore:SharedObject;
```

At this time, when the game is run, we can face two cases:

1. The game has never been run on the computer, so we have to somehow initialize the SharedObject.

2. The game has already been run on the computer, no matter if someone made an high score or not, no matter even if someone has played. In this case the SharedObject is initiazlied.

To make this, we need to add this code to `Main` function:

```
public function Main() {
   sharedHiScore = SharedObject.getLocal("hiscores");
   if (sharedHiScore.data.score==undefined) {
     sharedHiScore.data.score = 0;
     trace("No High Score found");
   }
   else {
     trace("Current High Score: "+sharedHiScore.data.score);
   }
   sharedHiScore.close();
   placeSpaceship();
   playLevel();
   addEventListener(Event.ENTER_FRAME,onEnterFrm);
   stage.addEventListener(MouseEvent.CLICK,onMouseCk);
}
```

Let's see its meaning:

```
sharedHiScore = SharedObject.getLocal("hiscores");
```

`getLocal` method returns a reference to a locally persistent SharedObject (in this case `hiscores`) that is available only on the current client. If the SharedObject does not already exist, `getLocal` method creates one.

```
if (sharedHiScore.data.score==undefined) { ... }
```

When looking at `score` value inside `hiscores` SharedObject, if it's `undefined` it means there isn't any variable called `score` in `hiscores` SharedObject or there isn't any `hiscores` SharedObject at all.

```
sharedHiScore.data.score = 0;
trace("No High Score found");
```

In this case we need to initialize `score` variable in `hiscores` SharedObject. We'll set it to zero. At the same time, we print a message in the Output window saying we did not find any high score.

```
else { trace("Current High Score: "+sharedHiScore.data.score); }
```

If we found a high score, we show it in the Output window.

```
sharedHiScore.close();
```

When we are done with the SharedObject, we have to close it. `close` method does this job.

Now, when the player dies, we have to check his score with the SharedObject high scores and eventually update it. The last part of `die` function must be changed this way:

```
private function die():void {
    var glow:GlowFilter=new GlowFilter(0x00FFFF,1,10,10,6,6);
    spaceship.filters=new Array(glow);
    removeEventListener(Event.ENTER_FRAME,onEnterFrm);
    stage.removeEventListener(MouseEvent.CLICK,onMouseCk);
    trace("Your score: "+score);
    sharedHiScore = SharedObject.getLocal("hiscores");
    trace("Current hiscore: "+sharedHiScore.data.score);
    if (score>sharedHiScore.data.score) {
      trace("CONGRATULATIONS!! NEW HISCORE");
      sharedHiScore.data.score = score;
    }
    sharedHiScore.close();
}
```

As you can see, the SharedObject is opened once again, and its `score` variable is compared with `score` class level variable. As you can see, both variables can have the same name because they refer to different classes. Then if needed we update the SharedObject and finally we close it.

Test the movie and the first time you will see in the Output window:

No High Score found

Now play a game, and if when you die you scored, let's say, 18, you will see in the Output window:

Your score: 18

Current hiscore: 0

CONTRATULATIONS!! NEW HISCORE

At this time you must close and restart the game as it does not provide a "replay", and once you restart it (you can also restart you computer if you want) you will see:

Current High Score: 18

The game remembered the latest high score you made.

Summary

The most important things you learned during this chapter are the capability of adding filters on the fly to your DisplayObjects and the feature of saving data on your computer using SharedObjects. You can manage any kind of save game with SharedObjects, such as the latest level beaten, the amount of gold the player owns, or any other kind of information.

Where to go now

To provide a better experience to players, you could place some dynamic text fields showing the current level and the score, as well as the high score. Then you can add some lines to onMouseCk function, you can make the player restart the game if he clicks the mouse when the game is over. You only have to reset the score, the level, and the variable that states the game is over.

7
Bejeweled

Bejeweled is the first "modern" (its first release was in 2001) game to be discussed in this book. I chose to dedicate the last three chapters of this book to modern games to show you how most modern successful casual games are still relatively easy to code, meaning in this niche of market good ideas prevail over game complexity. Millions of copies of Bejeweled have been sold, and its Facebook version is played by a million people every month.

The game is played on a 8x8 grid with 64 gems of seven different kinds placed over it. The objective is to swap one gem with an adjacent gem to form a horizontal or vertical streak of three or more gems. These gems then disappear and new ones fall from the top to fill in gaps.

In this chapter you will code a fully working Bejeweled prototype learning these techniques:

- `do while` loop, to create loops with at least one iteration
- DisplayObjects `visible` property, to quickly make objects invisible
- strings `split` method, to split a string into an array of substrings using a given separator
- `with` statement, to define a default object to be used in the script

This time we'll skip game design because there is a lot of work to do. Anyway, throughout this book you've already seen how to make a good game design document, so it won't be a problem to do it on your own.

Creating documents and objects

Create a new file (**File | New**) then from **New Document** window select **Actionscript 3.0.** Set its properties as width to 640px, height to 480px, background color to #000033 (a dark blue), and frame rate to 30. Also define the Document Class as Main and save the file as bejeweled.fla.

We are using two objects: one with seven frames containing all gems, called gem_mc, and one for the square that will indicate the gems we are selecting, called selector_mc.

All assets will be drawn with registration point at 0,0 and designed to fit in a 60x60 tile.

In bejeweled.fla, create two new Movie Clip symbols and call them selector_mc and gem_mc. Set them as exportable for ActionScript and leave all other settings at their default values, just like you did in previous chapters.

Then draw something like this:

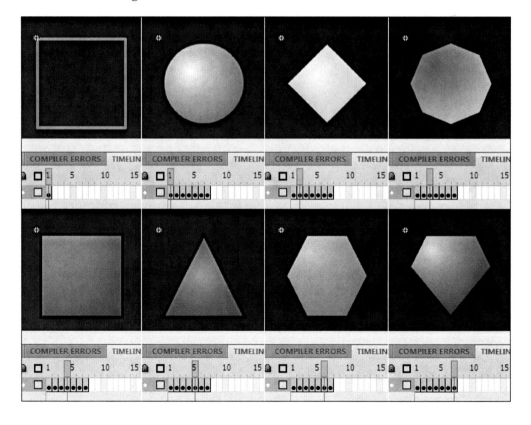

In the upper left corner you can see selector_mc, while the remaining pictures represent the seven gems used in the game.

Placing the gems

Placing the gems on stage may seem just a matter of adding some random DisplayObjects to Display List, but you'll see that we'll find ourselves in trouble very soon.

The idea: We are going to populate the array and physically place the jewels in the same script, so we'll fill the array with random integer numbers between 0 and 6, to represent each of the possible jewels. At the same time, we'll place a gem in the proper position and show the proper frame.

The development: You already know what we need to place the jewels as it's the same concept as placing cards, mines, crates, or whatever kind of asset in a tile-based game. Anyway, let's recap once again. We need:

- a two-dimensional array to represent the game field
- a DisplayObject to act as a container for all jewels
- an instance of gem_mc object

A couple of for loops will populate the array with random numbers, as gem_mc objects will be placed on the stage.

Without closing bejeweled.fla, create a new file and from **New Document** window select **ActionScript 3.0 Class**. Save this file as Main.as in the same path you saved bejeweled.fla. Then write:

```
package {
  import flash.display.Sprite;
  import flash.events.MouseEvent;
  public class Main extends Sprite {
    private var jewels:Array=new Array();
    private var gemsContainer:Sprite=new Sprite();
    private var gem:gem_mc;
    public function Main() {
      jewelsInit();
    }
    private function jewelsInit():void {
      addChild(gemsContainer);
      for (var i:uint=0; i<8; i++) {
        jewels[i]=new Array();
        for (var j:uint=0; j<8; j++) {
          jewels[i][j]=Math.floor(Math.random()*7);
```

```
            gem = new gem_mc(jewels[i][j],i,j);
            gemsContainer.addChild(gem);
        }
      }
    }
  }
}
```

First, I am importing the required classes for this game, such as `Sprite` and `MouseEvent` since the game will be controlled by the mouse.

Then we need three class level variables: `jewels` is the array that will contain game field data, `gemsContainer` is the DisplayObject that will contain all gems, and `gem` is a `gem_mc` instance, that is the gem itself.

In `Main` function, the constructor, we only call `jewelsInit` function which will handle initial jewels placement.

This function is very simple, as it only adds `gemsContainer` to Display List, then creates and populates an 8x8 two-dimensional array with random integer numbers between 0 and 7. As a new `jewels` element is added, a new `gem_mc` instance is created.

The only thing you haven't seen before is `gem_mc` constructor, that wants three arguments: the value of the gem itself, its row position and its column position.

Obviously `gem_mc` class will manage gems appearance and position.

Without closing `bejeweled.fla`, create a new file and from **New Document** window select **ActionScript 3.0 Class**. Save this file as `gem_mc.as` in the same path you saved `bejeweled.fla`. Then write:

```
package {
  import flash.display.MovieClip;
  public class gem_mc extends MovieClip {
    public function gem_mc(val:uint,row:uint,col:uint) {
      gotoAndStop(val+1);
      name=row+"_"+col;
      x=col*60;
      y=row*60;
    }
  }
}
```

Notice the class extends `MovieClip` as it has a timeline. As you can see, it just shows the proper frame according to `val` value, and places the gem considering we are playing in squared tiles with 60 pixel sides.

I also gave a name to this DisplayObject, to make it easily selectable once needed. The name is made by the row number followed by an underscore, followed by column number. You already saw this concept during the making of Minesweeper.

Test the movie and you will see your game field filled with gems. That's when bad news comes into play. Test the movie a couple more times, and you will be playing a game like this one:

What's wrong? We already have three or more adjacent gems of the same kind in a row or in a column.

In Bejeweled, the game field starts with no more than two adjacent gems of the same kind, as it's up to the player switching gems to make successful streaks.

Placing the gems for real

Preventing the game field from starting with successful streaks means coding all the required routines to see if a given gem is part of a successful streak. There is a lot to code, but the good news is the functions to check for successful streaks that we are about to write are the same as we will use when the player starts swapping gems.

The idea: When it's time to place a gem, check if the gem we are about to place will form a successful streak. In this case, keep generating random gems until it's no longer part of a streak. Finally place the gem.

The development: Checking for a successful streak is not different from checking for victory in Connect 4. We can even say it's easier since we only have to look horizontally and vertically, without caring about diagonals.

Following the concepts seen during the making of Connect 4, let's start creating some basic functions.

The first function we need is one that tells us if there is a certain gem in a given row and column, assuming row and column values can even be wrong.

Let's call it `checkGem` and make it return `true` if there is a `gem` in the `row-th` row and `col-th` column, `false` elsewhere.

```
private function checkGem(gem:uint,row:int,col:int):Boolean {
  if (jewels[row]==null) {
    return false;
  }
  if (jewels[row][col]==null) {
    return false;
  }
  return gem==jewels[row][col];
}
```

It just checks for `jewels[row][col]` value to be equal to `gem` once we verified it's not a `null` value. We can have `null` values when we try to look for a gem in an illegal position, which is outside the populated array.

What can we do with this function? We can build other functions to check whether a given gem is part of a streak or not.

We know a gem is a part of a streak when there are at least other two adjacent gems of the same kind horizontally or vertically. So it's easy to create a function to see if the gem is part of a horizontal streak.

Given a row and a column position, we will keep counting gems at its left and at its right until we find a gem that does not match, or an illegal position.

This is `rowStreak` function, with `row` and `col` arguments representing the position of the gem to check, it returns the number of matching gems.

```
private function rowStreak(row:uint,col:uint):uint {
  var current:uint=jewels[row][col];
  var streak:uint=1;
  var tmp:int=col;
  while (checkGem(current,row,tmp-1)) {
    tmp--;
    streak++;
  }
  tmp=col;
  while (checkGem(current,row,tmp+1)) {
```

```
      tmp++;
      streak++;
   }
   return (streak);
}
```

Let's give it a brief look:

```
   var current:uint=jewels[row][col];
```

Saving in `current` variable the value of `jewels[row][col]` array, that is the gem we will look for.

```
   var streak:uint=1;
```

`streak` variable will keep count of the streak. It's set at `1` because the starting gem itself is a part of the streak.

```
   var tmp:int=col;
```

`tmp` is just a temporary variable to save `col` value as we will change it during the script and we want to save its original value for a later use.

```
   while (checkGem(current,row,tmp-1)) { ... }
```

This `while` loop scans the gems on the left. Since `tmp` is the column value, decreasing it means moving one column left. This is what we do inside the loop:

```
   tmp--;
   streak++;
```

`tmp` value is decreased to look more at the left, and `streak` is increased as if we are inside the loop, it means we found a matching gem.

Once we exit the loop, `tmp` value is restored to `col` value and we start scanning on the right in the same way.

At the end of the function, `streak` value is returned.

In the same way we can code `colStreak` function, that checks for vertical streaks.

```
   private function colStreak(row:uint,col:uint):uint {
      var current:uint=jewels[row][col];
      var streak:uint=1;
      var tmp:int=row;
      while (checkGem(current,tmp-1,col)) {
         tmp--;
         streak++;
      }
```

```
    tmp=row;
    while (checkGem(current,tmp+1,col)) {
      tmp++;
      streak++;
    }
    return (streak);
}
```

At this time, we can determine when a gem is part of a successful streak in a row or in a column.

To complete the set of functions, we just need another one that tells us if a gem in a given position is part of a streak, no matter if horizontal or vertical.

That's what isStreak function does. It just checks if there is a horizontal or a vertical successful streak, that is a streak longer than two gems.

```
private function isStreak(row:uint,col:uint):Boolean {
    return rowStreak(row,col)>2||colStreak(row,col)>2;
}
```

Once we know when we have a streak, we also can prevent jewelsInit function to generate one. We'll simply force the generation of a random gem until it's not part of a successful streak.

Change jewelsInit function this way:

```
private function jewelsInit():void {
    addChild(gemsContainer);
    for (var i:uint=0; i<8; i++) {
      jewels[i]=new Array();
      for (var j:uint=0; j<8; j++) {
        do {
          jewels[i][j]=Math.floor(Math.random()*7);
        } while (isStreak(i,j));
        gem = new gem_mc(jewels[i][j],i,j);
        gemsContainer.addChild(gem);
      }
    }
}
```

Now test the movie, and you won't see any successful streak.

The key lies in the `do while` loop used in the function.

The `do while` loop works in the same way as a `while` loop, with the exception that the code block is executed at least once, because the `while` condition is checked at the end of the block.

We are ready to play.

Selecting a gem

Now the player must be able to select gems since he's supposed to swap them to form streaks.

The idea: When the player clicks, we can detect mouse coordinates, check if he clicked inside the game area and know which gem he selected.

The development: You already drew the selector, so it's just a matter of placing the selector in the proper tile when the player clicks the mouse.

First we need a new class level variable to create a `selector_mc` instance.

```
private var jewels:Array=new Array();
private var gemsContainer:Sprite=new Sprite();
private var gem:gem_mc;
private var selector:selector_mc=new selector_mc();
```

Notice how I already used the constructor `new selector_mc()` to have it ready to be used.

Now, in `Main` constructor function, we have to add it to Display List and add a listener to be triggered once the player clicks the mouse.

```
public function Main() {
  jewelsInit();
  addChild(selector);
  selector.visible=false;
  stage.addEventListener(MouseEvent.CLICK,onClick););
}
```

The script does not show anything you don't already know, excluding we want the selector to be invisible when the game starts, because the player still has to click.

There are lots of ways to make a DisplayObject invisible. For instance, we could set its `alpha` property to zero, or place it outside the visible area acting on `x` and `y` properties.

This time we'll use a new way to make it invisible, setting its `visible` property to `false`.

What's the difference between setting `visible` property to `false` and setting the `alpha` property to `0`? DisplayObjects that are not visible are disabled, this means if you set a button to not visible, it cannot be clicked.

When the player clicks the mouse, we must ensure he's clicking inside the game area. Game area is made by a 8x8 grid of tiles, and each tile is a square with a 60 pixel side, so the whole game area is a square that measures 60 x 8=480 pixels.

Once we know the player clicked inside the game area, we can place the selector and make it visible.

This is `onClick` function:

```
private function onClick(e:MouseEvent):void {
  if (mouseX<480&&mouseX>0&&mouseY<480&&mouseY>0) {
    var selRow:uint=Math.floor(mouseY/60);
    var selCol:uint=Math.floor(mouseX/60);
    selector.x=60*selCol;
    selector.y=60*selRow;
    selector.visible=true;
  }
}
```

The `if` statement checks for the mouse to be inside the game area, then a couple of variables are created:

```
var selRow:uint=Math.floor(mouseY/60);
```

selRow represents the row of the selected gem and it's the floor of the mouse y-coordinate divided by 60 (tile size).

In the same way, selCol is the column of the selected gem.

Once we know selected gem's row and column starting from mouse coordinates, it's easy to move the selector to its proper place:

```
selector.x=60*selCol;
selector.y=60*selRow;
```

Finally it's time to show it.

```
selector.visible=true;
```

Setting visible property to true will make it visible, in the correct place.

Test the movie, and click on a gem. The selector will place around such gem.

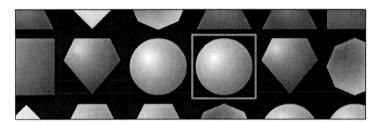

But in Bejeweled the player doesn't just select gems. He must swap them.

Preparing to swap gems

Not all gems can be swapped. To tell the truth, very few gems can, since a gem can only be swapped with one of its adjacent gems, horizontally or vertically.

The idea: When a gem is selected, and the player clicks on another gem, we must check if the gems are adjacent. If they aren't, then deselect the previously selected gem and select the new one. If they are adjacent, then we are ready to swap them.

The development: Everything runs around the concept of "being adjacent", so we need a function to determine if two gems are adjacent.

Let's express this concept in everyday words: two gems are adjacent if they are on the same column and the first gem is right under or right below the second, or they are on the same row and they are next to each other.

Translated into AS3 it sounds this way:

```
private function isAdjacent(row1:int,col1:int,row2:int,col2:int):
Boolean {
  if ((row1==row2+1||row1==row2-1)&&col1==col2) {
    return true;
  }
  return (col1==col2+1||col1==col2-1)&&row1==row2;
}
```

`isAdjacent` function wants four arguments: the row and the column of both gems, and returns `true` if they are adjacent, false otherwise.

Notice how I placed `return true` inside the `if` statement. When a function executes a `return`, it ends. So, if the script enters in the `if` statement and finds the first `return`, it will never execute the second one, as it would if the script could continue its execution.

Another, more optimized way to code `isAdjacent` would be:

```
isAdjacent(row1:int,col1:int,row2:int,col2:int):Boolean {
  return Math.abs(row1-row2)+Math.abs(col1-col2)==1
}
```

Now we have to keep track of the currently selected gem, if any, to know what to do when the player clicks on a gem. Two class level variables called `pickedRow` and `pickedCol` will store the row and the column of the picked gem.

```
private var jewels:Array=new Array();
private var gemsContainer:Sprite=new Sprite();
private var gem:gem_mc;
private var selector:selector_mc=new selector_mc();
private var pickedRow:int=-10;
private var pickedCol:int=-10;
```

Look how their initial values are `-10`. Since at the beginning of the game there isn't any selected gem, I assigned `pickedRow` and `pickedCol` an impossible value of my choice.

From now on, when both variables are set at `-10`, it means there isn't any picked gem.

You could also define a constant called something like NONE_PICKED and set it at `-10` to make the code more readable.

Now when the player clicks the mouse, the script should act this way:

- If there isn't any picked gem, place the selector on the clicked gem and set it as picked
- If there is already a picked gem, check if the picked and the clicked gem are adjacent
- If they are adjacent, prepare to swap gems, remove the selector and set no gem as picked
- If they aren't, move the selector on the clicked gem and set it as picked

Change onClick function this way:

```
private function onClick(e:MouseEvent):void {
   if (mouseX<480&&mouseX>0&&mouseY<480&&mouseY>0) {
     var selRow:uint=Math.floor(mouseY/60);
     var selCol:uint=Math.floor(mouseX/60);
     if (! isAdjacent(selRow,selCol,pickedRow,pickedCol)) {
       pickedRow=selRow;
       pickedCol=selCol;
       selector.x=60*pickedCol;
       selector.y=60*pickedRow;
       selector.visible=true;
     } else {
       trace("going to swap gems");
       pickedRow=-10;
       pickedCol=-10;
       selector.visible=false;
     }
   }
}
```

Then test the movie, and try to pick some gems. The game will behave as in this picture:

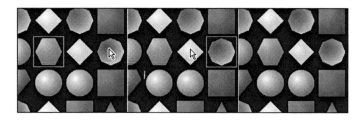

From left to right, the orange gem is picked and the player clicks on the green gem, that is not adjacent. So the green gem becomes picked, and when the player clicks on the yellow gem, that is adjacent, in the Output window you will see.

```
going to swap gems
```

Let's see how the script does work:

```
if (! isAdjacent(selRow,selCol,pickedRow,pickedCol)) { ... }
```

This `if` statement is the core of the function: it checks for the clicked and the selected gems not to be adjacent. If there isn't any picked gem, `pickedRow` and `pickedCol` are set to `-10`, so `isAdjacent` function will be forced to return `false`. If there is a picked gem, `isAdjacent` will tell us if it's adjacent to the selected gem.

```
pickedRow=selRow;
pickedCol=selCol;
```

If they aren't adjacent, or there wasn't any picked gem, set `pickedRow` and `pickedCol` to respectively `selRow` and `selCol`. This means the just clicked gem turns into a picked gem. Also, the selector is placed on such a gem.

```
else {
    trace("going to swap gems");
    pickedRow=-10;
    pickedCol=-10;
    selector.visible=false;
}
```

This is the code that will be executed when the clicked and the picked gems are adjacent: the debug string shown previously is prompted on the Output window; `pickedRow` and `pickedCol` are set to `-10` as there are no gems picked anymore, and the selector is made invisible.

Now you are ready to swap gems.

Swapping gems

Swapping gems is the key of the game, as this allows the player to create successful streaks.

The idea: It takes two steps to swap two gems:

- swapping their values in the array
- swapping the position of their DisplayObjects

As you may see, once you know the two gems can be swapped, it's very easy.

The development: As usual we are making a set of functions to do the dirty jobs and keeping our main functions clear and easy to read.

First, we need a function to swap two elements in `jewels` array.

```
private function swapJewelsArray(row1:uint,col1:uint,row2:uint,col2:
uint):void {
  var tmp:uint=jewels[row1][col1];
  jewels[row1][col1]=jewels[row2][col2];
  jewels[row2][col2]=tmp;
}
```

The function is so easy that there's no need to comment it.

Another, more interesting function we are about to create will swap the gem DisplayObjects.

```
private function swapJewelsObject(row1:uint,col1:uint,row2:uint,col2:
uint):void {
  with (gemsContainer.getChildByName(row1+"_"+col1)) {
    x=col2*60;
    y=row2*60;
    name="tmp";
  }
  with (gemsContainer.getChildByName(row2+"_"+col2)) {
    x=col1*60;
    y=row1*60;
    name=row1+"_"+col1;
  }
  gemsContainer.getChildByName("tmp").name=row2+"_"+col2;
}
```

Basically it's the same old concept used to swap any kind of object, with a temporary object saving the first object we will overwrite, just as you saw when you coded `swapJewelsArray` function.

Another interesting thing in `swapJewelsObject` function is the `with` statement.

`with` sets its parameter as the default object to be used during all its block of code, reducing the amount of code to be written and consequently preventing errors.

This means this code:

```
with (gemsContainer.getChildByName(row1+"_"+col1)) {
  x=col2*60;
  y=row2*60;
  name="tmp";
}
```

is the same as this one:

```
gemsContainer.getChildByName(row1+"_"+col1).x=col2*60;
gemsContainer.getChildByName(row1+"_"+col1).y=row2*60;
gemsContainer.getChildByName(row1+"_"+col1).name="tmp";
```

but is a lot easier to read.

With these two brand new functions, swapping gems is very easy. Just use them to swap gems when previously you wrote "going to swap gems":

```
private function onClick(e:MouseEvent):void {
  if (mouseX<480&&mouseX>0&&mouseY<480&&mouseY>0) {
    var selRow:uint=Math.floor(mouseY/60);
    var selCol:uint=Math.floor(mouseX/60);
    if (! isAdjacent(selRow,selCol,pickedRow,pickedCol)) {
      pickedRow=selRow;
      pickedCol=selCol;
      selector.x=60*pickedCol;
      selector.y=60*pickedRow;
      selector.visible=true;
    } else {
      swapJewelsArray(pickedRow,pickedCol,selRow,selCol);
      swapJewelsObject(pickedRow,pickedCol,selRow,selCol);
      pickedRow=-10;
      pickedCol=-10;
      selector.visible=false;
    }
  }
}
```

Test the movie, select a gem and click on an adjacent gem like in this picture:

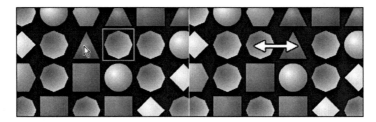

Gems will swap, and the selector will disappear. Now you can swap all adjacent gems.

At this time, normally I'd write a paragraph about smooth movement, but there is still a lot to do, and you should be able to do it by yourself as you are dealing with smooth movements since the first chapters.

Rather, we'll focus on an issue, that is, in Bejeweled you can't swap any couple of adjacent gems, because the mandatory condition to let you swap gems is at least one of the swapped gems forms a successful streak.

Swapping gems for real

We already have everything we need to swap gems only when a successful streak will be made, so this will be a five minutes walk. Take a break because the hardest is yet to come.

The idea: When you are about to swap two gems, check if the game field with the swapped gems has a successful streak. Only in this case, proceed swap the gems.

The development: Creating a script to foresee if two swapped gems would form a successful streak would be a bit complicated as it would require more temporary variables to come into play, so we will follow a simpler approach.

When the player swaps two adjacent gems, we will update `jewels` array to effectively swap the gems. Then we'll check for successful streaks. If a successful streak is found, we'll update the gems DisplayObjects to make the player see the swapped gem, restoring `jewels` array to its initial status otherwise.

How will we be able to restore `jewels` array if we did not save it anywhere? It is done by simply swapping its elements again, to make them return in the initial place.

Change `onClick` function this way:

```
private function onClick(e:MouseEvent):void {
  if (mouseX<480&&mouseX>0&&mouseY<480&&mouseY>0) {
    var selRow:uint=Math.floor(mouseY/60);
    var selCol:uint=Math.floor(mouseX/60);
    if (! isAdjacent(selRow,selCol,pickedRow,pickedCol)) {
      ...
    } else {
      swapJewelsArray(pickedRow,pickedCol,selRow,selCol);
      if (isStreak(pickedRow,pickedCol)||isStreak(selRow,selCol)) {
        swapJewelsObject(pickedRow,pickedCol,selRow,selCol);
```

```
    } else {
      swapJewelsArray(pickedRow,pickedCol,selRow,selCol);
    }
    pickedRow=-10;
    pickedCol=-10;
    selector.visible=false;
  }
 }
}
```

Once `jewels` array elements have been swapped, we check for successful streaks:

```
if (isStreak(pickedRow,pickedCol)||isStreak(selRow,selCol)) { ... }
```

As you can see, we are looking for a successful streak in both gem positions as any of them, if not both, can be part of a successful streak.

If we have a successful streak, we swap DisplayObjects too, otherwise we do another

```
swapJewelsArray(pickedRow,pickedCol,selRow,selCol);
```

to undo last move.

Test the game and you will be able to swap gems only if at least one of them will be part of a successful streak.

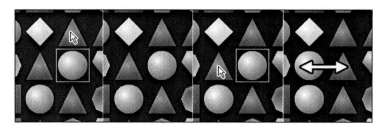

In the previous picture, the white gem is selected, then the player selects the above purple triangle to swap, but there wouldn't be any successful streak, so nothing happens. When the player selects the white gem and swaps it with the purple triangle on its left, a successful streak can be made, and gems are swapped.

Now, take a deep breath because we'll dive into troubles again.

Selecting which gems to remove

Once the player swapped two gems it means there is at least a successful streak, that is, there are at least three gems to remove. We need to know which gems have to be removed.

The idea: At this time it's important to know which one of the two swapped gems is part of a successful streak, or, if the player really made a good move, if both gems are part of a successful streak. Anyway, for every successful streak, we have to remove all gems included.

The development: To keep things easy, we are going to create a function that scans `jewels` array almost in the same way `rowStreaks` and `colStreaks` functions do. The main difference is we will save the names of the gems to be removed in an array, for a later use.

Create this new function, `removeGems`, that wants the row and the column as arguments of the gem we found being part of a successful streak.

```
private function removeGems(row:uint,col:uint):void {
  var gemsToRemove:Array=[row+"_"+col];
  var current:uint=jewels[row][col];
  var tmp:int;
  if (rowStreak(row,col)>2) {
    tmp=col;
    while (checkGem(current,row,tmp-1)) {
      tmp--;
      gemsToRemove.push(row+"_"+tmp);
    }
    tmp=col;
    while (checkGem(current,row,tmp+1)) {
      tmp++;
      gemsToRemove.push(row+"_"+tmp);
    }
  }
  if (colStreak(row,col)>2) {
    tmp=row;
    while (checkGem(current,tmp-1,col)) {
      tmp--;
      gemsToRemove.push(tmp+"_"+col);
    }
    tmp=row;
    while (checkGem(current,tmp+1,col)) {
      tmp++;
      gemsToRemove.push(tmp+"_"+col);
    }
  }
  trace("Will remove "+gemsToRemove);
}
```

As said, it's very similar to something like a merge of `rowStreaks` and `colStreaks` functions, with the difference we aren't increasing a counter variable anymore, but inserting gems' names into an array. `gemsToRemove` array will save all the names of the gems that we remove.

Once the function is ready, we just have to call it after any gems swap. We'll need to call it only once, if only one of the swapped gems is part of a successful streak, or twice, if both gems are part of a successful streak.

Change `onClick` function this way:

```
private function onClick(e:MouseEvent):void {
  if (mouseX<480&&mouseX>0&&mouseY<480&&mouseY>0) {
    var selRow:uint=Math.floor(mouseY/60);
    var selCol:uint=Math.floor(mouseX/60);
    if (! isAdjacent(selRow,selCol,pickedRow,pickedCol)) {
      pickedRow=selRow;
      pickedCol=selCol;
      selector.x=60*pickedCol;
      selector.y=60*pickedRow;
      selector.visible=true;
    } else {
      swapJewelsArray(pickedRow,pickedCol,selRow,selCol);
      if (isStreak(pickedRow,pickedCol)||isStreak(selRow,selCol)) {
        swapJewelsObject(pickedRow,pickedCol,selRow,selCol);
        if (isStreak(pickedRow,pickedCol)) {
          removeGems(pickedRow,pickedCol);
        }
        if (isStreak(selRow,selCol)) {
          removeGems(selRow,selCol);
        }
      } else {
        swapJewelsArray(pickedRow,pickedCol,selRow,selCol);
      }
      pickedRow=-10;
      pickedCol=-10;
      selector.visible=false;
    }
  }
}
```

As you can see I am calling for `removeGems` function only if I found a successful streak. At this point of the script, it's obvious I will find at least one successful streak, as the gems swap only if one of them forms a successful streak.

Test the movie and swap two gems.

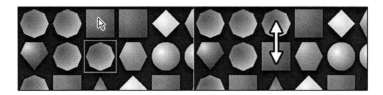

If you do something as in this picture, forming a successful streak with the three top-left rows, in the Output window you will see:

```
Will remove 0_2,0_1,0_0
```

Every successful streak of gems will populate `gemsToRemove` array, no matter the length of the streak.

Removing gems

We now have a list of gems to be removed, so it's time to remove them from the game.

The idea: Scan through the `gemsToRemove` array and remove all the gems.

The development: Removing a gem takes two steps: removing the gem DisplayObject from Display List, and update `jewels` array. This leads to a question: if `jewels` array contains element from 0 to 6 to represent different gem types, how can we code the "empty" status? We'll use -1 to say there isn't any gem in the `jewels` array.

The first thing to do is looping through the `gemsToRemove` array, and we'll do it using the `forEach` method as we did during the making of Astro-PANIC! although we used it on a Vector.

Indeed, `forEach` method works in the same way with arrays too. Add this line to `removeGems` function:

```
private function removeGems(row:uint,col:uint):void {
  ...
  gemsToRemove.forEach(removeTheGem);
}
```

Now for every element in the `gemsToRemove` array, `removeTheGem` function will be executed. Here we have to remove its DisplayObject and set its corresponding `jewels` element to -1.

Write `removeTheGem` function this way:

```
private function removeTheGem(element:String,index:int,arr:Array):void
{
  with (gemsContainer) {
    removeChild(getChildByName(element));
  }
  var coordinates:Array=element.split("_");
  jewels[coordinates[0]][coordinates[1]]=-1;
}
```

Did you see how many arguments? It's because of the `forEach` method structure, as you should remember from the making of Astro-PANIC!

As you can see, first I remove the gem with `removeChild`, then it's time to get row and column positions starting from a string with the name of the gem.

This means, we should find a way to manipulate a string like `3_6` in a way we know we are working on row `3`, column `6`.

`split` string method comes to our help, splitting a string into an array of substrings obtained as if the argument of `split` method were a separator.

Following the previous example, splitting `3_6` string using underscore (_) as argument would produce an array of two elements, containing `3` and `6`.

With this line:

```
var coordinates:Array=element.split("_");
```

we'll have gem's row and column values respectively in `coordinates[0]` and `coordinates[1]`. Finally we can set the proper `jewels` element at `-1` with:

```
jewels[coordinates[0]][coordinates[1]]=-1;
```

Test the movie and swap two gems. The successful streak will disappear.

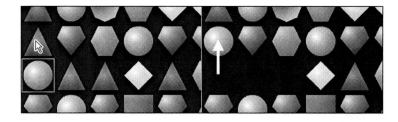

Now streaks are successfully removed, but above gems should fall down to fill the empty spaces.

Making gems fall

Once each gem is removed, we have to adjust the game field making the above gems fall down to fill empty spaces.

This is the last hard to develop feature you will encounter in this chapter. After managing with falling gems, making the rest of the game will be quite easy.

The idea: Starting from the bottom-most row, we must look for empty spaces. Once an empty space is found, all the gems (if any) in the same column above the empty space should fall down to fill the empty space.

The development: Obviously the need of adjusting the game field occurs only after some gems have been removed.

So the entire routine will be called at the end of removeGems function:

```
private function removeGems(row:uint,col:uint):void {
  ...
  adjustGems();
}
```

adjustGems function will handle falling gems. Here's how it should work:

- Scan jewels array from column to column starting from the bottom-most row.
- If an empty (-1) element is found, then look for the upper first non-empty element in the same column.
- If such non-empty element is found, swap it with the empty element found and adjust its DisplayObject position and name.

It seems harder than it really is. Let's check adjustGems function:

```
private function adjustGems():void {
  for (var j:uint=0; j<8; j++) {
    for (var i:uint=7; i>0; i--) {
      if (jewels[i][j]==-1) {
        for (var k:uint=i; k>0; k--) {
          if (jewels[k][j]!=-1) {
            break;
          }
        }
        if (jewels[k][j]!=-1) {
          trace("moving gem at row "+k+" to row "+i);
          jewels[i][j]=jewels[k][j];
          jewels[k][j]=-1;
          with(gemsContainer.getChildByName(k+"_"+j)){
```

```
        y=60*i;
        name=i+"_"+j;
      }
     }
    }
   }
  }
 }
```

First, notice how I am scanning `jewels` array to look for empty elements:

```
for (var j:uint=0; j<8; j++) {
  for (var i:uint=7; i>0; i--) {
    if (jewels[i][j]==-1) { ... }
  }
}
```

I am looping from column to column from the highest row index (7) back to the lowest (0). Once I find an empty element, I am sure there are no empty elements in the same column with a greater row index. That is, it's the lowest empty element in the column.

```
for (var k:uint=i; k>0; k--) {
  if (jewels[k][j]!=-1) {
    break;
  }
}
```

At this time, I look for the first element in the same column, with a smaller row index, that is not empty (different than -1). `break` ensures `k` value at the end of this `for` loop contains the row index of the first non-empty element, if any. It could have been done with a `while` loop, but I liked the idea of the triple `for` loop.

```
if (jewels[k][j]!=-1) { ... }
```

Now I am checking if I really found a non-empty element, or I just ended the `for` loop because `k` value reached 0. If I found a non-empty element, I swap `jewels` values and adjust the gem position in order to occupy the empty space I found.

Let me explain this with a picture sequence:

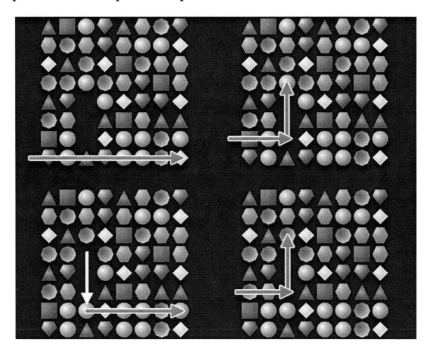

The red arrow indicates how the script scans the game field, look how it changes its direction once it has found an empty spot, and how the lowest gem is being placed in the empty spot.

Test the movie, and create some successful streak, horizontally or vertically.

Once the gems have been swapped and the streak disappears, the above gems (if any) fall down as if there was gravity.

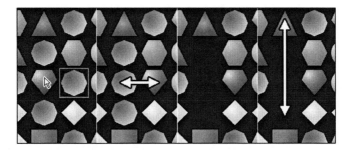

Now, we must somehow fill the empty spot falling gems cannot replace with some new gems.

Adding new gems

No matter if you make gems fall to fill empty places, or leave them as they are, when you remove some gems from the game field, you will need to replace them with new ones.

The idea: Once the gems have been removed and empty spaces have been filled with gems from above (if any), we must scan `jewels` array and create new gems wherever we find a -1.

The development: I told you this was easy, and this time we just need a couple of `for` loops. Obviously new gems will be created at the very end of the gems removal process, so we'll call the function to replace gems at the very end of `removeGems` function.

```
private function removeGems(row:uint,col:uint):void {
   ...
   replaceGems();
}
```

And `replaceGems` function is very easy as it just looks for empty spots where to add new gems.

```
private function replaceGems():void {
  for (var i:int=7; i>=0; i--) {
    for (var j:uint=0; j<8; j++) {
      if (jewels[i][j]==-1) {
        jewels[i][j]=Math.floor(Math.random()*7);
        gem=new gem_mc(jewels[i][j],i,j);
        gemsContainer.addChild(gem);
      }
    }
  }
}
```

I just want you to notice two things:

First, unlike in a game field creation, we don't check for new gems not to form a successful streak, as combos and bonuses can be assigned if new gems form a streak with existing ones.

Second, I look for new spots where new gems from the bottom of the gamefield can be placed. This will add realism to the game if you plan to make some kind of animations of falling gems. This way the lowest gems will be the first to fall.

Test the movie and remove some gems, and empty spots will be replaced by new gems.

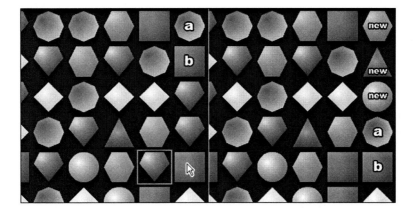

Congratulations! You are only one step away from completing the prototype.

Dealing with combos

Although gems are currently moved and added after a successful streak, we don't check if the falling-on added gems create some streaks and need to be removed. This is a very important feature in Bejeweled as it allows players to make combos and earn more points.

The idea: After any gem is moved or added, check for successful streaks.

The development: Gems are added with `replaceGems` function, and moved with `adjustGems`.

We simply have to include an `if` statement in both the functions to see if the last added/adjusted gem is part of a successful streak.

Change `replaceGems` function this way:

```
private function replaceGems():void {
  for (var i:int=7; i>=0; i--) {
    for (var j:uint=0; j<8; j++) {
      if (jewels[i][j]==-1) {
        jewels[i][j]=Math.floor(Math.random()*7);
        gem=new gem_mc(jewels[i][j],i,j);
        gemsContainer.addChild(gem);
        if (isStreak(i,j)) {
          trace("COMBO");
```

```
        removeGems(i,j);
      }
    }
  }
}
```

and in the same way, this is how `adjustGems` function should be:

```
private function adjustGems():void {
  for (var j:uint=0; j<8; j++) {
    for (var i:uint=7; i>0; i--) {
      if (jewels[i][j]==-1) {
        for (var k:uint=i; k>0; k--) {
          if (jewels[k][j]!=-1) {
            break;
          }
        }
        if (jewels[k][j]!=-1) {
          jewels[i][j]=jewels[k][j];
          jewels[k][j]=-1;
          with(gemsContainer.getChildByName(k+"_"+j)){
            y=60*i;
            name=i+"_"+j;
          }
          if (isStreak(i,j)) {
            trace("COMBO");
            removeGems(i,j);
          }
        }
      }
    }
  }
}
```

Test the game and play. If you are lucky, sometimes you should see

`COMBO`

appearing in your Output window. Now, something for the lazy players.

Giving hints

Sometimes a player can't see the next move to do, so they need a hint. We must code a routine to give them such a hint.

The idea: We have plenty of space on the right of the game field, so the game will give a hint when you click on the right of the game field. How can we give the hint?

For each gem, starting from top-left to bottom-right, we'll see if swapping it with the gem at its right (if any) or with the gem below (if any) gives a streak. To make you see the code works, the script will show all possible hints.

The development: In onClick function, when the player does not click in the game field, we will start the routine to give hints. We already said we can't foresee the game field with swapped gems, so we will physically swap gems twice, making the second swap act like an undo, just like you did when you swapped gems manually.

Change onClick function this way:

```
private function onClick(e:MouseEvent):void {
   if (mouseX<480&&mouseX>0&&mouseY<480&&mouseY>0) {
      ...
   } else {
     for (var i:uint=0; i<8; i++) {
       for (var j:uint=0; j<8; j++) {
         if (i<7) {
           swapJewelsArray(i,j,i+1,j);
           if (isStreak(i,j)||isStreak(i+1,j)) {
             trace(i+","+j+" -> "+(i+1)+","+j);
           }
           swapJewelsArray(i,j,i+1,j);
         }
         if (j<7) {
           swapJewelsArray(i,j,i,j+1);
           if (isStreak(i,j)||isStreak(i,j+1)) {
             trace(i+","+j+" -> "+i+","+(j+1));
           }
           swapJewelsArray(i,j,i,j+1);
         }
       }
     }
   }
}
```

The whole code is very intuitive; anyway we'll see together how it works:

```
for (var i:uint=0; i<8; i++) {
  for (var j:uint=0; j<8; j++) {
    ...
  }
}
```

This is the classical couple of `for` loops to scan through the array.

```
if (i<7) { ... }
```

Since I want to swap each gem with the one at its right, I have to ensure that I am not on the rightmost column.

```
swapJewelsArray(i,j,i+1,j);
```

Swapping gems

```
if (isStreak(i,j)||isStreak(i+1,j)) { ... }
```

Checking if at least one of the swapped gems forms a streak

```
trace(i+","+j+" -> "+(i+1)+","+j);
```

writing the hint on the Output window

```
swapJewelsArray(i,j,i+1,j);
```

Swapping back gems.

The rest of the code follows the same concept applied to vertical swapping.

Test the movie and in a situation like this one:

you will get these hints:

```
2,6 -> 3,6

4,5 -> 4,6

5,1 -> 6,1

5,2 -> 6,2

6,2 -> 6,3

6,5 -> 7,5
```

These are all and the only possible moves. Enjoy your Bejeweled game.

Summary

During the making of Bejeweled you learned how to code the prototype of a top selling game. Besides the new technical concepts you saw, I would like you to note how successful games are often built upon simple prototypes, with stunning graphics and polished gameplay. Coding these kind of games is nothing you can't do, no matter how many copies they sell.

Where to go now

It's clear the most interesting missing feature is the smooth movement. To add it, you will need an ENTER_FRAME listener because it's the easiest way you can manage gems movements and disappearings. I would point you to this script I published on my blog: bit.ly/dJNPq2. Here you will find a complete yet quite unreadable code (it was created to make the entire game in less than 2KB) of a Bejeweled game with some kind of movement. With the concepts learned in this chapter and that code, you should be able to create your perfect Bejeweled game.

8
Puzzle Bobble

Puzzle Bobble is an arcade puzzle game featuring the characters and the overall look and feel of the popular Bubble Bobble arcade game.

The player controls something like a cannon that cannot be moved but only rotated, loaded with a randomly colored bubble.

Once the player fires, the fired bubble moves along a straight line, eventually bouncing off the sides of the game area, until it reaches the top of the game area or touches another bubble.

Player's goal is clearing the stage by forming chains of three or more adjacent bubbles of the same color. Bubbles forming part of this chain, as well as bubbles hanging from them are removed from the stage.

Basically Puzzle Bobble is a "match three and remove" tile-based game just like Bejeweled, but the interesting feature is the way the tiles are placed in the game field. We aren't dealing with square tiles but with hexagonal tiles, and this will affect both the way we'll draw the game field and the gameplay.

In this chapter you will code a fully working Puzzle Bobble prototype learning these techniques:

- Detecting when the player releases a key
- Detecting when more than one key has been pressed
- Rotating DisplayObjects
- Drawing circles
- Handling non-squared tiles

This time too we are going to skip the game design as it's something you already mastered.

Creating documents and assets

Create a new file (**File | New**) then from **New Document** window select
Actionscript 3.0. Set its properties as width to 640px, height to 480px, background
color to #000033 (a dark blue), and frame rate to 30. Also define the Document Class
as Main and save the file as puzzlebobble.fla.

There will be two actors in this movie: the cannon and the bubbles. We will draw
bubbles with six different colors in a Movie Clip called bubble_mc, while the cannon
will be drawn in a Movie Clip called cannon_mc.

Create these two symbols and make them exportable for ActionScript, as usual.

These are the assets I created:

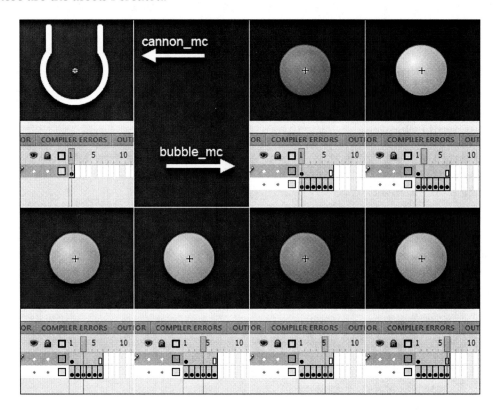

Bubbles are 36x36 pixel circles with registration point in their center. The cannon
is large enough to contain a bubble inside it, and its registration point is in its
center too.

You are free to draw them as you want, just remember during the whole game
creation I will be referring to 36x36 tiles.

Placing and moving the cannon

We are shooting bubbles with the cannon, so it will be the first thing to be added in the game.

The idea: The cannon must be placed in the bottom of the screen, in the middle of the game field. Players will be able to rotate it with LEFT and RIGHT arrow keys.

The development: Before we start coding we have to create Main class.

Without closing puzzlebobble.fla, create a new file and from **New Document** window select **ActionScript 3.0 Class**. Save this file as Main.as in the same path you saved puzzlebobble.fla.

At this time we'll also import all required classes, like KeyboardEvent and Event.

I am going to store into two constants the rotation speed of the cannon and the radius of the bubbles, as I know I'll be using these values a lot during the making of this game.

Write this code in Main.as:

```
package {
  import flash.display.Sprite;
  import flash.events.KeyboardEvent;
  import flash.events.Event;
  public class Main extends Sprite {
    private const ROT_SPEED:uint=2;
    private const R:uint=18;
    private var cannon:cannon_mc;
    private var left:Boolean=false;
    private var right:Boolean=false;
    public function Main() {
      placeCannon();
      stage.addEventListener(KeyboardEvent.KEY_DOWN,onKDown);
      stage.addEventListener(KeyboardEvent.KEY_UP,onKUp);
      addEventListener(Event.ENTER_FRAME,onEFrame);
    }
  }
}
```

There is nothing new, so I am giving you only a brief overview of the code.

ROT_SPEED is the rotation speed of the cannon, measured in degrees/frame.

R is the radius of the bubbles. I had to use a one letter variable for a page layout purpose, and I want you to remember using one letter variables is not a good practice, especially the class level variables. You should change it with BUBBLE_RADIUS or something else with a clear meaning.

cannon is the cannon_mc instance, while left and right are Boolean variables that will tell us if left and right keys are being pressed. I am introducing a new way to handle keys being pressed, that you'll want to use when there could be more than one single key pressed.

In my function we call placeCannon function that will obviously place the cannon on the stage, and we set the listeners. Notice there is a new listener, the latest in the script, KeyboardEvent.KEY_UP.

KEY_UP is triggered when the user releases a key. Now the big question is: why should I check for the player to release keys? All in all, the cannon is moved by pressing the keys, not by releasing them.

You're right, but using only KEY_DOWN listener will allow us only to get the latest key pressed. This means if the player presses LEFT arrow, we can know the player is pressing such arrow, but if the player presses RIGHT arrow without releasing LEFT key, KEY_DOWN will detect the latest key pressed RIGHT but there's no way to know whether LEFT arrow is still pressed or not.

This will make your life impossible when you are making games when more keys can be pressed at the same time.

Anyway, at the moment let's place the cannon. Add placeCannon function:

```
private function placeCannon():void {
  cannon=new cannon_mc();
  addChild(cannon);
  cannon.y=450;
  cannon.x=R*8;
}
```

The function just constructs and adds to Display List the cannon. Then y property is set to 450 to place the cannon in the bottom end of the stage, while x property is set to R*8, which means the cannon is aligned with the end of the fourth bubble. Since we have eight bubbles for each row, it's in the middle of the game area.

onKDown and onKUp functions will just assign true or false to left and right variables according to which key has been pressed or released.

onKDown function will set such variables to true if LEFT or RIGHT arrow keys are being pressed:

```
private function onKDown(e:KeyboardEvent):void {
  switch (e.keyCode) {
    case 37 :
      left=true;
      break;
    case 39 :
      right=true;
      break;
  }
}
```

While onKUp will set them to false once they are released:

```
private function onKUp(e:KeyboardEvent):void {
  switch (e.keyCode) {
    case 37 :
      left=false;
      break;
    case 39 :
      right=false;
      break;
  }
}
```

This way we can know at any time if LEFT arrow, RIGHT arrow or both are pressed.

You already know what 37, 38, 39, and 40 key codes stand for. To make the code more readable, you can import flash.ui.Keyboard and use constants called Keyboard.LEFT, Keyboard.RIGHT, Keyboard.UP, and Keyboard.DOWN rather than 37, 39, 38, and 40 respectively.

At this time onEFrame function just updates cannon rotation according to left and right values:

```
private function onEFrame(e:Event):void {
  if (left) {
    cannon.rotation-=ROT_SPEED;
  }
  if (right) {
    cannon.rotation+=ROT_SPEED;
  }
}
```

Test the movie, and you will be able to rotate the cannon counterclockwise pressing LEFT arrow, and clockwise pressing RIGHT arrow. Try to press LEFT and RIGHT arrows together to see the cannon stop, because the two opposite rotations will nullify.

Notice how I rotate the cannon using `rotation` property.

`rotation` sets the rotation property of a DisplayObject in degrees from its original orientation. You can rotate it clockwise with values from `0` to `180` and counterclockwise with values from `0` to `-180`.

Any value outside `-180` - `180` range will be adjusted to fit in such a range, so for instance `-190` is equal to `170`, and `190` is equal to `-170`.

Drawing the game field

Although it's not necessary to literally "draw" the game field, doing it will help us to deal with this particular kind of tile-based game. We know we are dealing with hexagonal tiles, but since hexagons can be drawn inside a circle, we will simplify the script drawing circular tiles.

The idea: We will draw on the stage the circular tiles that will define the game field. This will make us see where bubbles should be placed.

The development: As usual we need a DisplayObject to act as a container for everything related to game field. A new class level variable called `bubCont` will do this job:

```
private const ROT_SPEED:uint=2;
private const RADIUS:uint=18;
private var cannon:cannon_mc;
private var left:Boolean=false;
private var right:Boolean=false;
private var bubCont:Sprite;
```

Then the first thing `Main` function has to do is placing the container. We'll delegate this task to a function called `placeContainer`.

```
public function Main() {
  placeContainer();
  ...
}
```

`placeContainer` function has to add the container to Display List and draw the 11x8 tile environment. Add this function:

```
private function placeContainer():void {
  bubCont=new Sprite();
  addChild(bubCont);
  bubCont.graphics.lineStyle(1,0xffffff,0.2);
  for(var i:uint=0;i<11;i++){
    for(var j:uint=0;j<8;j++){
      bubCont.graphics.drawCircle(R+j*R*2,R+i*R*2,R);
    }
  }
}
```

It's just a couple of `for` loops to iterate through a tile-based environment like you already did during the development of almost every game examined in this book.

The only difference is we aren't drawing squares, but circles.

`drawCircle` method draws a circle. As with all `graphics` methods, you have to set a line style before you can call it, unless the default style is ok to use. I am doing it some lines above, with:

```
bubCont.graphics.lineStyle(1,0xffffff,0.2);
```

`drawCircle` wants three arguments, respectively the horizontal position of the center, in pixels, relative to the registration point of the parent DisplayObject, the vertical position, assigned with the same concept, and the radius, in pixels.

This line

```
bubCont.graphics.drawCircle(R+j*R*2,R+i*R*2,R);
```

will draw the series of circles. Remember `R` is the radius of the bubbles, and it will be the same for the circles.

Test the movie and you will see all circles forming the game field.

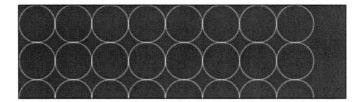

Everything worked fine, except some circles aren't placed in the right place.

Counting lines from top to bottom starting from zero, even lines are drawn correctly, while odd lines are not.

Circles in odd lines must be shifted by R pixels to the right and there can only be seven circles.

We must be able to draw alternate rows

Drawing the game field with alternate rows

In odd rows, there can be only seven circles, shifted by R pixels on the right.

The idea: Check whether we are drawing an odd or an even row. Then if we are drawing an even row, draw circles in the same way you just drew, if we are drawing an odd row, shift circles' center by R pixels on the right and don't draw the last circle.

The development: Change `placeContainer` function this way:

```
private function placeContainer():void {
  bubCont=new Sprite();
  addChild(bubCont);
  bubCont.graphics.lineStyle(1,0xffffff,0.2);
  for (var i:uint=0; i<11; i++) {
    for (var j:uint=0; j<8; j++) {
      if (i%2==0) {
        bubCont.graphics.drawCircle(R+j*R*2,R+i*R*2,R);
      } else {
        if (j<7) {
          with (bubCont.graphics) {
            drawCircle(2*R+j*R*2,R+i*R*2,R);
          }
```

```
                }
              }
            }
          }
        }
```

As we enter the couple of `for` loops, we check if `i` is an even number using the modulo operator. In this case, we are drawing circles in the same old way.

If it's not, we check if `j` (representing the number of circles in the same row) is less than 7 as we don't want to draw the eighth circle, then we draw the circles shifting them by `R` pixels on the right.

Don't worry about the `with` statement as I was forced to use it in order to write the code without line breaks.

I suggest you to replace this code:

```
with (bubCont.graphics) {
    drawCircle(2*R+j*R*2,R+i*R*2,R);
}
```

with this single line:

```
bubCont.graphics.drawCircle(2*R+j*R*2,R+i*R*2,R);
```

Notice how the x-coordinate of the circle center is `R+j*R*2` for the even rows and `2*R+j*R*2` for the odd, and the difference is `R`, just as we wanted.

Test the movie and you will have your set of alternate rows.

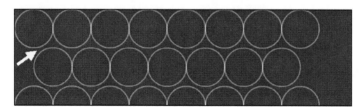

And here comes another problem. Do you see those gaps between circles of different rows, shown by the arrow?

That's not the right way to draw the game field. The vertical distance among rows must be less than `R`. We have to determine it.

Drawing the game field according to Pythagoras

We must find the right vertical distance among rows to let the game field render properly.

The idea: We'll use Pythagorean Theorem to determine the vertical distance.

The distance between two circles must always be 2*R, but circles placed on odd rows are shifted to the right by R pixels. So what's the vertical distance?

In the following picture you will see the desired result:

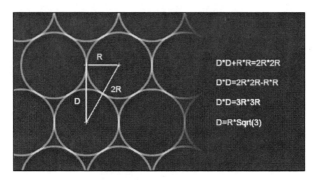

If we build a right triangle whose hypotenuse is the distance between two circles (cyan line) and the legs are respectively the amount of pixel odd rows circles are shifted to the right (green line), the other leg (yellow line) represents the vertical distance.

Follow the formulas shown in the picture and you will find the vertical distance is determined by R multiplied by the square root of 3.

The development: We need a new class level constant I called D for a book layout purpose (you should call it something like VERTICAL_DISTANCE) which will store the value of the vertical distance according to the R value, so you should add it after R has been declared.

```
private const ROT_SPEED:uint=2;
private const R:uint=18;
private const D:Number=R*Math.sqrt(3);
private var cannon:cannon_mc;
private var left:Boolean=false;
private var right:Boolean=false;
private var bubCont:Sprite;
```

Then you just need to change the vertical coordinate of circle origins from `R+i*R*2` to `R+i*D`. Change `placeContainer` function this way:

```
private function placeContainer():void {
  bubCont=new Sprite();
  addChild(bubCont);
  bubCont.graphics.lineStyle(1,0xffffff,0.2);
  for (var i:uint=0; i<11; i++) {
    for (var j:uint=0; j<8; j++) {
      if (i%2==0) {
        bubCont.graphics.drawCircle(R+j*R*2,R+i*D,R);
      } else {
        if (j<7) {
          with (bubCont.graphics) {
            drawCircle(2*R+j*R*2,R+i*D,R);
          }
        }
      }
    }
  }
}
```

Now test the movie and you will finally have your game field properly rendered.

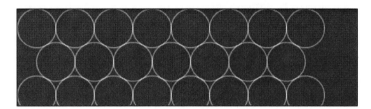

Now everything is ready to fire some bubbles. First, let's load them into the cannon.

Loading the cannon with a bubble

First, we have to load the cannon with a bubble.

The idea: Create a bubble and place it into the cannon.

The development: We need a variable to create a `bubble_mc` instance, so add `bubble` class level variable.

```
private const ROT_SPEED:uint=2;
private const R:uint=18;
private const D:Number=R*Math.sqrt(3);
private var cannon:cannon_mc;
private var left:Boolean=false;
private var right:Boolean=false;
private var bubCont:Sprite;
private var bubble:bubble_mc;
```

Once the container has been drawn and the cannon has been placed, we can place the bubble. Delegate it to `loadBubble` function in `Main` constructor.

```
public function Main() {
    placeContainer();
    placeCannon();
    loadBubble();
    stage.addEventListener(KeyboardEvent.KEY_DOWN,onKDown);
    stage.addEventListener(KeyboardEvent.KEY_UP,onKUp);
    addEventListener(Event.ENTER_FRAME,onEFrame);
}
```

What should `loadBubble` function do? We only need to create a new `bubble_mc` instance, add it to Display List and place it inside the cannon, showing a random frame. This is `loadBubble` function:

```
private function loadBubble():void {
    bubble = new bubble_mc();
    addChild(bubble);
    bubble.gotoAndStop(Math.floor(Math.random()*6))+1;
    bubble.x=R*8;
    bubble.y=450;
}
```

Bubble's `x` and `y` properties are the same as cannon ones, to place it exactly inside the cannon, while the frame shown is a random number between 1 and 6.

Notice how I did not add the bubble to `bubCont` game field container because a bubble is not part of the game field until it stops in a place.

Test the movie and watch your rotating cannon loaded with a bubble.

The color of the bubble should change every time you test the movie as it's randomly picked.

The player is now ready to fire.

Firing the bubble

To fire the bubble, the player must press UP arrow key.

The idea: Detect when the player presses UP arrow key, and then calculate the horizontal and vertical speed of the bubble according to the cannon's rotation.

The development: This part has some similarities with the enemy ships' movement you dealt with during the making of Astro-PANIC!

Before we start checking for the UP arrow key, we'll define the bubble speed and some other variables. Let's make a couple of new declarations:

```
private const ROT_SPEED:uint=2;
private const R:uint=18;
private const D:Number=R*Math.sqrt(3);
private const DEG_TO_RAD:Number=0.0174532925;
private const BUBBLE_SPEED:uint=10;
private var cannon:cannon_mc;
private var left:Boolean=false;
private var right:Boolean=false;
private var bubCont:Sprite;
private var bubble:bubble_mc;
private var fire:Boolean=false;
private var vx,vy:Number;
```

BUBBLE_SPEED is the speed of the bubble, in pixels per frame. It's way slower than the original game speed and it's definitely too slow if you want to have an enjoyable game, but it will allow us to understand what happens to the bubble once it has been fired. Once you completed the game, you should raise the value from 10 to 15.

DEG_TO_RAD is the ratio between degrees and radians, that is, PI/180. For instance, if you want to convert 45 degrees into radians, you will have to multiply 45 by DEG_TO_RAD. Converting degrees to radians is very important as cannon rotation is measured in degrees, while trigonometry methods such as Math.cos and Math.sin work with radians.

fire is the classic variable to determine whether the player is firing or not.

vx and vy are the horizontal and vertical speed of the bubble, to be calculated according to BUBBLE_SPEED and cannon rotation.

We also have to add a new case to the switch statement in onKDown function to check if the key pressed is UP arrow key:

```
private function onKDown(e:KeyboardEvent):void {
  switch (e.keyCode) {
    case 37 :
      ...
    case 39 :
      ...
    case 38 :
      if (! fire) {
        fire=true;
        var radians=(cannon.rotation-90)*DEG_TO_RAD;
        vx=BUBBLE_SPEED*Math.cos(radians);
        vy=BUBBLE_SPEED*Math.sin(radians);
      }
      break;
  }
}
```

Once the player presses UP arrow key (case 38), if he's not already firing, then set fire to true, get the cannon rotation in radians and calculate vx and vy using trigonometry in the same way you calculated horizontal and vertical speed of enemy spaceships during the making of Astro-PANIC!

Notice I am subtracting 90 from cannon rotation since when the cannon is heading up, its real rotation is zero degrees while the effective rotation to vertically fire a bubble should be -90.

In the picture, you can see the different angle systems; on the left the one used by the cannon rotation and on the right the angles as Flash manages them.

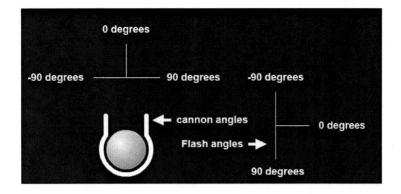

That's why we have to subtract 90 to cannon rotation. Once we know the player fired and the horizontal and vertical speeds of the bubble, we have to update bubble's position in onEFrame function adding these lines at the end:

```
private function onEFrame(e:Event):void {
   ...
   if (fire) {
     bubble.x+=vx;
     bubble.y+=vy;
   }
}
```

We can do it just by adding vx and vy to x and y properties respectively.

Test the movie and press UP arrow key to fire the bubble.

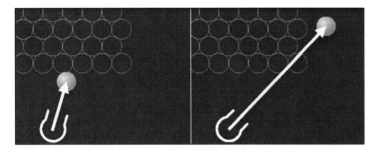

Everything works fine, but the bubble flies out of the game area and never stops.

Letting bubble bounce and stop

To make a complete shooting routine, bubble must bounce off game field sides and stop once it touches the upper side.

The idea: To make bubble bounce off game field sides, we have to check if the bubble is leaving the game field to the left or right side. In both cases, inverting the horizontal speed will make the bubble bounce off. When it's about to leave the game field to the upper side, we have to stop its movement.

The development: We only need to make some changes to `onEFrame` function, as it's the one and only one that handles bubble movement. The concept is very simple to the one developed to make enemy spaceships bounce off the game area during the making of Astro-PANIC! so it does not need that much commenting:

```
private function onEFrame(e:Event):void {
   ...
  if (fire) {
    bubble.x+=vx;
    bubble.y+=vy;
    if (bubble.x<R) {
      bubble.x=R;
      vx*=-1;
    }
    if (bubble.x>R*15) {
      bubble.x=R*15;
      vx*=-1;
    }
    if (bubble.y<R) {
      bubble.y=R;
      fire=false;
    }
  }
}
```

The new code has been added in the block of code executed if `fire` variable is `true`.

```
if (bubble.x<R) { ... }
```

Since `bubble_mc` DisplayObject has the registration point at 0,0 if its horizontal position is less than R (its radius) this means the bubble is leaving the game field to the left.

```
bubble.x=R;
```

Keeping the bubble completely inside the game field

```
vx*=-1;
```

Inverting horizontal position.

The same concept is applied when the bubble is leaving the game area to the right, while when it's leaving to the top—we just adjust its vertical position and set `fire` to `false`. Now the bubble won't move anymore.

Test the movie and shoot some bubbles with an angle so they have to bounce off game field sides. Then they'll stop at the very top of the game field.

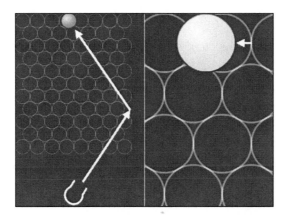

Now we have to face a new problem: Puzzle Bobble is a tile-based game, and this means bubbles cannot be placed anywhere, they should be inside their cells.

This does not happen, as you can see from the previous picture, with the green bubble not absolutely aligned with its cell.

Adjusting bubble position and reloading

The final step of firing a bubble is adjusting its final position so that it perfectly fits inside a cell. Only at this time we can load another bubble into the cannon.

The idea: Once the bubble reached the top of the game field, we have to place it in the closest cell available. Then, we'll place a new randomly colored bubble into the cannon, allowing the player to shoot again and starting the game loop again.

The development: When the bubble reaches the top of the game area, we'll call a new function to delegate the parking process of the bubble.

Change `onEFrame` function to execute only a function called `parkBubble`, when the bubble is about to leave the game field to the top.

```
private function onEFrame(e:Event):void {
   ...
 if (fire) {
     ...
   if (bubble.y<R) {
      // remove everything else
      parkBubble();
    }
  }
}
```

`parkBubble` function finds the closest column (that is, the closest horizontal cell) to the bubble.

```
private function parkBubble():void {
  var col:uint=Math.floor(bubble.x/(R*2));
  var placed_bubble:bubble_mc = new bubble_mc();
  bubCont.addChild(placed_bubble);
  placed_bubble.x=(col*R*2)+R;
  placed_bubble.y=R;
  placed_bubble.gotoAndStop(bubble.currentFrame);
  removeChild(bubble);
  fire=false;
  loadBubble();
  trace("adjusted bubble to fit at column "+col);
}
```

To find the closest column, you just need to find the highest integer lower than the division of the horizontal position of the bubble by the tile width, that is, `R*2`, this way:

```
var col:uint=Math.floor(bubble.x/(R*2));
```

Then, we have to create a new bubble, that will be a copy of the current one, and add it to Display List:

```
var placed_bubble:bubble_mc = new bubble_mc();
bubCont.addChild(placed_bubble);
```

Notice this time the new bubble is added as a child of `bubCont` DisplayObject.

The new bubble will be placed inside the just found column and will show the same frame (that is the same bubble color) as the current one. We do it with these three lines:

```
placed_bubble.x=(col*R*2)+R;
placed_bubble.y=R;
placed_bubble.gotoAndStop(bubble.currentFrame);
```

Notice how `y` property is set to `R` because I know I am placing the bubble on the first row.

Finally the current bubble is removed from Display List, `fire` is set to `false` to let the player fire again and the `loadBubble` function is called again to load another bubble into the cannon.

Test the movie and fire some bubbles: they will all fit in a cell.

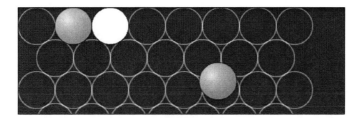

Moreover, the debug message in the Output window in this case will say (assuming the first bubble is the white one):

```
adjusted bubble to fit at column 2
adjusted bubble to fit at column 1
```

But obviously there must be another problem: bubbles do not stack, and if you fire a bubble in a cell already occupied by another bubble, this will just overlay it.

Allowing bubbles to stack

It's time to let the bubbles stack, which means we have to make them solid, so they can't overlay anymore.

The idea: When the bubble is moving, check if it collides with the bubbles already placed in the game field. In this case, find the closest available cell at once, without waiting for the bubble to leave the game field to the top.

The development: We are working with collisions between circles, so we'll use Pythagorean Theorem to see if the two bubbles collide.

Let's create a new function called `collide` that wants a bubble as argument and will return `true` if it collides with the fired bubble, and `false` otherwise.

It's the same concept we used to check for collisions between enemy and player spaceships in the making of Astro-PANIC!

```
private function collide(bub:bubble_mc):Boolean {
  var dist_x:Number=bub.x-bubble.x;
  var dist_y:Number=bub.y-bubble.y;
  return Math.sqrt(dist_x*dist_x+dist_y*dist_y)<=2*R;
}
```

Notice this time I used `sqrt` method, but you know rewriting the last line this way:

```
return dist_x*dist_x+dist_y*dist_y<=(2*R)*(2*R);
```

increases performances.

Once we are able to know whether the fired bubble is colliding with other bubbles, it's time to check for collisions at each frame, until it reaches the top of the game field.

Modify `onEFrame` function by adding this code at the end of the block of code to be executed if `fire` is `true`.

```
private function onEFrame(e:Event):void {
  ...
  if (fire) {
    ...
    if (bubble.y<R) {
      parkBubble();
    } else {
      for (var i:uint = 0; i<bubCont.numChildren; i++) {
        var tmp:bubble_mc;
        tmp=bubCont.getChildAt(i) as bubble_mc;
        if (collide(tmp)) {
          parkBubble();
          break;
        }
      }
    }
  }
}
```

The new code begins with `else` because it will be executed only if the bubble did not reach the top of the game area.

```
for (var i:uint = 0; i<bubCont.numChildren; i++) { ... }
```

Looping through all `bubCont` DisplayObject children means looping through all bubbles placed on the game field.

Next two lines assign the `i-th` placed bubble to `tmp` variable. I had to write the code in two lines for a layout purpose, but you may want to write it this way:

```
var tmp:bubble_mc=bubCont.getChildAt(i) as bubble_mc;
```

The core of the script is the check for collisions:

```
if (collide(tmp)) {
  parkBubble();
  break;
}
```

If there is a collision, call `parkBubble` function to make the bubble fit into the closest cell and break the cycle as there is no point in continuing to look for collisions.

Unfortunately, `parkBubble` function was made to work properly only when the bubble is about to leave the stage to the top, that is when it's on the first row.

And, even worse, you know horizontal cell positions vary, as cells in odd rows are shifted to the right by R pixels.

We need to heavily rewrite the function:

```
private function parkBubble():void {
  var row:uint=Math.floor(bubble.y/D);
  var col:uint;
  if (row%2==0) {
    col=Math.floor(bubble.x/(R*2));
  } else {
    col=Math.floor((bubble.x-R)/(R*2));
  }
  var placed_bubble:bubble_mc = new bubble_mc();
  bubCont.addChild(placed_bubble);
  if (row%2==0) {
    placed_bubble.x=(col*R*2)+R;
  } else {
    placed_bubble.x=(col*R*2)+2*R;
  }
  placed_bubble.y=(row*D)+R;
  placed_bubble.gotoAndStop(bubble.currentFrame);
  removeChild(bubble);
  fire=false;
  loadBubble();
}
```

Let's see what we are doing:

```
var row:uint=Math.floor(bubble.y/D);
```

Now the first thing is determining the row. The concept is the same applied to the column, but we must know which row we are working on to adjust horizontal position.

```
var col:uint;
```

Declares the variable that will store column number

```
if (row%2==0) { ... }
```

If the row is even, the column is calculated in the same way as before.

```
else {
   col=Math.floor((bubble.x-R)/(R*2));
}
```

otherwise column value is determined in a very similar manner, just shifting the horizontal position by R pixels on the left (look how R is subtracted to x property).

The same concept is applied when it's time to place the parked bubble, there are two similar ways to place it, one for the even rows (same as in the previous example), and one for odd rows.

Finally, y property is calculated in a way that fits for each row, this way:

```
placed_bubble.y=(row*D)+R;
```

Test the movie and you will be able to shoot bubbles that will stack like in the original game.

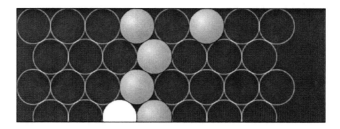

Probably you will notice it's a bit hard to place bubbles in some spots as they seem to react too much to collisions. This happens because in `collide` function we wanted bubbles not to touch any other bubble with a perfect collision detection.

You will make the game a bit more playable if you change this line:

```
return Math.sqrt(dist_x*dist_x+dist_y*dist_y)<=2*R;
```

this way:

```
return Math.sqrt(dist_x*dist_x+dist_y*dist_y)<=2*R-4;
```

Subtracting some pixels from the collision detection. This will make the fired bubble pass more easily through stacked bubbles.

Unfortunately, video games live in a strange world. We worked hard to let the player place the bubbles, and now we'll have to work twice as hard to let him/her remove it from the game.

Detecting bubble chains

When the player forms a chain of at least three bubbles of the same color, they have to disappear from the game.

Before we make them disappear we have to detect if we have chains.

The idea: Once a new bubble is placed on the game field, we can use a variant of the flood fill algorithm that we used during the creation of Minesweeper to check if the bubble is a part of a chain.

The development: We worked on the visual part of the game until now. It's time to add some code to be executed behind the scene to check for chains.

First, we need to save the game field status in an array, and we'll need another array to store all bubbles that are part of a chain. Add two new class level variables:

```
private const ROT_SPEED:uint=2;
private const R:uint=18;
private const D:Number=R*Math.sqrt(3);
private const DEG_TO_RAD:Number=0.0174532925;
private const BUBBLE_SPEED:uint=10;
private var cannon:cannon_mc;
private var left:Boolean=false;
private var right:Boolean=false;
private var bubCont:Sprite;
private var bubble:bubble_mc;
private var fire:Boolean=false;
private var vx,vy:Number;
private var fieldArray:Array;
private var chainArray:Array;
```

`fieldArray` is the array representing the field.

`chainArray` will store all bubbles that are part of a chain.

During the execution of `placeContainer` function we will set up `field_array` array too.

```
private function placeContainer():void {
   fieldArray=new Array();
   bubCont=new Sprite();
   addChild(bubCont);
   bubCont.graphics.lineStyle(1,0xffffff,0.2);
   for (var i:uint=0; i<11; i++) {
      fieldArray[i]=new Array();
      for (var j:uint=0; j<8; j++) {
         if (i%2==0) {
            bubCont.graphics.drawCircle(R+j*R*2,R+i*D,R);
            fieldArray[i][j]=0;
         } else {
            if (j<7) {
               with (bubCont.graphics) {
                  drawCircle(2*R+j*R*2,R+i*D,R);
                  fieldArray[i][j]=0;
               }
            }
         }
      }
   }
}
```

There is really nothing to explain here as it's just an array initialization just like the ones you made each time in a tile-based game.

And like all tile-based games, there are a couple of functions that we will need to deal with the array to manage them.

This is the famous `getValue` function; you've already met it during the making of various tile-based games.

```
private function getValue(row:int,col:int):int {
   if (fieldArray[row]==null) {
      return -1;
   }
   if (fieldArray[row][col]==null) {
      return -1;
   }
   return fieldArray[row][col];
}
```

It will return the value of `fieldArray[row][col]` or `-1` if the value does not exist, that is `row` or `col` have an illegal value.

The second function we are creating is useful to see if a bubble is part of a chain. So main question is: when is a bubble part of a chain? When it has the same color we are looking for and it's not already a part of the chain.

Now let's imagine that we store the chain in `chainArray` array writing in each element, a string made of the row number followed by a comma followed again by the column number.

`isNewChain` function wants the row and the column as arguments to watch, and the color to check.

```
private function isNewChain(row:int,col:int,val:uint):Boolean {
    return val == getValue(row,col)&&chainArray.indexOf(row+","+col)==-
1;
}
```

It will return `true` if the color to check is the same as the one stored in the field array at `fieldArray[row][col]` and there isn't any element in `chainArray` that contains the string made by the concatenation of `row`, comma (`,`), and `col`.

With these two functions, it's easy to scan for all matching bubbles in a recursive way, starting from the position of the last placed bubble.

Follow me during the creation of `getChain` function, which is the most difficult part of this chapter:

```
private function getChain(row:int,col:int):void {
    chainArray.push(row+","+col);
    var odd:uint=row%2;
    var match:uint=fieldArray[row][col];
    for (var i:int=-1; i<=1; i++) {
        for (var j:int=-1; j<=1; j++) {
            if (i!=0||j!=0) {
                if (i==0||j==0||(j==-1&&odd==0)||(j==1&&odd==1)) {
                    if (isNewChain(row+i,col+j,match)) {
                        getChain(row+i,col+j);
                    }
                }
            }
        }
    }
}
```

It wants two arguments representing the row and the column to start scanning, that obviously will initially be the row and the column of the bubble the player just fired.

```
chainArray.push(row+","+col);
```

The examined bubble itself is part of the chain, so we are inserting it into `chainArray` array with `push` method. Notice the string we are inserting, as explained before.

```
var odd:uint=row%2;
```

This is a temporary variable that can take two values: `1` if the row is odd and `0` if it's even.

```
varmatch:uint=fieldArray[row][col];
```

Storing on `match` variable the value of `fieldArray` array at the row and column given by the arguments,

```
for (var i:int=-1; i<=1; i++) {
  for (var j:int=-1; j<=1; j++) {
    if (i!=0||j!=0) {
      if (i==0||j==0||(j==-1&&odd==0)||(j==1&&odd==1)) { ... }
    }
  }
}
```

This combination of `for` loops and `if` statements scan for all neighbor tiles of the one at `row`, `col` according to this picture:

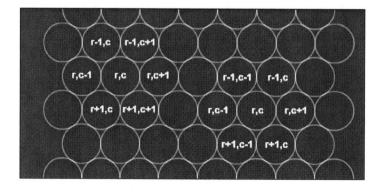

Note how the neighbors' coordinates vary if the bubbles are on an even or odd row.

To detect for bubble chains, is a concept very similar to the flood fill I described during the making of Minesweeper, only this time I am flood filling the same colored bubbles from a starting point.

```
if (isNewChain(row+i,col+j,match)) {
  getChain(row+i,col+j);
}
```

And for each of the neighbor tiles, if it's part of the chain, then execute `getChain` function on this tile too, recursively scanning for its neighbor tiles.

Once the execution of `getChain` function is over, `chainArray` will contain the list of all bubbles that form a chain with the starting bubble, or just the starting bubble itself if there's no chain.

Now we just have to add some lines at the end of `parkBubble` function:

```
private function parkBubble():void {
  . . .
  placed_bubble.y=(row*D)+R;
  placed_bubble.gotoAndStop(bubble.currentFrame);
  fieldArray[row][col]=bubble.currentFrame;
  chainArray=new Array();
  getChain(row,col);
  trace("chain: "+chainArray);
  removeChild(bubble);
  fire=false;
  loadBubble();
}
```

One last effort and we are done:

```
fieldArray[row][col]=bubble.currentFrame;
```

Obviously we have to save the current frame of the bubble in `fieldArray` array, to store the value of the bubble.

```
chainArray=new Array();
```

Initializes `chainArray` to have an empty, clean array where the chain can be stored.

```
getChain(row,col);
```

Calls the core function of this part, `getChain`.

```
trace("chain: "+chainArray);
```

Writes some output to ensure everything worked perfectly.

Test the movie and shoot some bubbles. For each bubble, you will see the chain with that bubble included.

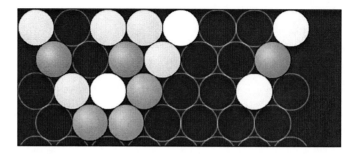

In this case, when you place the third purple bubble, assuming it's the leftmost one, you will see in the output window:

```
chain: 3,1,3,2,2,3
```

Which means we have a chain of three elements: 3,1, 3,2 and 2,3.

Now, we have to remove those bubbles.

Removing the chain

Once we find a chain, bubbles in that chain have to be removed from the game field.

The idea: When we have a chain of three or more bubbles, we have to physically remove the bubbles and clear the corresponding elements in fieldArray array.

The development: We already have an array with all the bubbles to remove. Let's start calling bubbles in the same way when we create them. Add this line to parkBubble function:

```
private function parkBubble():void {
  var row:uint=Math.floor(bubble.y/D);
  var col:uint;
  if (row%2==0) {
    col=Math.floor(bubble.x/(R*2));
  } else {
    col=Math.floor((bubble.x-R)/(R*2));
  }
  var placed_bubble:bubble_mc = new bubble_mc();
  bubCont.addChild(placed_bubble);
  if (row%2==0) {
    placed_bubble.x=(col*R*2)+R;
```

```
  } else {
    placed_bubble.x=(col*R*2)+2*R;
  }
  placed_bubble.y=(row*D)+R;
  placed_bubble.gotoAndStop(bubble.currentFrame);
  placed_bubble.name=row+","+col;
  ...
}
```

Calling the bubble in the same way we inserted the strings into `chainArray` array will allow us to easily remove them calling by their names. Add these lines to `parkBubble` function:

```
private function parkBubble():void {
  ...
  getChain(row,col);
  if (chainArray.length>2) {
    for (var i:uint=0; i<chainArray.length; i++) {
      with (bubCont) {
        removeChild(getChildByName(chainArray[i]));
      }
      var coords:Array=chainArray[i].split(",");
      fieldArray[coords[0]][coords[1]]=0;
    }
  }
  removeChild(bubble);
  fire=false;
  loadBubble();
}
```

Test the movie, and you will be able to remove chained bubbles. What happened?

When we calculated the chain with `getChain` function, first we need to know if the chain is made by three or more bubbles, so we are looking at `chainArray` length:

```
if (chainArray.length>2) { ... }
```

If the chain is longer than two (that is, three or more) bubbles, then we have to scan through `chainArray` array to see which bubbles we are going to remove:

```
for (var i:uint=0; i<chainArray.length; i++) { ... }
```

Now it's time to remove bubbles from the Display List:

```
with (bubCont) {
  removeChild(getChildByName(chainArray[i]));
}
```

Naming the bubbles in the same way we added strings in `chainArray` array does the trick.

Then we only need to update `fieldArray` elements, turning them to zero.

```
var coords:Array=chainArray[i].split(",");
fieldArray[coords[0]][coords[1]]=0;
```

Test the movie and you will be able to remove bubbles when you make a chain.

Let's make things harder: look at this picture and tell me what should you do with the cyan bubble after red chain has been removed.

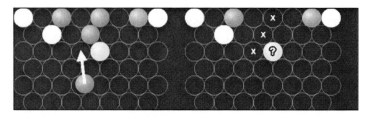

Bubbles which remain unchained have to be removed.

Removing unlinked bubbles

The last step to a Puzzle Bobble prototype is removing unchained bubbles.

The idea: Everything turns around the concept of connected bubbles. We can say a bubble is connected when it's on the highest row or when it's adjacent to at least one connected bubble. With this in mind, each bubble which is not adjacent to at least one connected bubble must be removed.

The development: We need a new array to keep track of all connections. Let's create it as a class level variable and call it `connArray`. It will be used in a kind of flood fill for connected bubbles.

```
private const ROT_SPEED:uint=2;
private const R:uint=18;
private const D:Number=R*Math.sqrt(3);
private const DEG_TO_RAD:Number=0.0174532925;
private const BUBBLE_SPEED:uint=10;
private var cannon:cannon_mc;
private var left:Boolean=false;
private var right:Boolean=false;
private var bubCont:Sprite;
```

```
private var bubble:bubble_mc;
private var fire:Boolean=false;
private var vx,vy:Number;
private var fieldArray:Array;
private var chainArray:Array;
private var connArray:Array;
```

Let's start creating a simple function that will tell us if in a given game field position a bubble exists and it's in `connArray`.

```
private function isNewConnection(row:int,col:int):Boolean {
   return getValue(row,col)>0&&connArray.indexOf(row+","+col)==-1;
}
```

The meaning is easy: we see if we have a bubble with `getValue` and we look for its name in `connArray` array. If both conditions are satisfied, the function returns `true`.

We are now ready to develop the core function of this section.

```
private function getConnections(row:int,col:int):void {
   connArray.push(row+","+col);
   var odd:uint=row%2;
   for (var i:int=-1; i<=1; i++) {
      for (var j:int=-1; j<=1; j++) {
         if (i!=0||j!=0) {
            if (i==0||j==0||(j==-1&&odd==0)||(j==1&&odd==1)) {
               if (isNewConnection(row+i,col+j)) {
                  if (row+i==0) {
                     connArray[0]="connected";
                  } else {
                     getConnections(row+i,col+j);
                  }
               }
            }
         }
      }
   }
}
```

It looks a bit confused, so I'll explain it line by line.

```
connArray.push(row+","+col);
```

First, we insert the bubble itself in the array. It's the basic of all recursive functions.

```
var odd:uint=row%2;
```

This is the safe old way to have `odd` equal to 1 if we are working on an odd row, and equal to zero if we are on an even row.

```
for (var i:int=-1; i<=1; i++) {
  for (var j:int=-1; j<=1; j++) {
    if (i!=0||j!=0) {
      if (i==0||j==0||(j==-1&&odd==0)||(j==1&&odd==1)) { ... }
    }
  }
}
```

And this is the combination of `for` loops and `if` statements to scan for adjacent bubbles that you've already met when we looked for bubble chains.

```
if (isNewConnection(row+i,col+j)) { ... }
```

This is how we check if the adjacent bubble is a new connection or it's a bubble we already know is connected with the bubble we are examining. We aren't just looking for adjacent bubbles, but for adjacent bubbles which are in the highest row, and we can check for it this way:

```
if (row+i==0) { ... }
```

If `row+1` is equal to zero, we have an adjacent bubble which is in the highest row, so the bubble we are examining cannot be unlinked. We will insert a special value in the first element of `connArray` array just to let us remember we are dealing with a linked bubble.

```
connArray[0]="connected";
```

You can use anything you want, I've inserted the string connected because I want the world to know I found a linked bubble. But what happens if there aren't adjacent bubbles in the highest row?

```
else {
  getConnections(row+i,col+j);
}
```

We just call `getConnections` function recursively to adjacent bubbles. If the current bubble does not have adjacent bubbles in the highest row, maybe one of its neighbors has.

We are now able to create a function called `removeNotConnected` which will scan the entire game field looking for unconnected bubbles.

```
private function removeNotConnected():void {
  for (var i:uint=1; i<11; i++) {
    for (var j:uint=0; j<8; j++) {
```

```
      if (getValue(i,j)>0) {
        connArray=new Array();
        getConnections(i,j);
        if (connArray[0]!="connected") {
          with (bubCont) {
            removeChild(getChildByName(i+"_"+j));
          }
          fieldArray[i][j]=0;
        }
      }
    }
  }
}
```

Let's see how it works. The couple of `for` loops scan for the entire game array, looking for bubbles with `getValue` function. When we find a bubble (that is, when `getValue` function returns a value greater than zero), the core of the function is executed:

```
connArray=new Array();
getConnections(i,j);
```

First, we clear and initialize `connArray` array, then we populate it with `getConnections` function. At this time, the first element of `connArray` should be `connected`.

```
if (connArray[0]!="connected") { ... }
```

If it's not `connected`, we can say we are dealing with an unconnected bubble and we have to remove it.

```
with (bubCont) {
   removeChild(getChildByName(i+"_"+j));
}
```

This is how I am removing the bubble. Again, I used `with` for a layout purpose, it's not mandatory (and it's quite a malpractice to tell the truth). Now the field itself needs to be cleared:

```
fieldArray[i][j]=0;
```

Finally, if we have a chain longer than two bubbles, that is we are about to remove some bubbles from the game field, we have to call removeNotConnected function to clear the game field from unconnected, floating bubbles.

```
private function parkBubble():void {
  . . .
  if (chainArray.length>2) {
    for (var i:uint=0; i<chainArray.length; i++) {
      with (bubCont) {
        removeChild(getChildByName(chainArray[i]));
      }
      var coords:Array=chainArray[i].split("_");
      fieldArray[coords[0]][coords[1]]=0;
    }
    removeNotConnected();
  }
  removeChild(bubble);
  fire=false;
  loadBubble();
}
```

Test the movie and create a chain which leaves some unconnected bubbles, like the white one in the picture:

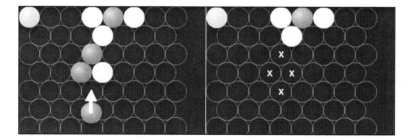

Once red bubbles have been removed, the white unconnected bubble is removed too.

And that's your Puzzle Bobble prototype ready to be played.

Summary

Puzzle Bobble uses hexagonal tiles rather than square tiles, and as you learned during the making of this prototype, this requires some extra coding when you are looking for adjacent cells or when you are placing actors in your game field. Anyway, using hexagonal tiles opens your game design to a wide range of puzzle and strategic games.

Where to go now

If you noticed the whole game is played on the left edge of the stage, it's because I would like you to develop a multiplayer game, with the split screen technique. This means player one plays on the left of the stage, and player two plays on the right.

The way I showed you to handle key presses allows you to have another player controlling the cannon with a different set of keys, let's say A and S to rotate the cannon and W to fire.

9

BallBalance

BallBalance is not a classic in videogames history, it's just a Flash game I made and got sponsored by Kongregate.

You can play it at http://www.kongregate.com/games/triqui/ballbalance

Drop spheres on the balance. Every sphere has a set weight so drop them wisely. Spheres affect the balance according to their distance from the fulcrum. Match three or more spheres of the same color horizontally or vertically (and diagonally in this prototype, although in the original game you can't) to make them disappear. Let the balance hit the ground and it is game over.

It's a quite simple game I want you to make. During the making of this game you won't see new techniques or methods, but you'll improve your skills anyway because you'll see the making of an original game from scratch. Moreover, I will be giving you only a brief explanation of the code, as you should already have the basics to replicate this game.

Also, the way I will explain the making of this game is a bit different than what you are used to seeing in the book. There isn't any "the idea" and "the development" paragraphs. I am only creating the game in the same way I created it three years ago. Obviously this approach frequently leads to errors and programming malpractice, so you should always make a good game design as described throughout this book, anyway sometimes it's good to let fingers run on the keyboard and just experiment.

On your marks. Ready. Go!

Creating files and assets

Create a new file (**File | New**) then from **New Document** window select **Actionscript 3.0**. Set its properties as width to 640px, height to 480px, background color to #000033 (a dark blue) and frame rate to 30. Also define the Document Class as Main and save the file as ballbalance.fla.

There are three actors in this game: the fulcrum, the balance, and the spheres. We will draw the spheres with six different colors in a Movie Clip called ball_mc.

Spheres have a radius of 25 pixels and the registration point in their center. Also, a dynamic text field called weight, capable of hosting numbers from 1 to 5, is placed in the middle of the sphere.

The fulcrum is a 60x50 triangle with the registration point in the middle of its base, called fulcrum_mc.

The balance, called balance_mc, is a grid made by six rows by eight columns. Each tile has a 50 pixel side, and its registration point is in the middle of its base, between the fourth and the fifth column.

Create these three symbols and make them exportable for ActionScript, as usual.

Here are the actors I drew:

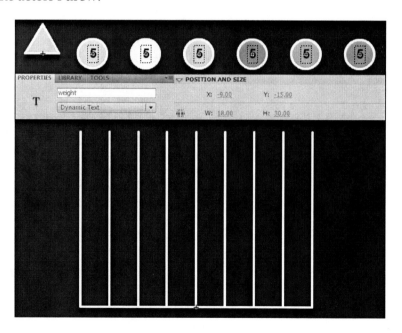

Let's start coding.

Adding the balance

Let's prepare the gamefield and initialize the game array. We will place the fulcrum in the bottom of the gamefield, horizontally centered, and the balance over the fulcrum. Then we'll create a 6x8 array filled with zeros.

Without closing `ballbalance.fla`, create a new file and from **New Document** window select **ActionScript 3.0 Class**. Save this file as `Main.as` in the same path you saved `ballbalance.fla`. This is the content of `Main.as`:

```
package {
  import flash.display.Sprite;
  import flash.events.Event;
  import flash.events.MouseEvent;
  public class Main extends Sprite {
    private var balance:balance_mc=new balance_mc();
    private var gameArray:Array;
    public function Main() {
      prepareArray();
      buildBalance();
    }
    private function buildBalance():void {
      var fulcrum:fulcrum_mc = new fulcrum_mc();
      addChild(fulcrum);
      fulcrum.x=320;
      fulcrum.y=480;
      addChild(balance);
      balance.x=320;
      balance.y=430;
    }
    private function prepareArray():void {
      gameArray = new Array();
      for (var i:uint=0; i<6; i++) {
        gameArray[i]=new Array();
        for (var j:uint=0; j<8; j++) {
          gameArray[i].push(0);
        }
      }
    }
  }
}
```

There's nothing to say about `prepareArray` function as it fills `gameArray` with zeros just as you are used to seeing, while `buildBalance` function places the fulcrum on the ground (the very bottom of the stage) and the balance over it.

Unlike previous games, the first row, the one with index zero, isn't the topmost but the bottommost. Keep this in mind during the making of this game.

Test the movie and you will see your balance ready to be filled with colored spheres.

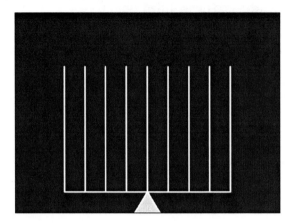

Now, let's make the player choose where to drop spheres.

Choosing where to drop spheres

The player has to be able to choose where to drop spheres with the mouse. Moving the mouse over a column will make the sphere place at the very top of the column. This way the player will select the column by placing a sphere over it.

This time we'll try a different approach to game mechanics. Rather than having a different set of functions to be called according to what's happening on stage, we'll manage the whole game in the function triggered by an ENTER_FRAME event. To let us know what's going on in our game, we'll use a variable called gameStatus that will take various values according to the state of the game. Let's add three new class level variables to Main class:

```
private var balance:balance_mc=new balance_mc();
private var gameArray:Array;
private var ball:ball_mc;
private var selCol:int;
private var gameStatus:String="placing";
```

ball will be used to create a ball_mc instance, to add a sphere to the game.

selCol is the column the player is going to select, that is the column where he will drop the sphere.

`gameStatus` is the state of the game. At the beginning its value is `placing` because we are placing a sphere. Note how I am using a string to describe the state. It would have been more correct if I'd used an integer to represent the various states of the game, with a set of constants to give them a meaningful name, this way:

```
private const PLACING:int=1;
private var gameStatus:int=PLACING;
```

Anyway, I did not want to create a lot of constants so I am using this faster and dirty way. You are free to follow my example or do the nice programmer and create a set of constants, one for every state of the game.

Since `gameStatus` comes into play every time an ENTER_FRAME event is triggered, we need to add the listener in `Main` constructor:

```
public function Main() {
  prepareArray();
  buildBalance();
  addEventListener(Event.ENTER_FRAME,onEnterFrm);
}
```

Now `onEnterFrm` will be called at every frame. Let's see how it's made:

```
private function onEnterFrm(e:Event):void {
switch (gameStatus) {
   case "placing" :
     addBall();
     gameStatus="moving";
     break;
   case "moving" :
     selCol=Math.floor((balance.mouseX+200)/50);
     if (selCol<0) {
       selCol=0;
     }
     if (selCol>7) {
       selCol=7;
     }
   ball.x=-175+selCol*50;
   break;
  }
}
```

The whole function is managed by the `switch` statement acting on `gameStatus` variable. As you can see, there are two cases: when `gameStatus` contains the string `placing` and when it contains `moving`. Again, feel free to define a constant called `MOVING`, assigning it a value of 2 (or anything you want, but different than 1 that should be `PLACING` value) and manage the `switch` using constants rather than strings.

Since `selCol` can never be both less than zero and greater than 7, this block

```
if (selCol<0) {
  selCol=0;
}
if (selCol>7) {
  selCol=7;
}
```

Could be rewritten this way:

```
if (selCol<0) {
  selCol=0;
}
else if (selCol>7) {
  selCol=7;
}
```

But as said we are just prototyping a playable concept, so we won't bother that much about being correct at scripting.

Anyway, let's see what happens when we enter in the `placing` case, which is our starting state. In this case, `addBall` function is called to add the sphere on the stage. This is `addBall` function:

```
private function addBall():void {
  ball=new ball_mc();
  balance.addChild(ball);
  ball.y=-325;
  ball.gotoAndStop(Math.ceil(Math.random()*6));
  ball.weight.text=Math.ceil(Math.random()*5).toString();
}
```

The function constructs and adds a sphere on the Display List as a child of `balance` DisplayObject, sets it at the very top of it, setting its `y` property at -325 (again, use a constant if you want), then a random color and a random weight are chosen. The random color is shown stopping the sphere's timeline to a frame between 1 and 6, while the weight is shown writing a number between 1 and 5 in the `weight` dynamic text of the sphere.

I only want you to note how I am using `ceil` method to return the ceiling of the expression. These two lines:

```
ball.gotoAndStop(Math.ceil(Math.random()*6));
ball.gotoAndStop(Math.floor(Math.random()*6)+1);
```

Will show the same frame, assuming the random number is the same.

The last thing I want you to note is the `y` property at -325. Is there a meaning behind this number or could it be 312 or 491? I've chosen a value which allowed me to place the sphere as if it were on a row above the balance, and which can be divided by 25, the sphere's radius. I'll use this feature to add smooth animations to falling spheres, later in this chapter.

Back to our `switch` statement, after adding the sphere on the stage with `addBall`, we change `gameStatus` giving it the value of `moving`. This means next time we'll enter the `switch` statement; we'll execute the code in `moving` case. I said "next time" because the `break` at the end of `placing` case prevents us from executing anything else inside the `switch` statement.

What happens in `moving` case?

```
selCol=Math.floor((balance.mouseX+200)/50);
```

This line is the core of the block. We detect the x mouse position inside `balance` DisplayObject and according to its registration point and column's width we know we are on the first column (column 0) when the mouse x position ranges from -200 to -151, on the second column (column 1) when the mouse x position ranges from -150 to -101, and so on. This value is assigned to `selCol` variable, and it represents the column the player is choosing to drop the sphere. Then the value is sanitized to let us have only values from 0 to 7, which represent legal column values, and finally with:

```
ball.x=-175+selCol*50;
```

The sphere is exactly placed over the column selected with the mouse.

You may ask why we are detecting x mouse position inside `balance` DisplayObject and not directly on the stage: that's because between the balance and the stage itself there is a different coordinate system, especially when the balance is rotated. That's why we are choosing the balance itself as a reference for x mouse position.

Test the movie, and you will see a random sphere with a random weight you can move with the mouse over the balance.

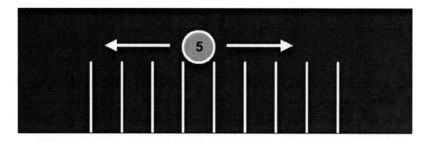

Now the player is able to select a column. Let's make him drop the sphere.

Dropping the spheres

The player will be able to drop the spheres by clicking with the mouse on the column he/she wants to drop a sphere. Once a sphere has been dropped, it will fall down until it touches the floor of the balance or another sphere.

We need another class level variable to store the position of the row where the sphere will drop, just like we are storing the position of the column with `selCol`. Add the new variable, called `selRow`.

```
private var balance:balance_mc=new balance_mc();
private var gameArray:Array;
private var ball:ball_mc;
private var selCol:int;
private var selRow:int;
private var gameStatus:String="placing";
```

Do you see something strange in these variable declarations? `selCol` and `selRow` have been defined as integers, but they will never take a value less than zero, so they should have been defined as unsigned integers, right? It's true, but Flash handles unsigned integers a bit slower than integers. So if you are looking for performances, always prefer integers over unsigned integers. It's not the case in our game that won't benefit from using integers in place of unsigned integers as it's not that CPU expensive, but keep this information in mind.

Back to our game, we said the player will drop the spheres with a mouse click, so we are going to add a listener in `Main` constructor:

```
public function Main() {
  prepareArray();
  buildBalance();
  addEventListener(Event.ENTER_FRAME,onEnterFrm);
  stage.addEventListener(MouseEvent.CLICK,onClick);
}
```

The player can click anywhere around the screen, that's why the listener has been added on the stage. Once the click has been detected, `onClick` function comes into play.

```
private function onClick(e:MouseEvent):void {
  if (gameStatus=="moving"&&gameArray[5][selCol]==0) {
    gameStatus="falling";
  }
}
```

Let's see when a sphere can be dropped in a column. There are two conditions that must be satisfied:

1. The player is moving the sphere, choosing a column
2. The column isn't already fully occupied by previously dropped spheres

Both conditions are included in the `if` statement. `gameStatus=="moving"` means the player is moving the ball above the balance, choosing where to drop it, and `gameArray[5][selCol]==0` means there is at least one free spot in the `selCol` column.

If a sphere can be dropped, then `gameStatus` takes the value `falling`.

What happens when the sphere is falling? Let's add this new case to the `switch` statement in `onEnterFrm` function:

```
case "falling" :
  ball.y+=12.5;
  if ((ball.y-25)%50==0) {
    selRow = -1*(ball.y+25)/50;
    if (selRow==0||gameArray[selRow-1][selCol]!=0) {
      var placedBall:ball_mc = new ball_mc();
      balance.addChild(placedBall);
      placedBall.x=ball.x;
      placedBall.y=ball.y;
      placedBall.gotoAndStop(ball.currentFrame);
```

```
        placedBall.weight.text=ball.weight.text;
        placedBall.name=selRow+"_"+selCol;
        gameArray[selRow][selCol]=placedBall.currentFrame;
        balance.removeChild(ball);
        gameStatus="checking";
      }
   }
   break;
```

Making spheres fall is the key of the game, so I am explaining it line by line:

```
ball.y+=12.5;
```

Moves the sphere down by 12.5 pixels, which is a value that divides its initial position, -325. Moving the sphere by a non-integer amount of pixels can seem a nonsense as in the screen there aren't half pixels, but we'll leave it to Flash to interpolate and approximate pixel movements, we just want to move the sphere by any value that can divide 25, which is the radius of the sphere. The smaller the value, the slower the animation.

```
if ((ball.y-25)%50==0) { ... }
```

Acting on y property and keeping in mind the sphere's registration point which is in the middle, it checks if the sphere is perfectly aligned to a row. This means we aren't in a frame that merely performs a smooth movement but the sphere reached a new row. It's time to see if it should stop or continue falling.

```
selRow = -1*(ball.y+25)/50;
```

And this is how the current row is determined. It's basically the distance between the bottom of the ball and the vertical registration point of the balance, divided by 50 which is the tile's size.

```
if (selRow==0||gameArray[selRow-1][selCol]!=0) { ... }
```

This `if` statement checks whether the sphere should stop falling or not. The sphere will stop if at least one of these two conditions is satisfied:

1. The sphere is on the ground of the balance that is at row zero.

2. The sphere is immediately above another sphere.

Once we enter the `if` statement, it means the sphere should stop falling.

```
var placedBall:ball_mc = new ball_mc();
```

At this time we create a new `ball_mc` instance to represent the sphere that we will swap with the falling one to make it lie in its position.

```
balance.addChild(placedBall);
```

The new sphere is now added to Display List as a child of `balance` DisplayObject.

```
placedBall.x=ball.x;
placedBall.y=ball.y;
placedBall.gotoAndStop(ball.currentFrame);
placedBall.weight.text=ball.weight.text;
```

These lines make the new `placedBall` sphere look exactly the same as the falling sphere.

```
placedBall.name=selRow+"_"+selCol;
```

Gives a unique name to the sphere, according to its position. As you've seen during this book, this will help us to locate the sphere when it's time to remove it.

```
gameArray[selRow][selCol]=placedBall.currentFrame;
```

`gameArray` now is updated, placing the sphere color (actually the frame it's showing) in the element corresponding to the current row and column.

```
balance.removeChild(ball);
```

At this time we don't need the falling sphere anymore, and we remove it from Display List.

```
gameStatus="checking";
```

Everything seems to be ready for us to set `gameStatus` to `placing` and add a new sphere to the game, but before we must check for sphere chains. So we set `gameStatus` to `checking` although we haven't written any code for a `checking` case. Don't worry as the switch will simply do nothing once the sphere touches the ground.

Test the movie and drop a sphere.

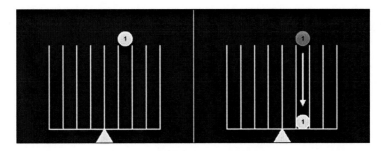

You will see the sphere falling down with a smooth animation, then the game stops. We must now check for chains.

Stacking spheres

When the player forms a chain of three or more spheres of the same color, they must disappear. Throughout this book you learned how to manage adjacent tiles in tile-based games a lot of times, in a lot of different ways. I'm showing you another way, just to make you understand how the same things can be made in a lot of ways when you know a language.

We'll start adding a new class level variable called `chainArray` that is the array that will contain the chains.

```
private var balance:balance_mc=new balance_mc();
private var gameArray:Array;
private var chainArray:Array;
private var ball:ball_mc;
private var selCol:int;
private var selRow:int;
private var gameStatus:String="placing";
```

With this new variable, we can code the `checking` case to add to the `switch` statement in `onEnterFrm` function:

```
case "checking" :
  chainArray = new Array();
  gameStatus="placing";
  for (var i:uint=0; i<6; i++) {
    for (var j:uint=0; j<8; j++) {
      if (gameArray[i][j]!=0) {
        checkForChains(i,j);
      }
    }
  }
      break;
```

The first thing the block of code does is intialize `chainArray`. Now the array is empty and clean, and we'll fill it with sphere chains, if any.

At the moment we are setting `gameStatus` to `placing` again because this is the state we are going to use if we don't find any chain.

The couple of `for` loops scan through `gameArray` elements looking for a sphere, that is, an element whose value is different than zero. For every `gameArray` element different than zero, `checkForChains` function is executed, passing `i` (the row) and `j` (the column) as arguments. There's room for optimization in these two loops, as we know for sure unmoved spheres cannot be part of a chain, and at this time only the sphere we just dropped can be part of it. Anyway, I am leaving this optimization to you as I need a quick way to scan for chains when more than one sphere will be falling, as you will discover later in this chapter.

Before talking about `checkForChains`, let's create the little function we made every time we needed to return an array value only if it exists or -1 otherwise. This time the function is called `checkBall` but it's just a copy/paste of the same function we found in every tile-based game built throughout this book.

```
private function checkBall(row:int,col:int):int {
  if (gameArray[row]==null) {
    return -1;
  }
  if (gameArray[row][col]==null) {
    return -1;
  }
  return gameArray[row][col];
}
```

We are almost ready to code `checkForChains` function, which checks for successful chains, but we still need another couple of functions. Chains can be made horizontally, vertically, or in both diagonals, and each of the four possible directions will have a dedicated function that will check for a chain starting from a specific sphere. The concept isn't that different from the one we developed during the making of Connect Four.

Let's see the function to check for horizontal chains:

```
private function checkHorizontal(row:uint,col:uint):void {
  var current:uint=gameArray[row][col];
  var streak:Array=[row.toString()+"_"+col.toString()];
  var tmpCol:int=col;
  while (checkBall(row,tmpCol-1)==current) {
    streak.push(row.toString()+"_"+(tmpCol-1).toString());
    tmpCol--;
  }
  tmpCol=col;
  while (checkBall(row,tmpCol+1)==current) {
    streak.push(row.toString()+"_"+(tmpCol+1).toString());
    tmpCol++;
```

```
    }
    if (streak.length>2) {
      gameStatus="removing";
      chainArray=chainArray.concat(streak);
    }
  }
```

`checkHorizontal` function will check for a horizontal chain starting from a sphere located at a specific row and column, as you can see looking at its arguments.

Let's see how it works:

```
var current:uint=gameArray[row][col];
```

Saves in a variable called `current` the color of the current sphere.

```
var streak:Array=[row.toString()+"_"+col.toString()];
```

Creates a new array called `streak` that contains the names of the spheres in the chain. Obviously the checked sphere itself is a part of the chain, so `streak` array will initially contain the name of the checked sphere.

```
var tmpCol:int=col;
```

Stores `col` argument value into a temporary variable called `tmpCol`. We have to play a bit with this value, so using a temporary variable prevents the original value from being somehow overwritten and getting lost.

```
while (checkBall(row,tmpCol-1)==current) { ... }
```

This `while` loop scans the row to the left and continues its iteration as long as the colors of the spheres it found are the same as the current sphere we're checking.

```
streak.push(row.toString()+"_"+(tmpCol-1).toString());
```

If the sphere has the same color, then we need to push in `streak` array its name, as it's a part of the chain.

```
tmpCol--;
```

Finally `tmpCol` is decreased to look one sphere further on the left.

```
tmpCol=col;
while (checkBall(row,tmpCol+1)==current) {
  streak.push(row.toString()+"_"+(tmpCol+1).toString());
  tmpCol++;
}
```

Once we are done with the checking on the left side, we must check for spheres of the same color on the right side. First, we reset `tmpCol` value, and then another `while` loop will scan the spheres on the right of the checked sphere in the same way we just did on the left.

```
if (streak.length>2) { ... }
```

At the end of both `while` loops, after we finished scanning on the left and on the right of the initial sphere, `streak` array will contain the names of all the spheres in the chain. Since a chain must be made by at least three spheres, we are checking `streak`'s length to be greater than 2.

```
gameStatus="removing";
chainArray=chainArray.concat(streak);
```

In this case, `gameStatus` takes removing value as we found a chain and we must remove it. At the same time, `streak` elements are added to `chainArray` array with `concat` method, which concatenates the elements specified in the parameter with the elements in the caller array.

In the same way we just managed horizontal chains, `checkVertical` looks for vertical chains, eventually inserting the names of the spheres forming part of the chain in `chainArray` array. This time the argument that needs to be saved is `row`, copied in `tmpRow` variable.

```
private function checkVertical(row:uint,col:uint):void {
  var current:uint=gameArray[row][col];
  var streak:Array=[row.toString()+"_"+col.toString()];
  var tmpRow:int=row;
  while (checkBall(tmpRow-1,col)==current) {
    streak.push((tmpRow-1).toString()+"_"+col.toString());
    tmpRow--;
  }
  tmpRow=row;
  while (checkBall(tmpRow+1,col)==current) {
    streak.push((tmpRow+1).toString()+"_"+col.toString());
    tmpRow++;
  }
  if (streak.length>2) {
    gameStatus="removing";
    chainArray=chainArray.concat(streak);
  }
}
```

Diagonals' chains too are dealt in the same way, with checkDiagonal and checkDiagnoal2 functions. This is checkDiagonal:

```
private function checkDiagonal(row:uint,col:uint):void {
  var tmpStr:String;
  var current:uint=gameArray[row][col];
  var streak:Array=[row.toString()+"_"+col.toString()];
  var tmpRow:int=row;
  var tmpCol:int=col;
  while (checkBall(tmpRow-1,tmpCol-1)==current) {
    tmpStr=(tmpRow-1).toString()+"_"+(tmpCol-1).toString()
    streak.push(tmpStr);
    tmpRow--;
    tmpCol--;
  }
  tmpCol=col;
  tmpRow=row;
  while (checkBall(tmpRow+1,tmpCol+1)==current) {
    tmpStr=(tmpRow+1).toString()+"_"+(tmpCol+1).toString()
    streak.push(tmpStr);
    tmpRow++;
    tmpCol++;
  }
  if (streak.length>2) {
    gameStatus="removing";
    chainArray=chainArray.concat(streak);
  }
}
```

It's exactly the same concept, except we need to save both the row and the column in temporary variables. checkDiagonal2 follows the same concept.

```
private function checkDiagonal2(row:uint,col:uint):void {
  var tmpStr:String;
  var current:uint=gameArray[row][col];
  var streak:Array=[row.toString()+"_"+col.toString()];
  var tmpRow:int=row;
  var tmpCol:int=col;
  while (checkBall(tmpRow+1,tmpCol-1)==current) {
    tmpStr=(tmpRow+1).toString()+"_"+(tmpCol-1).toString();
    streak.push(tmpStr);
    tmpRow++;
    tmpCol--;
  }
  tmpCol=col;
```

```
      tmpRow=row;
      while (checkBall(tmpRow-1,tmpCol+1)==current) {
        tmpStr=(tmpRow-1).toString()+"_"+(tmpCol+1).toString();
        streak.push(tmpStr);
        tmpRow--;
        tmpCol++;
      }
      if (streak.length>2) {
        gameStatus="removing";
        chainArray=chainArray.concat(streak);
      }
    }
```

Calling these four functions will fill `chainArray` array with every sphere that forms a chain with the sphere we just dropped. Let's see how we can use them in `checkForChains` function:

```
    private function checkForChains(row:uint,col:uint):void {
      checkHorizontal(row,col);
      checkVertical(row,col);
      checkDiagonal(row,col);
      checkDiagonal2(row,col);
      if (gameStatus=="removing") {
        for (var i:uint = 0; i <chainArray.length - 1; i++) {
          for (var j:uint = i + 1; j <chainArray.length; j++){
            if (chainArray[i]===chainArray[j]) {
              chainArray.splice(j, 1);
            }
          }
        }
      }
    }
```

First, I am calling all the four functions to find all the chains. Then, if `gameStatus` is `removing`, this means we found at least a chain, since the only lines which will set `gameStatus` to `removing` are executed if a horizontal, vertical or diagonal chain has been found. In this case we have to remove duplicate elements in `chainArray` array.

How can there be duplicate elements? It's simple; just think about dropping a sphere which forms both a horizontal and a vertical chain: the sphere itself will be placed twice in `chainArray` array, the first time when we check for horizontal chains, and the second time when we check for vertical chains.

There's nothing new in these two `for` loops. Just remember `===` operator means "strictly equal to", that is the two values must be absolutely equal.

Test the game and you will be able to drop and stack spheres.

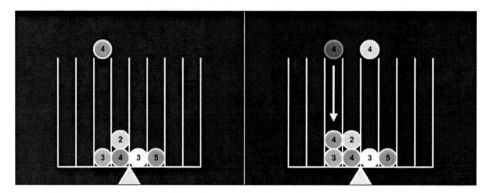

Unfortunately nothing happens when you make a chain, since the code to execute when `gameStatus` is equal to `removing` has yet to be written.

Removing spheres

What happens when `gameStatus` is `removing`? Here it is another case to add to our big `switch` statement in `onEnterFrm` function:

```
case "removing" :
  for (i=0; i<chainArray.length; i++) {
    with (balance) {
      getChildByName(chainArray[i]).alpha-=0.2;
      if (getChildByName(chainArray[i]).alpha<0) {
        removeChild(getChildByName(chainArray[i]));
        var parts:Array=chainArray[i].split("_");
        gameArray[parts[0]][parts[1]]=0;
        gameStatus="adjusting";
      }
    }
  }
  break;
```

The meaning of this code should be quite clear: the `for` loop scans for all elements in `chainArray` array, which are the names of the spheres to remove.

Every child of `balance` DisplayObject with the name corresponding to each element in `chainArray` array will have its `alpha` property decreased by 0.2, and as result the player will see spheres forming the chain fade away.

Once they are completely invisible, the spheres are removed from Display List, `gameArray` corresponding element is set to zero (empty spot) and `gameState` is set to `adjusting`.

Don't worry about this new game state at the moment, and test the movie. You will be able to create a chain and watch it disappear.

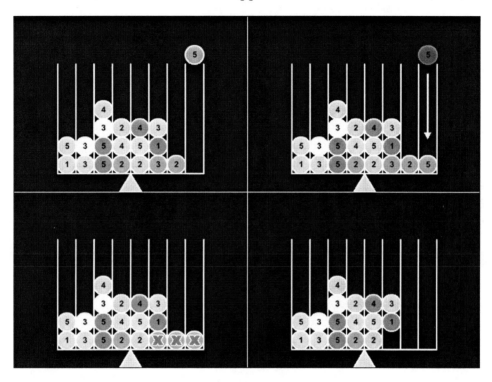

As you can see from this picture, once a chain is made, spheres disappear. But it's not over yet, as floating spheres should fall down to fill the empty gaps.

Adjusting floating spheres

Floating spheres must be treated like falling spheres. We have to make them fall and check if they form a chain. Let's see the last case to add to the `switch` statement in `onEnterFrm` function:

```
case "adjusting" :
  var adjusted:Boolean=false;
  for (i=1; i<6; i++) {
    for (j=0; j<8; j++) {
      if (gameArray[i][j]!=0&&gameArray[i-1][j]==0) {
```

```
                 adjusted=true;
                 with (balance) {
                   getChildByName(i+"_"+j).y+=12.5;
                   if((getChildByName(i+"_"+j).y-25)%50==0){
                     getChildByName(i+"_"+j).name=(i-1)+"_"+j;
                     gameArray[i-1][j]=gameArray[i][j];
                     gameArray[i][j]=0;
                   }
                 }
               }
             }
           }
         }
         if (! adjusted) {
           gameStatus="checking";
         }
         break;
```

First, I need a Boolean variable called `adjusted` to tell the script if all spheres have been adjusted. It starts with `false` because we assume there is still at least one sphere to adjust.

The couple of `for` loops scans for the entire `gameArray` array except the lowest row (look how i variable starts with 1), then the key of the process is this `if` statement:

```
if (gameArray[i][j]!=0&&gameArray[i-1][j]==0) { ... }
```

This `if` statement checks if there is a sphere (`gameArray[i][j]`) over an empty hole (`gameArray[i-1][j]==0`).

In this case we set `adjusted` to `true` because we found a sphere to adjust, then we move down the sphere to be adjusted by 12.5 pixels to make a smooth animation in the same way we did when we managed a falling sphere, then with this `if` statement:

```
if((getChildByName(i+"_"+j).y-25)%50==0){ ... }
```

We check if the sphere is still performing the animation or it reached the place below its starting position, again just as we've already done when dealing with a falling sphere.

```
getChildByName(i+"_"+j).name=(i-1)+"_"+j;
gameArray[i-1][j]=gameArray[i][j];
gameArray[i][j]=0;
```

In this case we update sphere's name as it changed its position, and `gameArray` too as we have to place a hole (zero) in the starting position of the sphere, and the color of the sphere (`gameArray[i][j]`) where the sphere fell.

Finally, if we did not adjust any sphere, we set gameStatus to checking to see if adjusted spheres formed a chain.

Test the movie, and play the game. You will be able to make chains and combos.

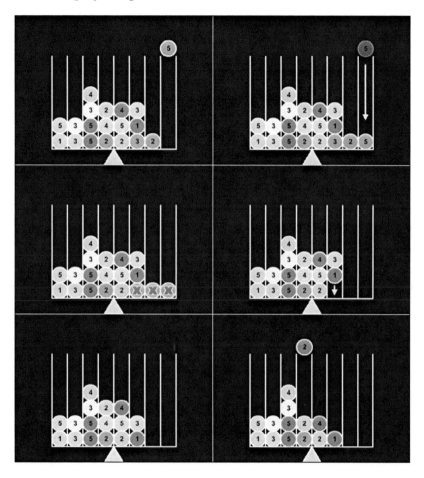

In the previous picture, the orange sphere forms a chain, all orange spheres in the chain are removed, then the purple and the cyan floating spheres fall down, and when the cyan sphere forms another chain, the new chain is removed and only when there aren't more chains to remove or spheres to adjust, the player is able to place another sphere. All of this with smooth animations.

At this time, the prototype is completed as you can play with all features, but the balance still does not move.

Moving the balance

At this time we should feature a fulcrum simulation. There's some physics concepts you should know, try to google for "fulcrum" to know more information.

We aren't looking for a complete simulation of a fulcrum, so multiplying the weight of the spheres by the distance, in columns, from the center will be enough. I won't care about row position in this script; anyway you are free to do it if you think this can improve the quality of the game.

At the end of `onEnterFrm` function after the `switch` statement add this code:

```
private function onEnterFrm(e:Event):void {
  switch (gameStatus) {
  ...
  }
  var weight:int=0;
  for (i=0; i<6; i++) {
    for (j=0; j<8; j++) {
      if (gameArray[i][j]!=0) {
        var tmpBall:ball_mc;
        tmpBall=balance.getChildByName(i+"_"+j) as ball_mc;
        var tmpWeight:uint=int(tmpBall.weight.text);
        if (j<=3) {
          weight+=(j-4)*tmpWeight;
        }
        else {
          weight+=(j-3)*tmpWeight;
        }
      }
    }
  }
  balance.rotation+=weight/100;
}
```

Then test the movie and you will be playing on a moving balance. Try not to make it rotate that much while you make chains.

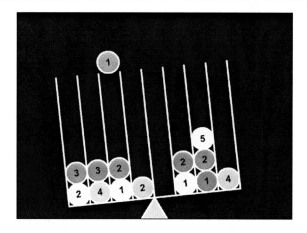

Let's take a look at the code:

```
var weight:int=0;
```

A new variable called `weight` is created, with its initial value at zero. Then the whole `gameArray` array is scanned, and for every sphere found, we check for its weight looking at its `weight` dynamic text field and save its content in a variable called `tmpWeight`.

Then, this `if then else` statement:

```
if (j<=3) {
  weight+=(j-4)*tmpWeight;
} else {
  weight+=(j-3)*tmpWeight;
}
```

Ensures the weight is multiplied by -4 if we are on the leftmost column (column zero), then -3, -2 and -1 for the second, third, and fourth columns, then by 1, 2, 3, and 4 respectively for the fifth to eighth columns.

Finally balance rotation is updated according to the weight.

```
balance.rotation+=weight/100;
```

The weight is divided by 100 to keep the game playable, or rotation will be too strong.

And your BallBalance prototype is completed.

Summary

What can I say! During the writing of this book, I've taken you by the hand through the creation of some of the most popular games in videogames history, and although I don't know you, I'm already missing you. Tomorrow I won't be writing anything you can find in this book, and I'm feeling a bit like when the summer is over. I dedicated six months of my life to this book, so I am taking it with some kind of sadness. Anyway, I just hope you enjoyed following me throughout this book.

See you around.

Where to go now

There are two things you should do: first, managing the "next" feature as in the making of Tetris, then you could try to manage the "game over" status, when the balance rotates more than a certain amount of degrees (I would suggest 15) or when it's completely filled by spheres.

Where to Go Now

Once you code a game, your work isn't over. Game developing starts before you write the game itself and ends after you have added the last line of code.

I want you to have this list of links that you can't miss if you want to be a respected game developer:

`http://www.flashmindmeld.com/`: 60 tips from 60 experts about what makes or breaks a successful Flash game.

`http://www.mochimedia.com/`: the most complete all in one service for Flash game developers, featuring among other things monetizing with advertising and social features.

`http://www.newgrounds.com/`: one of the most important Flash game portals. Make your game get a good score in this portal, and you can consider it a success.

`http://www.kongregate.com/`: another important Flash game portal, with a built-in social network. Add badges and rewards to your game and you'll get a lot of plays in this site, which also shares revenues with developers.

`http://armorgames.com/`: one of the first and most important Flash game portals which also sponsors the best games around the web. Catch their attention and you can be sure your game rocks.

`http://www.box2dflash.org/`: free open source rigid body physics engine for Flash.

`http://www.flare3d.com/`: commercial 3D engine for Flash, the most impressive among its competitors.

`http://www.flashgamelicense.com/`: community which connects developers with sponsors, to let you make money with your Flash game.

`http://flashgamedistribution.com/`: get your game distributed in every known portal in just a few clicks.

`http://www.kindisoft.com/`: software house that developed secureSWF, the best tool to protect your SWF files against decompilers.

`http://playtomic.com/`: the most complete and powerful analytics system for your Flash game. Endless possibilities of tracking what's happening in your game and who's playing it.

And finally, my blog, `http://www.emanueleferonato.com/`: here you will find daily posts about indie game developing and related topics.

Index

About Packt Publishing

Packt, pronounced 'packed', published its first book "*Mastering phpMyAdmin for Effective MySQL Management*" in April 2004 and subsequently continued to specialize in publishing highly focused books on specific technologies and solutions.

Our books and publications share the experiences of your fellow IT professionals in adapting and customizing today's systems, applications, and frameworks. Our solution based books give you the knowledge and power to customize the software and technologies you're using to get the job done. Packt books are more specific and less general than the IT books you have seen in the past. Our unique business model allows us to bring you more focused information, giving you more of what you need to know, and less of what you don't.

Packt is a modern, yet unique publishing company, which focuses on producing quality, cutting-edge books for communities of developers, administrators, and newbies alike. For more information, please visit our website: www.packtpub.com.

Writing for Packt

We welcome all inquiries from people who are interested in authoring. Book proposals should be sent to author@packtpub.com. If your book idea is still at an early stage and you would like to discuss it first before writing a formal book proposal, contact us; one of our commissioning editors will get in touch with you.

We're not just looking for published authors; if you have strong technical skills but no writing experience, our experienced editors can help you develop a writing career, or simply get some additional reward for your expertise.